# Behavioral Insights in Cybersecurity

*Behavioral Insights in Cybersecurity: A Guide to Digital Human Factors* by Dr. Dustin S. Sachs is a timely and essential resource for cybersecurity professionals, leaders, and organizational strategists seeking to understand the powerful role of human behavior in shaping digital security outcomes.

Bridging the gap between behavioral science and cybersecurity, this book challenges the traditional reliance on purely technical defenses and explores why human error accounts for up to 95% of cybersecurity breaches. Drawing from psychology, cognitive science, and organizational behavior, Dr. Sachs provides a compelling framework for rethinking how individuals, teams, and systems interact in high-stakes digital environments.

Through real-world examples and practical strategies, the book examines how cognitive biases, decision fatigue, stress, and cultural dynamics influence security performance. Leaders will learn to recognize and mitigate biases like availability and confirmation bias, implement structured decision-making processes, and foster cultures that prioritize security without sacrificing usability or autonomy.

This book introduces the "Technology Strategy Needs Pyramid," a human-centric model that moves beyond compliance to build mature, resilient, and ethically grounded cybersecurity ecosystems. From designing intuitive interfaces and leveraging behavioral analytics to implementing AI-driven adaptive defenses and ethical nudging, Dr. Sachs equips readers with actionable tools to align human tendencies with security goals.

Whether addressing insider threats, social engineering, or the limitations of legacy awareness training, *Behavioral Insights in Cybersecurity* advocates for a holistic approach that integrates technology, behavior, and culture. It is a must-read for cybersecurity leaders seeking to create sustainable, secure environments where people are not the weakest link—but the strongest asset.

This book is not just a guide—it's a call to reimagine cybersecurity leadership through the lens of human behavior, ethics, and strategic decision-making.

**Security, Audit and Leadership Series**

*Series Editor:* Dan Swanson, Dan Swanson and Associates, Ltd., Winnipeg, Manitoba, Canada.

The scope and mandate for internal audit continues to evolve each year, as does the complexity of the business environment and speed of the changing risk landscape in which it must operate. The fundamental goal of this exciting series is to produce leading-edge books on critical subjects facing security and audit executives and practitioners. Key topics addressed include Leadership, Cybersecurity, Security Leadership, Privacy, Strategic Risk Management, Auditing IT, Audit Management and Leadership, and Operational Auditing.

Evidence-Based Cybersecurity: Foundations, Research, and Practice
*By Pierre-Luc Pomerleau, David Maimon*

Operational Auditing: Principles and Techniques for a Changing World
*By Hernan Murdock*

The Security Leader's Communication Playbook: Bridging the Gap between Security and the Business
*By Jeffrey W. Brown*

The CISO 3.0: A Guide to Next-Generation Cybersecurity Leadership
*By Walt Powell*

Securing Talent: Building and Retaining High-Performance Cybersecurity Teams
*By Kevin Lynn McLaughlin*

Digitalization and Women's Rights: Volume 1
*By Muharrem Kılıç and Sezer Bozkus Kahyaoglu*

Analysis of Threat Perceptions: NATO and Türkiye's Cyber Terrorism Policies
*By Mehmet Emin Erendor*

Members, Methods, and Measures: Unlocking the Secrets of IT Leadership
*By Thomas E. Armstrong*

Philosophy.exe: The Techno-Philosophical Toolkit for Modern Minds
*By Matthias Muhlert*

Guardians of the Digital Age: Securing the Future
*By Elçin Biren*

Ironwill 360° Leadership: A Blueprint for Level 5 Unicorn Leadership
*By Douglas P. Pflug*

Behavioral Insights in Cybersecurity: A Guide to Digital Human Factors
*By Dustin S. Sachs*

# Behavioral Insights in Cybersecurity

## A Guide to Digital Human Factors

Dustin S. Sachs

CRC Press
Taylor & Francis Group
Boca Raton London New York

CRC Press is an imprint of the
Taylor & Francis Group, an **informa** business

Designed cover image: Shutterstock Image ID 2422220481

First edition published 2026
by CRC Press
2385 NW Executive Center Drive, Suite 320, Boca Raton FL 33431

and by CRC Press
4 Park Square, Milton Park, Abingdon, Oxon, OX14 4RN

*CRC Press is an imprint of Taylor & Francis Group, LLC*



ISBN: 978-1-032-99826-8 (hbk)
ISBN: 978-1-032-99853-4 (pbk)
ISBN: 978-1-003-60634-5 (ebk)

DOI: 10.1201/9781003606345

Typeset in Sabon
by codeMantra

For Product Safety Concerns and Information please contact our EU representative:
GPSR@taylorandfrancis.com.
Taylor & Francis Verlag GmbH, Kaufingerstraße 24, 80331 München, Germany.

**To Mandy,**

Your unwavering love, patience, and belief in me are the foundation on which all this stands. You are my compass, my calm, and my greatest partner in every sense of the word.

**And to Max,**

May you always chase curiosity with courage, and may this book remind you that even the most complex problems can be tackled with passion and persistence. You inspire me every day to be better, for you and because of you.

# Contents

# Forewords

Cybersecurity is more than just technology—it is inherently a human challenge. Over two decades in cybersecurity have repeatedly shown me that while technological defenses have grown increasingly robust and sophisticated, the human factor remains persistently vulnerable. I've witnessed firsthand how even the most fortified technological environments falter when human behaviors are overlooked. With this realization, cybersecurity practitioners, behavioral scientists, and organizational leaders must urgently recognize the significance of human psychology as a critical element of security strategy. It is this very nexus between human behavior and cybersecurity that Dr. Dustin S. Sachs effectively explores in this timely and necessary book.

The field of cybersecurity today stands at an inflection point. High-profile cyber incidents frequently dominate the headlines, from major ransomware attacks crippling critical infrastructure to breaches exposing millions of sensitive records. An unsettling commonality emerges in nearly all such cases: despite cutting-edge tools and sophisticated defensive architectures, cyber adversaries often exploit human error or behavioral vulnerabilities. Incidents involving organizations such as Colonial Pipeline, SolarWinds, and MGM Resorts underscore a recurring theme: technology alone is insufficient. These cases demonstrate vividly that the human element—psychological vulnerabilities, cognitive biases, and decision-making patterns—cannot remain an afterthought.

Through years of experience leading cybersecurity efforts within complex environments, I've seen organizations invest heavily in the latest tools yet underestimate or even neglect the human factors that can render their defenses ineffective. Security awareness programs often rely heavily on compliance-driven approaches that, while well intentioned, fail to drive lasting behavioral change. Employees quickly tire of rote, repetitive training, becoming immune to warnings about phishing emails, social engineering attacks, or even basic password hygiene. What I've observed repeatedly is that awareness without understanding is ineffective. Behavioral insights, however, offer a transformative approach: they bridge the gap between knowing what security measures should be followed and genuinely believing in and internalizing those measures.

What Dr. Sachs provides in this book is a powerful argument backed by practical, actionable guidance. He goes beyond theoretical psychology to address the daily, real-world challenges practitioners face, translating behavioral science into concrete tools and strategies. Rather than merely exhorting readers to adopt better behaviors, Dr. Sachs meticulously illustrates how to effectively align security initiatives with natural human tendencies. The book's approach does not rely on punitive policies or complex technical hurdles; instead, it harnesses subtle yet impactful psychological nudges to steer behaviors toward more secure outcomes.

At a strategic level, leaders and decision-makers reading this book will find clear pathways toward fostering genuine cultural transformation. Dr. Sachs highlights a truth familiar to experienced cybersecurity professionals but often missed in broader conversations: cybersecurity is fundamentally a cultural issue. The practical steps offered here enable leaders to integrate security seamlessly into organizational culture, moving beyond a compliance checklist and cultivating a resilient, security-aware workforce.

What makes this book particularly compelling and relevant is its timing. As technology evolves rapidly—with emerging trends like AI-driven cybersecurity defenses, sophisticated biometric authentication, and pervasive remote work arrangements—human vulnerabilities evolve just as quickly. Cyber adversaries today are not only technically savvy but also experts at exploiting predictable human behaviors. Phishing attempts have grown more convincing, social engineering attacks more targeted, and ransomware demands more psychologically manipulative. The traditional approach to cybersecurity awareness training, which emphasizes punitive or restrictive measures, often fails precisely because it misunderstands or overlooks human psychology.

This book arrives at a crucial moment, filling an essential gap by providing cybersecurity practitioners with the tools to adapt their security strategies to human behavior instead of battling against it. By applying insights from behavioral science, Dr. Sachs demonstrates that cybersecurity can become an intuitive aspect of an organization's culture rather than an imposed burden. This shift from reactive compliance to proactive engagement not only strengthens an organization's defensive posture but also significantly enhances long-term resilience.

"Behavioral Insights in Cybersecurity" is not merely a useful addition but a necessary cornerstone in modern cybersecurity education and practice. It uniquely equips practitioners, scientists, and leaders with the capability to harness behavioral insights effectively. For those committed to building resilient, adaptable security cultures, Dr. Sachs's work is indispensable.

This book is more than an endorsement of behavioral science in cybersecurity—it is a call to action for leaders and practitioners across industries. It invites us to rethink our approach, embrace the human element fully, and forge a future where cybersecurity measures resonate naturally with human behavior.

The insights Dr. Sachs shares here have the potential not just to change individual behaviors but to transform entire organizational cultures, making cybersecurity practices intuitive, sustainable, and truly resilient. This timely and impactful contribution to cybersecurity literature deserves careful reading, thoughtful reflection, and decisive action by everyone dedicated to safeguarding our digital future.

Josiah Dykstra, PhD
April 2025

When we consider strengthening our digital defenses, our thoughts often turn to the latest threat intelligence, sophisticated AI, and robust technological safeguards. This is understandable, given our hyper-evolving world and our industry's natural inclination toward technical controls. But my 17 years of community building and leadership roles working at the intersection of technology, cybersecurity, and critical infrastructure have taught me that the most crucial component of our security strategy isn't groundbreaking technology or massive budgets but something much more powerful: people.

You are holding a guide that delves into the criminally undervalued, yet absolutely vital, topic of the human impact of cybersecurity. Cybersecurity isn't solely about algorithms and protocols; it's about people—the individuals who develop, manage, and defend our systems; and its even about those who may unintentionally (or intentionally) compromise those systems.

Our obsession with process, technology, and profit has come at the expense of the people pillar of our industry's core framework. It is worth noting and also fitting that in the People, Process, Technology (PPT) framework, people come first. We've spent billions advocated for strong passwords and cautious clicking, often in a manner that may have elicited more sighs than genuine behavioral change. But what if the industry's spending habits were aligned with a different perspective on cybersecurity? **A Perspective where truly resilient cybersecurity programs built on strong team cultures where humility, empathy, and kindness aren't just abstract concepts but core operational values?**

Creating such a culture isn't about idealistic notions; it's about **intentional, pervasive leadership**. It requires us to engage in **self-reflection**. Are we genuinely **self-aware** of our own biases and how they might influence our decision-making and how we respond to incidents, feedback, and members of our teams? When pressure is high, do we have the emotional maturity and control to stay true to our core values? As this book expertly explores, human psychology significantly impacts our successes and failures in cybersecurity, and it's up to us as leaders to understand why these qualities are key to the security posture of an organization. For example:

- When leaders are willing to **admit mistakes** and approach challenges with **humility**, they foster an environment where learning and growth are encouraged, not penalized. This cultivates a culture of transparency, where team members feel secure in raising concerns and contributing their diverse viewpoints.
- Embracing **vulnerability** as a leadership approach may seem counterintuitive, yet it is incredibly effective for strengthening relationships and building trust within a team. When we demonstrate our human side, we encourage others to do the same, leading to a more connected and supportive atmosphere.

As Dr. Sachs and I have discussed in past Op-Eds, successful cybersecurity leadership involves more than just managing risks; it's about influencing behaviors and fostering a strong culture. Recruiters should seek out individuals who possess qualities like curiosity, thoughtfulness, and humility. Leaders should cultivate these qualities by emulating them, celebrating them, and highlighting instances where desired outcomes were made possible in part by the team's culture and value system.

This book, ***Behavioral Insights in Cybersecurity: A Guide to Digital Human Factors***, isn't just another technical or leadership resource. It's a guide to understanding the human factors that underpin all our cybersecurity endeavors and how to harness this knowledge to be a more well-rounded and effective cybersecurity leader. It's a call to adjust our focus, not away from technology but toward a more balanced approach that recognizes the accretive impact of harnessing human psychology and aligns our resources and decision-making to this belief.

As you read through these pages, I encourage you to think honestly about your own behaviors and approach to life. Not just what you do but the underlying reason behind why you do it. Self-reflection and growth aren't easy. In fact, it can be difficult and uncomfortable. But from one imperfect human to another, I can promise you that leaning into compassion, empathy, humility, and kindness will not only make you more successful in the workplace but will make life infinity happier and fun. And at the end of the day, isn't that what it's all about?

**Parham Eftekhari**
EVP, Communities, CyberRisk Alliance
Founder and Chairman, Institute for Critical Infrastructure Technology

# Author Biography

**Dr. Dustin S. Sachs,** DCS, CISSP, CCISO, is a leading voice at the intersection of cybersecurity and behavioral science. With over two decades of experience securing critical infrastructure and advising global enterprises, Dr. Sachs brings a unique blend of technical expertise and psychological insight to the evolving challenges of digital security. He currently serves as Chief Technologist and Senior Director of Programs at CyberRisk Alliance, where he spearheads strategic initiatives that empower cybersecurity professionals through community-driven learning and innovation.

An award-winning cybersecurity practitioner, academic, and thought leader, Dr. Sachs holds a Doctorate in Computer Science with a specialization in Cybersecurity and Information Assurance. His research explores decision-making in cyber supply chain risk and the psychological drivers behind organizational security behavior. He has served in key roles at Fortune 500 companies, led high-impact third-party risk programs, and taught graduate-level cybersecurity courses, all while contributing to national cybersecurity discourse through leadership roles in ISC², Information System Audit and Controls Association (ISACA), and Federal Bureau of Investigation (FBI) InfraGard.

Dr. Sachs is passionate about demystifying human error and transforming it into strategic advantage. His work challenges traditional, compliance-heavy security models, advocating instead for human-centric approaches that foster resilience, accountability, and adaptive security cultures. Whether designing frameworks, advising Chief Information Security Officers (CISOs), or mentoring the next generation of cybersecurity professionals, his mission is clear: to make cybersecurity not only stronger but smarter.

When he's not exploring the psychology of digital risk, Dr. Sachs is a devoted husband and father, endlessly inspired by curiosity, connection, and the pursuit of lifelong learning.

Chapter 1

# Introduction to Behavioral Science and Cybersecurity

## LEARNING OBJECTIVES

This chapter provides a foundational understanding of the intersection between human behavior and cybersecurity, focusing on:

- The relationship between human behavior and cybersecurity vulnerabilities.
- The role decision-making plays in preventing cyber incidents.
- How behavioral science can mitigate human factors in cybersecurity.
- Strategies to integrate behavioral insights with technological defenses.
- The influence of organizational culture on cybersecurity practices.

## DEFINING BEHAVIORAL SCIENCE IN CYBERSECURITY

In cybersecurity, technical solutions are often emphasized as the first line of defense. However, many breaches occur due to human factors rather than technological failures. For cybersecurity professionals, understanding and influencing behavior is as crucial as deploying firewalls or encryption protocols. Behavioral science provides a lens through which cybersecurity leaders and practitioners can better comprehend how human actions and decision-making processes affect organizational security.

Behavioral science draws on psychology, sociology, and cognitive science to analyze the factors that drive human behavior in digital environments. Unlike strategies that focus solely on end users, behavioral insights can also guide cybersecurity professionals in their decision-making, team management, and policy implementation. The behaviors of those responsible for designing, monitoring, and enforcing cybersecurity measures can significantly influence organizational risk. By integrating behavioral science into their practices, cybersecurity leaders can address challenges such as cognitive biases in risk assessment, stress-induced errors in incident response, and ineffective communication during security training. Behavioral science

DOI: 10.1201/9781003606345-1

enables a more nuanced approach to leadership, policy design, and the development of security cultures that minimize vulnerabilities.

Cybersecurity professionals are not immune to cognitive biases, systematic patterns of deviation from rational judgment. For instance, the availability heuristic may cause a professional to overestimate the likelihood of familiar threats, such as phishing, while underestimating less common but equally critical risks (Tversky & Kahneman, 1973). Similarly, confirmation bias can lead a professional to favor evidence that supports preconceived notions, potentially overlooking vulnerabilities that contradict their assumptions. These biases can subtly influence decision-making, leading to blind spots in risk assessments, ineffective prioritization of security controls, and missed opportunities for proactive defense. Recognizing and mitigating these biases is essential for more accurate threat modeling and informed cybersecurity leadership.

Recognizing these biases is crucial for cybersecurity leaders. For example, during risk assessments, professionals might over-prioritize high-profile incidents while neglecting more probable, less dramatic threats. Behavioral science provides tools to counteract these biases, such as structured decision-making frameworks that incorporate diverse perspectives and data-driven analysis. Leaders can mitigate the impact of biases by fostering an environment of open dialogue and critical evaluation. Encouraging team members to question assumptions and share alternative viewpoints can help counteract individual biases, leading to more balanced and accurate assessments.

Behavioral science emphasizes the importance of emotional regulation and resilience in high-stress environments. Incident response teams can benefit from training in techniques such as mindfulness and stress management to maintain focus and composure under pressure (Gross, 2013). Additionally, leaders can implement protocols that provide clear guidance during crises, reducing the cognitive load on team members and minimizing errors. Creating a culture of psychological safety, where team members feel supported and are able to express concerns, also helps mitigate the emotional toll of cybersecurity work. Behavioral science insights can guide leaders in fostering environments where professionals can perform optimally, even in the face of significant stressors (Edmondson, 1999).

Behavioral science underscores the importance of collective behavior in shaping team dynamics. Within cybersecurity teams, the actions and attitudes of leaders and senior members significantly influence overall behavior. For instance, if a leader prioritizes compliance with security protocols, team members are more likely to follow suit.

Leaders can use behavioral principles to cultivate a culture of accountability and vigilance. Publicly recognizing team members who demonstrate exemplary security practices or successfully mitigate risks sets a standard for others to emulate. Conversely, addressing lapses in a constructive manner ensures that team members understand the importance of adherence without fostering fear or disengagement.

Effective communication is central to cybersecurity, but technical jargon can hinder understanding and action, even among professionals. Behavioral science highlights the role of clear, concise messaging in facilitating comprehension and decision-making. For example, using plain language to describe the implications of a vulnerability, rather than relying on overly technical terms, ensures that all stakeholders grasp the urgency and importance of addressing the issue.

Behavioral science also informs how feedback is delivered within teams. Constructive, timely feedback encourages learning and adaptation, while overly critical or delayed feedback can demotivate team members (Edmondson, 1999). Leaders should aim to balance accountability with encouragement, fostering a collaborative and improvement-oriented environment.Cybersecurity policies often fail not because they lack technical rigor, but because they are misaligned with human behavior. Policies that are overly complex or inconvenient can lead to noncompliance, even among well-intentioned professionals. Behavioral science advocates for the development of human-centered policies that account for natural tendencies, cognitive limitations, and environmental factors (Thaler & Sunstein, 2008).

For example, instead of mandating frequent, complex password changes, which often result in professionals writing passwords down, organizations can encourage the use of password managers to simplify compliance. Similarly, policies that incorporate nudges, such as automatic reminders to update software, align with professionals' workflows and reduce friction. Cybersecurity leaders can also use behavioral science to anticipate resistance to new policies and address it proactively. Engaging team members in the policy development process fosters a sense of ownership and increases buy-in, leading to higher compliance rates.

## UNDERSTANDING THE HUMAN ELEMENT

Cybersecurity breaches often highlight end users as the weak link in the chain. However, the reality is far more nuanced. The strategies, systems, and leadership decisions implemented by cybersecurity professionals and senior organizational leaders significantly influence outcomes (Zimmermann & Renaud, 2019). These stakeholders design security policies, implement technologies, and establish organizational cultures that either mitigate or exacerbate risks. The focus is on how leaders and professionals can reshape the cybersecurity landscape by addressing the human element, highlighting the critical role of leadership in creating secure systems.

Studies consistently show that human behavior is the primary cause of cybersecurity breaches, with estimates suggesting that 85%–95% of incidents stem from human factors (Dawson & Thomson, 2018). Actions like password reuse, susceptibility to phishing attacks, and neglecting software updates illustrate how users' decisions often compromise security.

These behaviors, however, are symptoms of deeper systemic issues. Addressing them requires understanding key vulnerabilities: cognitive overload, habitual routines, and social engineering.

End users and cybersecurity professionals alike face cognitive overload when systems are poorly designed (Anderson et al., 2022). For users, overly complex policies and processes create frustration and increase the likelihood of mistakes. Alert fatigue, a condition where individuals ignore warnings due to desensitization, exemplifies this issue. Leadership must recognize that usability is not a luxury; it is a critical security feature.

Even cybersecurity teams are not immune. Security Information and Event Management (SIEM) systems, for instance, often overwhelm professionals with thousands of alerts daily (Buchler et al., 2018). High-profile breaches like the Equifax hack demonstrate the risks of failing to prioritize genuine threats amid noise. Leaders who neglect to streamline these systems or invest in automation tools that enhance prioritization inadvertently contribute to vulnerabilities.

End users often develop risky habits, such as reusing passwords or relying on insecure methods, out of convenience (Morgan et al., 2020). These habits are shaped, and sometimes reinforced, by the systems designed by cybersecurity teams. For example, if password policies mandate frequent changes without providing tools like password managers, users may resort to insecure shortcuts. Breaking these habits requires more than awareness campaigns; it demands structural changes. Default settings that prioritize security, like single sign-on (SSO) solutions, can guide users toward secure behaviors effortlessly. Leadership decisions must account for behavioral science to ensure that systems promote, not undermine, secure routines (McEvoy & Kowalski, 2019).

Organizational leaders play a pivotal role in setting the tone for cybersecurity practices through their priorities and investments (Corradini & Nardelli, 2019). Yet, many organizations continue to underfund behavioral research and user-centric security measures, focusing instead on technical solutions that fail to address human factors. This short-sighted approach shifts the burden of cybersecurity from professionals to end users. Leaders often measure success based on compliance metrics, such as meeting regulatory frameworks, rather than real-world behavioral outcomes (Hasib, 2021). Policies designed to satisfy checklists often leave organizations exposed to risks that the guidelines fail to address. This compliance-centric mindset creates systems that users struggle to navigate, increasing the likelihood of workarounds like writing down passwords or ignoring protocols.

Organizational incentives also drive behavior. Tight deadlines and productivity pressures often discourage employees from adhering to time-consuming security protocols (Triplett, 2022). Embedding security into workflows, rather than treating it as an add-on, can resolve this tension. Leadership must prioritize strategies that integrate behavioral cues, such as automated reminders and just-in-time prompts, into day-to-day operations.

Leadership plays a critical role in fostering a nonpunitive reporting culture (Zimmermann & Renaud, 2019). Employees should feel empowered to report potential threats without fear of reprimand. This requires clear policies, regular training, and an organizational culture rooted in trust. Leaders who prioritize these elements create resilient systems where employees become active defenders against social engineering attacks.

Behavioral science provides a framework for designing cybersecurity strategies that align with how people naturally think and act. For instance, nudge theory can guide users toward secure choices by making those options easier or more attractive (Morgan et al., 2020). Leaders who incorporate these principles into password policies, email filters, and other systems reduce the likelihood of errors.

Behavioral analytics can help leaders identify patterns of risky behavior and address them proactively (Triplett, 2022). Tracking how employees interact with security tools reveals usability issues that undermine compliance. By addressing these challenges, leaders can implement targeted interventions that enhance both security and usability. The narrative that end users are the primary cause of cybersecurity breaches oversimplifies the issue. While user behaviors like falling for phishing scams or reusing passwords are problematic, these actions often stem from systemic failures in strategy, design, and leadership. Cybersecurity professionals and senior leaders hold the most influence over these outcomes.

Addressing cognitive overload, fostering secure habitual routines, and combating social engineering through tailored training and supportive cultures require leaders to recognize that technology alone is insufficient. Human factors must be central to every strategy. Ultimately, leadership is the keystone of effective cybersecurity (Hasib, 2021). Organizations that invest in understanding and addressing human behavior, not just through technical solutions but through thoughtful, user-centric strategies, will be better equipped to navigate the evolving threat landscape. The responsibility for change lies not with the end user but with those designing the systems and strategies meant to protect them.

## THE IMPORTANCE OF SOUND DECISION-MAKING IN CYBERSECURITY

Sound decision-making is a cornerstone of effective cybersecurity leadership. For cybersecurity professionals and senior organizational leaders, the stakes are higher and the implications far-reaching. Decisions about resource allocation, incident response, and strategic investments determine an organization's resilience against cyber threats. This discussion focuses on the unique challenges leaders face in cybersecurity decision-making and outlines strategies to improve judgment and reduce risk.

Cybersecurity leaders routinely make decisions that balance risk management with organizational goals. Whether investing in advanced threat detection tools or prioritizing compliance over innovation, these decisions must align with long-term objectives. Leaders must evaluate trade-offs, such as whether to invest in cutting-edge technology or strengthen foundational defenses. The inherent uncertainty of cyber threats complicates these choices, requiring leaders to rely on both data-driven analysis and professional intuition.

Unlike operational-level decisions, leadership choices often involve ambiguous scenarios where information is incomplete or rapidly evolving. For example, during a live incident, leaders must decide whether to isolate a system or risk broader disruption. These high-pressure situations require leaders to draw on experience, trust their team's expertise, and prioritize actions that minimize potential harm. The decisions made by cybersecurity leaders often extend beyond the technical realm. A decision to publicly disclose a breach, for instance, has significant implications for brand reputation, regulatory compliance, and customer trust. Leaders must navigate the competing demands of transparency, legal requirements, and stakeholder communication, ensuring their decisions reflect the organization's values and priorities.

Authority bias manifests in leadership contexts when senior leaders disproportionately weigh advice from highly authoritative sources, such as well-known consultants or industry experts, without sufficiently scrutinizing the recommendations. This bias is rooted in the assumption that credibility equates to accuracy or relevance, even when the context may differ significantly. As a result, leaders may implement strategies that are popular or widely endorsed but poorly suited to their unique operational environment. This reliance on authority can lead to costly oversights, such as investing in solutions that align with trends rather than addressing specific organizational risks.

Availability bias affects cybersecurity leaders when recent high-profile attacks dominate their thinking. For example, after witnessing a ransomware epidemic in their industry, a leader might overinvest in ransomware-specific defenses while neglecting other vulnerabilities. This cognitive shortcut causes individuals to assess risk based on what is most memorable or emotionally charged rather than what is statistically likely or strategically important. This disproportionate focus on familiar risks can leave the organization exposed to less obvious threats, such as insider threats, supply chain compromises, or misconfigurations in overlooked systems.

Recognizing and mitigating cognitive biases is essential for sound leadership decision-making. Building a culture of constructive dissent, where diverse perspectives are encouraged, helps counterbalance biases. Leaders can also adopt structured decision-making frameworks, such as decision trees or risk matrices, to reduce reliance on intuition alone.

Effective decision-making in cybersecurity leadership relies on accurate and actionable threat intelligence. Leaders must ensure their teams collect, analyze, and contextualize data from multiple sources, including internal logs and external feeds. By integrating this intelligence into decision-making processes, leaders can anticipate threats and prioritize investments in the most relevant defenses.

Predictive analytics enhances decision-making by enabling leaders to model potential outcomes based on historical data and emerging trends. For instance, an analysis of past incidents might reveal patterns that inform proactive strategies. Predictive models can also highlight the potential impact of allocating resources to specific initiatives, such as increasing endpoint security or expanding cloud infrastructure monitoring. Data-driven decision-making must align with organizational goals to be effective. Leaders need to contextualize cybersecurity metrics, such as incident response times or patch management rates, within the broader business strategy. By linking cybersecurity performance to operational and financial outcomes, leaders can make more informed decisions that balance risk and growth.

Leadership decisions often depend on the collective judgment of teams, making it essential for leaders to understand the dynamics of group behavior. Applying behavioral psychology principles can help leaders optimize both team performance and the quality of decision-making processes. This includes recognizing cognitive biases that may skew judgment and leveraging strategies to mitigate their effects. For example, fostering a collaborative environment reduces the likelihood of groupthink and encourages innovative problem-solving during critical incidents, ultimately leading to more resilient outcomes.

Leaders can also employ behavioral nudges to guide their teams toward long-term security objectives and build a culture of proactive risk management. These subtle cues and reinforcements shape behavior without requiring top-down mandates, making them a powerful tool in complex organizational settings. For instance, implementing systems that reward proactive risk identification rather than reactive responses reinforces strategic thinking and builds trust in leadership. Over time, these nudges help establish behavioral norms that ensure decisions consistently align with the organization's overarching cybersecurity goals, enhancing both resilience and accountability.

Decision-making improves when leaders and their teams commit to continuous learning. Regular training on emerging threats, coupled with post-incident reviews, ensures that lessons from past decisions inform future actions. A culture of learning not only enhances individual competencies but also strengthens the organization's collective decision-making capabilities. Crisis scenarios, such as major breaches or ransomware attacks, test leadership decision-making under pressure. Preparation is key to navigating these high-stakes situations effectively. Developing and regularly rehearsing incident response plans ensures that leaders and their teams are ready to act decisively when an attack occurs.

In complex organizations, centralized decision-making can slow down responses to evolving threats. Leaders should empower their teams with clear guidelines and the authority to make decisions within their domains.

For example, allowing incident response teams to take immediate containment actions without waiting for executive approval ensures faster and more effective mitigation. Trust is a critical component of decision-making in cybersecurity leadership. Leaders must establish transparent communication channels with stakeholders, including the board, customers, and employees. By demonstrating accountability and openness, leaders foster trust that supports collaborative decision-making during challenging times.

Effective decision-making is the backbone of cybersecurity leadership, shaping an organization's ability to anticipate, mitigate, and respond to threats. By addressing cognitive biases, leveraging advanced analytics, and fostering a collaborative decision-making culture, leaders can make informed choices that align with both security priorities and business goals. Continuous learning and alignment with organizational values further strengthen the foundation for sound decisions. Ultimately, leaders who prioritize strategic, data-driven, and ethical decision-making will be better positioned to safeguard their organizations and maintain stakeholder trust in an increasingly volatile cyber environment.

## COGNITIVE OVERLOAD AND ITS IMPLICATIONS FOR CYBERSECURITY

Cognitive overload occurs when individuals are overwhelmed with excessive information or tasks, which impairs their ability to process and respond effectively. In cybersecurity, this phenomenon frequently presents itself as alert fatigue, where users become desensitized to the sheer volume of security warnings. As a result, important alerts may be missed or ignored altogether. For example, employees who constantly receive notifications about potential threats may start disregarding them, unintentionally increasing the risk of a security breach (Mikkelsen & Seljåsen, 2024; Nobles, 2022).

This overload is often compounded by the complexity of security protocols, such as lengthy password policies, frequent credential updates, or multifactor authentication procedures. While these controls are critical for protecting systems and data, they can inadvertently create barriers to compliance. Users may respond to these demands by finding workarounds, using weak passwords, or even avoiding the procedures altogether. Behavioral science suggests that simplifying security processes and emphasizing only the most critical alerts can significantly improve user engagement and compliance (Albalawi, 2018; Reeves et al., 2021; Yelizarov & Gamayunov, 2013).

To counteract cognitive overload, organizations should focus on designing systems that intelligently filter and prioritize information based on user roles and responsibilities. For instance, IT administrators can receive comprehensive threat intelligence reports, while end users are only alerted to actionable, relevant steps they need to take. This targeted approach helps prevent unnecessary cognitive strain and increases the likelihood of appropriate responses. Reducing complexity and tailoring communication to the needs of different user groups are essential strategies for managing cognitive overload and improving cybersecurity outcomes (Hadi, 2023; Yavuz, 2024).

## INTEGRATING BEHAVIORAL INSIGHTS WITH TECHNOLOGICAL DEFENSES

Effective cybersecurity strategies require a balanced integration of behavioral insights and technological measures to address both human and systemic vulnerabilities. Behavioral insights focus on the user's interaction with security systems, emphasizing simplicity and intuitive design to minimize errors caused by complex interfaces. For instance, user-centered design principles have proven effective in enhancing system usability, which subsequently improves adherence to security protocols (Grobler et al., 2021). By making systems more user-friendly, organizations can mitigate human errors, a common entry point for cyber threats.

The convergence of behavioral and technological strategies has shown significant potential in creating resilient cybersecurity ecosystems. For example, in critical sectors like finance and healthcare, the adoption of artificial intelligence (AI)-driven predictive tools coupled with user-friendly interfaces has not only strengthened defenses but also increased trust in digital systems (Ejjami, 2024). By focusing on both human factors and system robustness, these integrated measures reduce the risk of breaches and enhance the overall security posture of organizations. Moreover, as cybersecurity threats become more sophisticated, the role of continuous education and technological adaptation cannot be overstated. Systems that integrate real-time feedback and adaptive learning mechanisms ensure that users stay informed about the latest threats and countermeasures. Such systems encourage a proactive approach to cybersecurity, where users are not only participants but also key defenders in the security framework (Moonsamy et al., 2024). This participatory model creates a dynamic defense mechanism capable of adapting to new challenges.

Organizations that neglect the human dimension of cybersecurity risk undermining the effectiveness of even the most advanced technological measures. A holistic approach that combines user education, behavioral insights, and robust technology is essential for addressing modern cybersecurity challenges. By adopting this integrated model, organizations can build systems that are not only secure but also adaptive and user-centric, thereby achieving sustainable security in an ever-evolving digital environment (Sadik et al., 2020). Technological defenses, while indispensable, cannot fully mitigate risks without addressing the human element. Cybercriminals often bypass technical controls by exploiting human vulnerabilities, such as phishing or social engineering attacks. Even the most advanced systems are ineffective if users unknowingly compromise them (Haney et al., 2024; Pfleeger & Caputo, 2012).

Designing systems with cybersecurity professionals in mind, emphasizing intuitive interfaces and clear workflows, is critical for minimizing human errors. Tools like password managers and automated security updates reduce the cognitive burden on users, enabling secure behaviors without requiring constant vigilance. Studies by Groen et al. (2023) show that intuitive systems significantly improve compliance with security protocols. Similarly, Delvecchio et al. (2024) highlight the role of gamification in engaging users and promoting secure practices.

While technological solutions such as firewalls, intrusion detection systems, and encryption are critical to cybersecurity, they address only part of the risk landscape. Technology often assumes rational human behavior, overlooking the unpredictability of how users interact with systems. For example, even the most robust password policies can fail if users write passwords down or reuse them across platforms (Haney et al., 2024). This gap in technological defenses is particularly evident in cases of social engineering, where attackers manipulate human emotions to bypass security mechanisms (Bharath et al., 2024).

Furthermore, overreliance on technology can lead to complacency among users and organizations. When individuals perceive systems as foolproof, they may neglect basic security hygiene, such as enabling multifactor authentication or avoiding public Wi-Fi for sensitive transactions (Delvecchio et al., 2024). Behavioral science underscores the need to address these human vulnerabilities by integrating awareness and education alongside technological measures.

## CHAPTER SUMMARY

This chapter underscores the critical role of human behavior in the cybersecurity landscape, challenging the traditional focus on purely technological solutions. It emphasizes that while firewalls, encryption, and advanced threat detection systems are vital, they cannot fully address vulnerabilities stemming from human error. Behavioral science provides an essential lens to examine and mitigate these risks by exploring how cognitive biases, decision-making processes, and organizational dynamics influence security outcomes. Recognizing that 85%–95% of breaches are attributed to human factors highlights the pressing need to integrate behavioral insights into cybersecurity strategies.

This chapter introduces key concepts, including cognitive overload, habitual routines, and social engineering, which often undermine secure practices. Cognitive overload, for instance, impairs users' ability to respond effectively to security alerts due to the sheer volume of information or tasks they must process. Similarly, habitual routines, like reusing passwords, expose individuals to greater risks, while social engineering exploits psychological vulnerabilities such as trust or fear to manipulate behavior. By understanding these dynamics, organizations can design interventions that address the root causes of insecure actions.

Organizational culture emerges as a foundational element in shaping cybersecurity practices. A security-conscious culture, driven by leadership and reinforced through consistent messaging and training, fosters a proactive approach to risk management. Employees are more likely to adhere to secure practices when they see leadership modeling these behaviors and when security is integrated seamlessly into daily operations. Conversely, cultures that prioritize convenience over security often inadvertently encourage risky behaviors, such as bypassing protocols to save time or resources.

The importance of decision-making in cybersecurity is another focal point of this chapter. Everyday decisions, from clicking on a link to updating software, significantly impact an organization's security posture. Behavioral science reveals how heuristics and biases, such as authority bias or the tendency to underestimate risks, shape these decisions. Designing environments that nudge individuals toward secure actions and providing tools such as warning systems or decision aids can mitigate these vulnerabilities. Effective decision-making frameworks must account for the cognitive and emotional factors influencing users' choices under pressure.

By laying the groundwork for understanding the interplay between human behavior and cybersecurity, this chapter sets the stage for a comprehensive, human-centric approach to security. It argues for a hybrid model that combines technical defenses with behavioral interventions to create resilient systems. Behavioral science not only identifies vulnerabilities but also offers practical solutions, such as gamified training, personalized feedback, and user-friendly systems, to enhance both individual and organizational security. This holistic perspective positions organizations to address evolving cyber threats more effectively, emphasizing that the path to robust cybersecurity lies at the intersection of technology and human behavior.

## REFERENCES

Albalawi, T. F. (2018). Quantifying the effect of cognitive biases on security decision-making [Doctoral dissertation, Kent State University]. OhioLINK electronic theses and dissertations center. https://rave.ohiolink.edu/etdc/view?acc_num=kent1532529752353789

Anderson, A. B., Ahmad, A., & Chang, S. (2022). Competencies of cybersecurity leaders: A review and research agenda. *ICIS 2022 Proceedings*, Article 9. https://aisel.aisnet.org/icis2022/security/security/9

Bharath, V., Gururaj, H. L., Soundarya, B. C., & Girish, L. (2024). Introduction to social engineering: The human element of hacking. In H.L. Gururaj, V. Janhavi, V. Ambika (Eds.), *Social engineering in cybersecurity* (1st ed., pp. 1–25). CRC Press.

Buchler, N., Rajivan, P., Marusich, L. R., Lightner, L., & Gonzalez, C. (2018). Sociometrics and observational assessment of teaming and leadership in a cyber-security defense competition. *Computers & Security, 73*, 114–136. https://doi.org/10.1016/j.cose.2017.10.013

Corradini, I., & Nardelli, E. (2019). Building organizational risk culture in cyber security: The role of human factors. In T. Ahram, D. Nicholson (Eds.), *Advances in human factors in cybersecurity* (pp. 193–202). Springer. https://doi.org/10.1007/978-3-319-94782-2_19

Dawson, J., & Thomson, R. (2018). The future cybersecurity workforce: Going beyond technical skills for successful cyber performance. *Frontiers in Psychology*, *9*, 744. https://doi.org/10.3389/fpsyg.2018.00744

Delvecchio, T., Zeijlemaker, S., De Bernardis, G., & Siegel, M. (2024). Human-Centered Interface Design for a Dynamic Cyber-Risk Group-Based Training Game. *MIT Sloan Research Paper* No. 7131–24, https://dx.doi.org/10.2139/ssrn.4807480

Edmondson, A. C. (1999). Psychological safety and learning behavior in work teams. *Administrative Science Quarterly, 44*(2), 350–383. https://doi.org/10.2307/2666999

Ejjami, R. (2024). Enhancing cybersecurity through artificial intelligence: Techniques, applications, and future perspectives. *Journal of Next-Generation Research 5.0, 1*(1). https://doi.org/10.70792/jngr5.0.v1i1.5

Grobler, M., Gaire, R., & Nepal, S. (2021). User, usage and usability: Redefining human-centric cyber security. *Frontiers in Big Data, 4*, Article 583723. https://doi.org/10.3389/fdata.2021.583723

Groen, E. C. et al. (2023). Achieving usable security and privacy through human-centered design. In N. Gerber, A. Stöver & K. Marky (Eds.), *Human factors in privacy research* (pp. 83–113). Springer. https://doi.org/10.1007/978-3-031-28643-8_5

Gross, J. J. (Ed.). (2013). *Handbook of emotion regulation* (2nd ed.). Guilford Press.

Hadi, A. (2023). User-friendly cybersecurity: A review of integrating usability and cognitive cost in SSDLC (Master's thesis, University of South-Eastern Norway). Retrieved from https://hdl.handle.net/11250/3163723

Haney, J. M., Cunningham IV, C., & Furman, S. M. (2024). Towards integrating human-centered cybersecurity research into practice: A practitioner survey. In *Proceedings of the Symposium on Usable Security and Privacy (USEC) 2024. Internet Society*. https://doi.org/10.14722/usec.2024.23013

Hasib, M. (2021). *Cybersecurity leadership: Powering the modern organization.* Tomorrow's Strategy Today.

McEvoy, T. R., & Kowalski, S. J. (2019). Deriving cyber security risks from human and organizational factors: A socio-technical approach. *Complex Systems Informatics and Modeling Quarterly*, *18*, 47–64. https://doi.org/10.7250/csimq.2019-18.03

Mikkelsen, A., & Seljåsen, T. (2024). Mindful balancing: Avoiding alert fatigue in security operation centers (Master's thesis, University of Agder). Retrieved from https://hdl.handle.net/11250/3144826

Moonsamy, A., Ahmed, M., Guidetti, O., & Rashid, B. (2024). The human firewall: Mitigating ransomware risks in critical infrastructures through human-centric approaches. In M. Ahmed (Ed.), *Ransomware evolution* (1st ed., pp. 1–16). CRC Press.

Morgan, P. L., Asquith, P. M., Bishop, L. M., Raywood-Burke, G., Wedgbury, A., & Jones, K. (2020). A new hope: Human-centric cybersecurity research embedded within organizations. In A. Moallem (Ed.), *HCI for cybersecurity, privacy and trust* (pp. 206–216). Springer. https://doi.org/10.1007/978-3-030-50309-3_14

Nobles, C. (2022). Stress, burnout, and security fatigue in cybersecurity: A human factors problem. *Holistica Journal of Business and Public Administration, 13*(1), 49–72. https://doi.org/10.2478/hjbpa-2022-0003

Pfleeger, S. L., & Caputo, D. D. (2012). Leveraging behavioral science to mitigate cyber security risk. *Computers & Security, 31*(4), 597–611. https://doi.org/10.1016/j.cose.2011.12.010

Reeves, A., Delfabbro, P., & Calic, D. (2021). Encouraging employee engagement with cybersecurity: How to tackle cyber fatigue. *SAGE Open, 11*(1), 21582440211000049. https://doi.org/10.1177/21582440211000049

Sadik, S., Ahmed, M., Sikos, L. F., & Islam, A. K. M. N. (2020). Toward a sustainable cyber security ecosystem. *Computers, 9*(3), 74. https://doi.org/10.3390/computers9030074

Thaler, R. H., & Sunstein, C. R. (2008). *Nudge: Improving decisions about health, wealth, and happiness.* Yale University Press.

Triplett, W. J. (2022). Addressing human factors in cybersecurity leadership. *Journal of Cybersecurity and Privacy, 2*(3), 573–586. https://doi.org/10.3390/jcp2030029

Tversky, A., & Kahneman, D. (1973). Availability: A heuristic for judging frequency and probability. *Cognitive Psychology, 5*(2), 207–232. https://doi.org/10.1016/0010-0285(73)90033-9

Yavuz, Y. E. (2024). Alerting users to phishing threats: A comprehensive evaluation of warning techniques (Bachelor's thesis, Institut für Informatik, LMU Munich). https://yuemya.de/bachelorthesis

Yelizarov, A., & Gamayunov, D. (2013). Adaptive security event visualization for continuous monitoring. In *Late-Breaking Results, Project Papers and Workshop Proceedings of the 21st Conference on User Modeling, Adaptation, and Personalization* (Rome, Italy, June 10–14, 2013). Retrieved from https://ceur-ws.org/Vol-997/wuav2013_paper_10.pdf

Zimmermann, V., & Renaud, K. (2019). Moving from a 'human-as-problem' to a 'human-as-solution' cybersecurity mindset. *International Journal of Human-Computer Studies, 131*, 169–187. https://doi.org/10.1016/j.ijhcs.2019.05.005

Chapter 2

# Foundations of Behavioral Science

## LEARNING OBJECTIVES

- Explore key behavioral science theories relevant to decision-making in cybersecurity.
- Understand how cognitive biases and heuristics influence security behavior.
- Apply behavioral insights to mitigate risks associated with human errors in cybersecurity.

## OVERVIEW OF KEY THEORIES

Behavioral science provides a lens to examine how individuals and groups make decisions, often under uncertainty or with incomplete information. It emphasizes that decisions are rarely made in isolation but are influenced by psychological, social, and environmental factors (Kahneman, 2011; Simon, 1955). This understanding is critical for cybersecurity professionals, who must design systems and processes that account for the complexities of human behavior.

One foundational theory in behavioral science is bounded rationality, proposed by Herbert Simon. This theory challenges the traditional notion that humans make fully rational decisions by highlighting the limitations of cognitive capacity, available information, and time constraints (Simon, 1955). In cybersecurity, bounded rationality explains why individuals often choose weak passwords or postpone software updates, actions that reflect pragmatic rather than optimal choices (Acquisti et al., 2017). Recognizing these constraints allows organizations to develop user-friendly systems that align with natural decision-making patterns, such as automating critical security updates.

Another cornerstone is dual-process theory, which outlines two distinct modes of thinking: System 1 (fast, intuitive, and automatic) and System 2 (slow, deliberate, and analytical) (Kahneman, 2011). While System 1 is efficient for routine tasks, it is prone to errors when applied to complex


DOI: 10.1201/9781003606345-2

or unfamiliar situations. For instance, users may fall victim to phishing attacks because System 1 processes the email's apparent urgency without engaging System 2's critical evaluation (Greene & Paxton, 2009). By fostering awareness of these processes through training, cybersecurity professionals can encourage behaviors that engage System 2 thinking, leading to more secure decision-making.

Behavioral science also delves into how social and cultural norms influence decision-making. People often look to others for cues on appropriate behavior, a phenomenon known as social proof (Cialdini, 2009). In the context of cybersecurity, this can manifest in employees following unsafe practices they observe in colleagues, such as sharing login credentials or ignoring security policies. Organizations can counteract this tendency by cultivating a strong security culture where adherence to best practices is visibly modeled and rewarded.

Loss aversion, another critical concept, highlights how individuals tend to prioritize avoiding losses over acquiring gains (Tversky & Kahneman, 1991). This bias can lead to resistance against implementing new security measures if they are perceived as disruptive or costly. Cybersecurity leaders can address this by framing new policies in terms of potential losses prevented rather than costs incurred, making the benefits of compliance more salient to employees and stakeholders (Herath & Rao, 2009).

Additionally, the theory of planned behavior provides insights into how attitudes, subjective norms, and perceived behavioral control influence actions (Ajzen, 1991). For example, an employee's likelihood of adhering to security protocols may depend on their belief in the effectiveness of those protocols, the organizational culture's stance on security, and their confidence in their ability to comply (Ifinedo, 2012). By addressing these factors through education, positive reinforcement, and user-friendly tools, organizations can enhance adherence to security practices.

Understanding the interplay between individual decision-making and organizational context is essential. Behavioral science reveals that individuals often act based on perceived incentives and barriers (Cialdini, 2009). Cybersecurity strategies that align with these insights, such as gamifying compliance or simplifying reporting processes, can improve engagement and reduce errors. When systems are designed to minimize friction and accommodate human tendencies, they are more likely to be effective in mitigating risks.

Behavioral science provides a comprehensive framework for analyzing and improving decision-making in cybersecurity. By leveraging theories like bounded rationality, dual-process thinking, and social proof, professionals can anticipate and address the human factors that contribute to vulnerabilities. This holistic approach ensures that security measures are not only technically robust but also practical and user-centric, ultimately enhancing the overall resilience of organizations.

## COGNITIVE NEUROSCIENCE

Cognitive neuroscience is an interdisciplinary field that explores the underpinnings of neural processes and the role of the brain in mental functions (Li, 2023). The field blends the principles of psychology, which studies the mind and its processes, with those of neuroscience, which focuses on the nervous system. As a result, cognitive neuroscience seeks to understand how activities such as perception, memory, and decision-making are rooted in brain activity (Serra, 2021). Decision-making, as a complex cognitive function, has been an area of particular interest within cognitive neuroscience.

Cognitive neuroscience focuses on understanding the brain's role in decision-making by identifying specific neural pathways and brain regions activated during these processes (Li, 2023). Emotions, past experiences, biases, and external factors often shape our choices (Cains et al., 2022). By studying these neural underpinnings, researchers can gain insights into the reasons behind our decisions. Understanding the rationale behind decisions helps clarify how various internal and external elements influence our choices, providing a more profound comprehension of our decision-making mechanisms (Serra, 2021).

Within cybersecurity, strong decision-making and decision processes are paramount (Alecse, 2022). Whether it is a system administrator determining the best security protocols or a user deciding whether an email is trustworthy, continuous choices impact cybersecurity outcomes. Understanding the neural processes that drive these decisions can offer valuable insights (Alecse, 2022). For instance, recognizing that specific brain patterns correlate with risky decision-making might allow for better training or tools to help counteract these tendencies.

Just as software can have vulnerabilities, so too can the human mind. Cognitive neuroscience can unveil inherent biases or predispositions in decision-making that cyber-attackers might exploit (Cains et al., 2022). Phishing attacks, for example, often prey on cognitive biases by creating a sense of urgency or leveraging authority. Cybersecurity experts can develop more effective training programs and safeguards to protect against these psychological manipulations by understanding the neural basis of such biases (Cains et al., 2022).

In an age where cyber threats continue to evolve and become more sophisticated, integrating knowledge from cognitive neuroscience into cybersecurity strategies becomes critical (Andrade et al., 2022). Organizations can better equip their teams and users to recognize and respond to threats by understanding the brain's role in decision-making. Moreover, as cybersecurity increasingly incorporates artificial intelligence (AI) and machine learning (ML), insights from cognitive neuroscience might inform the development of algorithms that mimic human decision-making processes, leading to more robust and adaptive security solutions (Naik et al., 2021).

## DECISION THEORY

A key aspect of cognitive neuroscience is rooted in the theories behind how humans make decisions (Li, 2023). The discipline is not just a simple study of choice. It delves deeper into how and why certain decisions are made over others (Korteling et al., 2023). By understanding the factors and variables at play, decision theory aims to equip individuals and organizations with structured methods to arrive at optimal choices. The foundations of decision theory can be traced back to three key disciplines: probability, statistics, and economics (Serra, 2021).

Probability aids in understanding the uncertainties tied to decision-making, ensuring that choices are based not just on vague assumptions but on quantifiable risks (Serra, 2021). On the other hand, statistics allows for data analysis and past trends, giving decision-makers insights into potential outcomes and consequences of their choices (Serra, 2021). Finally, economics provides a framework for understanding the value and cost of decisions, ensuring that resources are allocated efficiently (Serra, 2021). Decision theory offers a comprehensive approach to decision-making by synthesizing principles from these three domains.

Decision theory acknowledges that decisions are often made in uncertain environments, with incomplete information and competing objectives (Yoon et al., 2021). Thus, methodologies and tools are designed to navigate these challenges (Fischhoff & Broomell, 2020). Addressing decision-making challenges ensures that choices are informed and aligned with goals and objectives. Whether for individuals facing everyday choices or organizations charting their future, decision theory aims to guide decision-makers toward better, more informed outcomes (Fischhoff & Broomell, 2020; Yoon et al., 2021).

### Rational Choice Theory

Rational choice theory suggests that individuals weigh the pros and cons of different options to select the most beneficial (Simon, 1955). It assumes people are logical decision-makers who thoroughly evaluate available information and potential results (Arellano et al., 2023; Berthet, 2021; Simon, 1955). Originally from economics, this concept is now applied in sociology, political science, and cybersecurity. People aim to maximize their benefits by making informed choices based on systematic analysis (Simon, 1955).

In cybersecurity, understanding attacker motivations requires a grasp of rational choice theory. Like any other rational actors, attackers weigh the potential gains (financial profit, political influence, or even personal satisfaction) against the risks (being caught, facing legal consequences, or encountering technical barriers) (Maalem Lahcen et al., 2020). Organizations can apply rational choice theory to bolster their cybersecurity defenses.

Organizations can make their systems less attractive targets by understanding the motivations and calculus of potential attackers. Protection and resilience can be achieved by increasing the costs for hackers, through advanced detection systems, legal consequences, or public exposure, or by decreasing the apparent benefits, such as encrypting sensitive data or isolating crucial information (Maalem Lahcen et al., 2020). The goal is to shift the hacker's rational assessment, making an attack seem less appealing.

Beyond external threats, rational choice theory can also shed light on internal cybersecurity issues, especially those related to user behavior (Moustafa et al., 2021). Employees, for instance, might skip specific security protocols if they perceive the immediate benefits (like saving time or effort) to outweigh the potential risks (a future, abstract threat of a security breach). Recognizing this rational calculation, companies can introduce more user-friendly security solutions (Moustafa et al., 2021). Organizations can also increase awareness about the practical consequences of security incidents, thus helping users reconsider the cost-benefit analysis in favor of secure behavior.

## Bounded Rationality

Proposed by Herbert Simon, bounded rationality challenges the classical economic assumption of fully rational decision-making. Classical models suggest that individuals have access to perfect information and unlimited cognitive resources to make optimal choices. However, Simon argued that real-world decision-making occurs under significant constraints, including limited knowledge, finite mental processing power, and time pressures that force individuals to settle for "good enough" solutions rather than optimal ones (Simon, 1955). This concept, known as "satisficing," highlights the gap between theoretical rationality and practical behavior.

In cybersecurity, bounded rationality provides critical insights into user behavior. For instance, users often create weak passwords, reuse them across platforms, or delay security updates. These actions are not inherently irrational; rather, they reflect an attempt to balance the perceived effort of compliance with the benefits of security (Acquisti et al., 2017). A user may feel that remembering a complex password is too burdensome or that updating their system can wait until it is more convenient. Such behaviors illustrate how individuals make trade-offs when faced with competing priorities.

Moreover, bounded rationality emphasizes the role of context in decision-making. Users' choices are influenced by their immediate environment and the information available to them at the time (Kahneman, 2011). For example, if an organization does not emphasize the importance of strong password policies or fails to communicate the risks of ignoring updates, employees may not perceive these actions as critical. Similarly, users may rely on their past experiences, such as never having experienced a breach, to justify their current practices, even if those practices increase vulnerability (Herley, 2009).

Understanding bounded rationality also helps explain why many security measures fail to achieve their intended results. Traditional approaches to cybersecurity often assume that users will comply with policies as long as they are aware of the risks. However, this ignores the cognitive limitations and situational factors that shape behavior (West, 2008). By acknowledging these constraints, cybersecurity professionals can design interventions that align with how people naturally think and act.

One practical application of bounded rationality is the use of tools that reduce cognitive load. For instance, password managers simplify the process of creating and storing complex passwords, alleviating the need for users to remember them. Automatic software updates similarly address the challenge of prioritizing security tasks by removing the need for active user involvement (Bonneau et al., 2012). These solutions recognize that users are more likely to engage in secure behaviors when the effort required is minimized.

Another approach involves restructuring the decision-making environment to promote better choices. This can include implementing default settings that enhance security, such as requiring two-factor authentication or encrypting data by default. Nudging users toward secure practices by presenting them as the easiest or most intuitive options leverages bounded rationality to achieve desired outcomes (Thaler & Sunstein, 2008). For example, making security settings highly visible and simple to configure encourages compliance without overburdening the user.

Additionally, education and awareness campaigns should account for bounded rationality by focusing on clear, actionable guidance rather than overwhelming users with technical details. Providing step-by-step instructions or illustrating potential risks through real-world scenarios can help bridge the gap between knowledge and action (Wash, 2010). Training sessions that incorporate simulated phishing exercises or gamified learning can also engage users in a way that resonates with their natural decision-making tendencies.

Ultimately, bounded rationality highlights the need for empathy and realism in cybersecurity design and policymaking. Expecting users to behave as fully rational actors is unrealistic and counterproductive. Instead, security strategies should focus on understanding the constraints under which decisions are made and crafting solutions that support users in making better choices. By integrating these principles, organizations can foster a more secure and user-friendly environment (Simon, 1955).

## Expected Utility Theory

Expected utility theory focuses on measuring the potential value of different actions. The measurement quantifies the benefit or value derived from a particular choice or decision (Andrade et al., 2022). By ascertaining the utility, decision-makers can better weigh the possible outcomes of their actions. Understanding the impacts of actions becomes crucial in fields like cybersecurity, where the stakes are high, and the potential outcomes are multifaceted (Andrade et al., 2022).

In cybersecurity, decisions can range from adjusting firewall settings to overhauling network architectures (Aurelien, 2021). Each decision carries with it potential advantages and drawbacks. Take, for instance, the implementation of a new phishing detection tool. Using the expected utility, an organization can assess the potential threats the tool can identify and prevent and then balance this benefit against budgetary and operational considerations. An analytical approach enables organizations to make decisions that optimize protection while efficiently using resources (Chambers, 2022).

Risk management is a cornerstone of effective cyber risk identification and appropriately treating identified risks (Goel et al., 2020). Expected utility theory offers an analytical lens in considering the actions to be taken. Consider an organization contemplating its network access policies. The organization can sculpt a policy that balances protection with operational efficiency by analyzing the utility derived from open network access, such as increased employee productivity and flexibility, against the potential risks, like vulnerability to breaches. Decisions about investing in additional protective measures, such as cyber insurance, can also be assessed using this theoretical approach, ensuring that actions align with the most beneficial outcomes (Rios Insua et al., 2021).

## Multi-Criteria Decision Analysis

While expected utility theory offers a robust approach to decision-making, certain situations demand consideration of multiple criteria simultaneously. Multi-Criteria Decision Analysis (MCDA) is a method that facilitates evaluation based on several criteria (Ganin et al., 2020). Particularly in cybersecurity, where decisions can have wide-ranging implications spanning different departments and objectives, MCDA's comprehensive approach becomes invaluable. For instance, a decision to enhance security protocols has implications beyond just protection; it might affect system performance, user experience, or even the organization's bottom line.

The essence of MCDA lies in its systematic methodology, which breaks down the decision-making process into distinct elements or steps (Ganin et al., 2020). The decision problem is initially defined, and potential alternatives are identified. Subsequently, relevant criteria are determined to serve as the basis for evaluating these alternatives. One of the pivotal steps in MCDA is using specific methods or tools, such as the Analytic Hierarchy Process (AHP) (Ganin et al., 2020). AHP simplifies the decision-making process by categorizing it into a hierarchy of more manageable subproblems, allowing each to be assessed independently. In situations where the decision-making process is clouded by uncertainties or ambiguities, techniques like fuzzy logic or set pair analysis can be employed (Ganin et al., 2020). These methods provide a means to navigate the inherent vagueness in real-world scenarios. Once all criteria are evaluated, the alternatives are ranked or prioritized, guiding decision-makers toward the most optimal choice (Ganin et al., 2020). MCDA offers a comprehensive and organized framework, ensuring that all relevant factors are considered in the decision-making process.

The selection of security solutions illustrates the strength of MCDA (Ganin et al., 2020). Many security tools are available in today's market, each with unique advantages and limitations. One software might excel in detecting and countering malware attacks, while another offers extensive real-time monitoring capabilities. However, another might stand out for its seamless integration features. Faced with such diverse options, organizations cannot afford a myopic view. Through MCDA, they can assess each solution against various criteria, ensuring that the final choice effectively bolsters security and aligns with the organization's broader goals and operational needs (Ganin et al., 2020).

## Decision Under Uncertainty

When discussing decisions under uncertainty, it is essential to understand that decision-makers often lack perfect information regarding outcomes or the probabilities of outcomes occurring (Fischhoff & Broomell, 2020). Cybersecurity provides a quintessential example of this. Organizations must defend against continuously evolving threats and often do so without a clear picture of where the next attack might come from or how it might manifest.

Herbert Simon's notion of "bounded rationality" emphasizes the limits of human cognitive capabilities (Simon, 1955). In the fast-paced world of cybersecurity, decision-makers cannot process all available information or foresee every potential outcome. They often resort to simplifying complex problems and might rely on existing protocols or previously used solutions. Simon's insights attempt to demonstrate that perfect decision-making is ideal, but real-world constraints can often lead to satisfaction rather than optimization (Arellano et al., 2023; Berthet, 2021; Simon, 1955).

John von Neumann's game theory, particularly the Minimax theorem, provides an essential framework for decision-making in adversarial contexts like cybersecurity (von Neumann & Morgenstern, 1944). Organizations must anticipate the strategies of attackers while formulating their defense mechanisms. In a landscape where attackers and defenders continuously adapt to each other's moves, game theoretic models can offer valuable insights into crafting strategies that minimize potential losses, even in the face of uncertainty.

## Decision Paradoxes

The concept of a decision paradox arises when the logical structure of a decision leads to a contradiction or an outcome that defies intuitive expectations. One classic example in decision theory is the Allais Paradox, where individuals' choices demonstrate inconsistencies with expected utility theory (Allais, 1979; Hofmann, 2022; Khrennikov, 2023; Levy, 2022). In cybersecurity, similar paradoxes can emerge. For instance, organizations might invest heavily in state-of-the-art security infrastructure but then neglect to enforce basic security protocols, like two-factor authentication. The inconsistency of prioritizing advanced measures while overlooking foundational ones represents a decision paradox where actions do not align with expressed values or objectives.

Daniel Ellsberg's research introduced the concept of ambiguity aversion, where people prefer risks with known probabilities over those with unknown probabilities (Ellsberg, 1961; Khrennikov, 2023). In cybersecurity, this could be manifested when an organization prioritizes defense against well-understood threats over newer, less-understood ones, even if the latter could be more damaging. The reluctance to engage with unfamiliar threats might leave significant vulnerabilities unaddressed.

Understanding and addressing decision paradoxes in cybersecurity is essential for a comprehensive defense strategy (Arellano et al., 2023; Jalali et al., 2019; Marchewka, 2022). If decision-makers are inconsistent in risk evaluations, certain threats may be over-prioritized, while others are unjustifiably ignored (White, 2023). The uneven allocation of resources might leave critical vulnerabilities exposed. Organizations must recognize these paradoxes and employ decision-making frameworks that ensure a balanced and consistent approach to cybersecurity threats (Fischhoff & Broomell, 2020).

## UNDERSTANDING DUAL-PROCESS THEORY FOR CYBERSECURITY PRACTITIONERS

Dual-process theory, conceptualized by psychologists Daniel Kahneman and Amos Tversky, is a vital framework for understanding how cybersecurity practitioners make decisions (Kahneman, 2011; Tversky & Kahneman, 1974). It delineates two cognitive systems: System 1 and System 2. System 1 is fast, intuitive, and automatic, often used for routine or well-practiced tasks, such as triaging alerts in familiar systems or recognizing common attack patterns (Kahneman, 2011). Conversely, System 2 is slow, deliberate, and analytical, engaging in tasks that require careful evaluation, such as investigating novel cyber threats or performing forensic analyses. These systems are complementary, with System 1 offering speed and efficiency, while System 2 provides depth and rigor (Evans & Stanovich, 2013).

For cybersecurity professionals, the ability to toggle between these two systems is critical. Routine operations like monitoring dashboards or following incident response protocols often depend on System 1 for efficiency. However, when faced with complex or unfamiliar scenarios, such as zero-day vulnerabilities or sophisticated phishing campaigns, System 2 must take precedence to ensure thoughtful and effective problem-solving

(Evans & Stanovich, 2013; Kahneman, 2011). Understanding when to rely on each system enables practitioners to optimize both speed and accuracy in their decision-making processes.

## System 1 Thinking

System 1 and System 2 thinking represent two distinct modes of decision-making processes in the human brain, a dual-process theory that has significantly influenced psychology, behavioral economics, and neuroeconomics (Kahneman, 2011; Li, 2023; Serra, 2021; Sharp et al., 2022). System 1 is often described as the brain's fast, automatic, intuitive approach, requiring little effort and no sense of voluntary control (Kahneman, 2011). For example, when one instantly recognizes a face in a crowd or understands simple sentences in one's native language, System 1 is at work. Conversely, System 2 is characterized by slower, more deliberate, and more effortful processing, requiring conscious thought and attention (Kahneman, 2011). Solving a complex mathematical problem or deciding after careful consideration engages System 2 processes. System 2 thinking is associated with the subjective experience of agency, choice, and concentration.

The interplay between these two systems is crucial for understanding human behavior, especially in decision-making and judgment (Fischhoff & Broomell, 2020; Kahneman & Frederick, 2005; Kahneman et al., 2021; Korteling & Toet, 2022; Korteling et al., 2023; Milkman et al., 2009). System 1 can lead to biases and heuristics that influence judgments and decisions in ways that are not always rational or optimal (Berthet, 2021). System 2, while capable of correcting these biases, often relies on System 1 for initial impressions and judgments, which it may or may not override (Carmichael, 2020). Critics of the dual-process theory argue that the distinction between System 1 and System 2 may be too simplistic and that the processes are more interconnected than previously thought (Ketchen Jr. & Craighead, 2022). Recent neuroeconomics and cognitive neuroscience research continue to explore the complex relationship between these two systems, suggesting that decision-making involves a dynamic interaction between automatic and controlled processes rather than a simple dichotomy (Korteling & Toet, 2022; Li, 2023; Serra, 2021; Sharp et al., 2022).

Understanding System 1 and System 2 thinking provides insight into human cognition and behavior and offers practical implications for various domains, including marketing, policymaking, and personal decision-making (Cox, 2023). By recognizing the influence of automatic, intuitive thinking, individuals and institutions can design better interventions and strategies to improve decision outcomes and behavioral patterns (Arellano et al., 2023). Exploring System 1 and System 2 thinking opens new avenues for research and application regarding the complexities of human decision-making (Panda, 2022). The existing literature emphasizes the need for a nuanced approach to analyzing behavior that accounts for both the automaticity of human cognition and the deliberative processes that can override or modify instinctual responses.

### Strengths of System 1 in Cybersecurity

System 1 is essential for handling the high-volume, repetitive tasks that are common in cybersecurity. Practitioners often face a deluge of alerts, requiring quick filtering and prioritization. For example, recognizing a pattern of failed login attempts or identifying a known malware signature leverages the automatic and intuitive capabilities of System 1 (Kahneman, 2011). These rapid assessments allow professionals to allocate their attention to incidents that warrant deeper analysis. In high-pressure environments, System 1's efficiency helps practitioners maintain operational momentum and address time-sensitive issues (Lundberg, 2015).

### Limitations of System 1 in Complex Scenarios

Despite its advantages, System 1 thinking has limitations that can be detrimental in cybersecurity. It relies heavily on heuristics, which, while useful for routine decisions, can lead to errors when applied to complex or unfamiliar threats (Kahneman, 2011). For example, an analyst might overlook a subtle anomaly in network traffic because it does not fit established patterns they recognize (Endsley & Kiris, 1995). Similarly, reliance on System 1 can make practitioners vulnerable to cognitive biases, such as confirmation bias, where they focus on evidence that supports their initial assumptions while ignoring contradictory data (Tversky & Kahneman, 1974).

### Implications for Incident Response

During an incident response, overreliance on System 1 can result in hasty actions that exacerbate the situation. For instance, an analyst might prematurely categorize an alert as a false positive based on superficial similarities to past events. Such snap judgments can delay the detection of advanced persistent threats (APTs) or lead to incomplete containment efforts (Groenendaal et al., 2022; Khusainov et al., 2022; Perry et al., 2024). Recognizing the limitations of System 1 is essential for practitioners to mitigate these risks and ensure a comprehensive response to incidents (Dekker, 2014).

## System 2 Thinking

System 2 is indispensable for addressing novel or complex cybersecurity challenges. It allows practitioners to methodically analyze intricate data, evaluate competing hypotheses, and identify subtle indicators of compromise. For example, during a forensic investigation, System 2 enables analysts to trace the origin of an intrusion by meticulously examining logs, correlating timestamps, and identifying patterns across disparate systems (Kahneman, 2011). This deliberate approach ensures that critical details are not overlooked, leading to more accurate assessments and effective mitigation strategies (Endsley & Kiris, 1995).

### Overcoming Barriers to System 2 Engagement

Engaging System 2 requires cognitive effort and time, resources that are often scarce in the fast-paced world of cybersecurity. Practitioners working under stress or facing alert fatigue may find it challenging to sustain the focus required for deliberate analysis. Multitasking, a common demand in security operations centers (SOCs), further inhibits System 2 activation, increasing the risk of errors (Dekker, 2014). To overcome these barriers, organizations must create conditions that support deep, analytical thinking, such as reducing unnecessary distractions and providing adequate time for complex investigations (Lundberg, 2015).

### Practical Strategies to Foster System 2 Thinking

Cybersecurity teams can implement specific practices to encourage System 2 engagement. Structured decision-making frameworks, such as the MITRE ATT&CK® framework or the Cyber Kill Chain, guide analysts through systematic processes, minimizing reliance on intuition (Hutchins et al., 2011). Additionally, tools that facilitate in-depth analysis, such as Security Information and Event Management (SIEM) systems and threat intelligence platforms, enable practitioners to access and correlate data efficiently (Ramakrishnan & Chittibala, 2024). By combining structured methodologies with supportive technologies, organizations can create an environment that prioritizes thoughtful, deliberate decision-making.

## DECISION FATIGUE

Decision fatigue is a psychological phenomenon that describes the decline in the quality of decisions made by an individual after a prolonged period of decision-making (Alecse, 2022; Pignatiello et al., 2020). The concept of decision fatigue is not exclusive to personal choices but extends to organizational decision-making processes. In cybersecurity, the implications of decision fatigue are particularly pronounced. Cybersecurity teams are constantly bombarded with alerts, many of which could be false positives (Chowdhury et al., 2019; Singh et al., 2023). These alerts require immediate attention and discernment to determine their legitimacy and potential threat level.

The continuous stream of decisions that cybersecurity teams must make can be overwhelming. For instance, with the rise of AI and ML in cybersecurity solutions, there is an increasing reliance on these technologies to detect threats like Android malware or vulnerable source code (Naik et al., 2021). However, these AI-based solutions often produce results that humans do not interpret easily (Giudici & Raffinetti, 2021). As a result, security operators may face tens of thousands of security alerts daily, many of which could be false positives (Chowdhury et al., 2019; Singh et al., 2023). The inundation of information can lead to alert fatigue, where the sheer volume of alerts can cause critical threats to be overlooked or misjudged.

Decision fatigue creates an opportunity for AI and other tools to aid decision-making (Booch et al., 2021; Brandtner, 2023;). For instance, traditional visualization tools might struggle to display the vast amount of data that need to be processed in cybersecurity. In contrast, data visualizations can assist in categorizing alerts. Innovative solutions, such as immersive analytics, have been explored to interact with complex dataset representations, aiming to provide more precise insights and reduce the chances of oversight (Brandtner, 2023).

A parallel can be drawn in the healthcare sector with clinical decision support systems (CDSS) (Panigutti et al., 2022). These systems are designed to prevent medication errors by providing alerts for potential drug-disease interactions. They, too, suffer from high rates of false positive alerts, leading to alert fatigue among healthcare professionals (Panigutti et al., 2022). Just as in cybersecurity, the consequences of overlooking a critical alert in healthcare can be severe, emphasizing the importance of effective and efficient decision-making processes.

In cybersecurity, organizations constantly face the risk of data breaches and other catastrophic consequences stemming from errors or oversights (Chowdhury et al., 2019). As the digital landscape evolves, so do cyber threats, becoming increasingly complex and challenging to detect. Decision fatigue is growing as security professionals grapple with overwhelming alerts and incidents (Chowdhury et al., 2019). In this dynamic environment, organizations must acknowledge the gravity of this issue and the potential impact on their cybersecurity efforts. Making sound decisions in the face of evolving threats is paramount to safeguarding sensitive data and systems.

## TRAINING CYBERSECURITY PRACTITIONERS TO LEVERAGE DUAL-PROCESS THINKING

Effective training programs for cybersecurity professionals should enhance both System 1 and System 2 capabilities. For System 1, practitioners can benefit from exercises that improve pattern recognition and intuitive responses to routine alerts. For example, repeated exposure to common attack signatures or phishing simulations can help analysts build mental models that improve their ability to quickly identify known threats (Kahneman, 2011). These exercises strengthen System 1 processes, enabling practitioners to respond with speed and confidence when handling familiar scenarios (McNeese & Hall, 2017).

To foster System 2 thinking, training should emphasize scenarios that require detailed analysis and critical reasoning. For instance, tabletop exercises simulating advanced threat scenarios, such as ransomware attacks or supply chain compromises, challenge practitioners to evaluate complex data, consider multiple perspectives, and make informed decisions under pressure (Bada & Sasse, 2019). By replicating real-world challenges, these exercises condition professionals to engage System 2 processes more effectively. Over time, this training improves their ability to navigate the unpredictable and evolving nature of cybersecurity threats (Mäses et al., 2021).

Feedback is a vital component of training programs that focus on dual-process thinking. After completing simulations or real-world incident reviews, practitioners should receive detailed feedback that highlights strengths and areas for improvement. For example, feedback might address how a reliance on System 1 led to premature conclusions or how engaging System 2 resulted in a more thorough analysis (Ganye & Smith, 2025). Encouraging practitioners to reflect on their cognitive processes not only enhances learning but also fosters greater self-awareness and adaptability (Andrade et al., 2022).

## THE ROLE OF TECHNOLOGY IN SUPPORTING DUAL-PROCESS THINKING FOR PRACTITIONERS

Technology can significantly enhance the efficiency of System 1 processes by automating repetitive and time-intensive tasks. Automated threat detection tools, such as endpoint detection and response (EDR) systems and intrusion detection systems (IDS), filter out low-priority alerts, allowing practitioners to focus on high-risk incidents (Hiruta et al., 2019). For example, ML algorithms can identify known attack patterns and flag them for immediate action, reducing the cognitive burden on analysts. By streamlining routine operations, technology ensures that System 1 is applied effectively without compromising accuracy (McNeese & Hall, 2017).

Advanced technologies, including AI and ML, augment System 2 processes by providing deeper insights and facilitating complex analyses. For instance, AI-powered tools can identify correlations in vast datasets, detect anomalies that might elude human observation, and generate actionable intelligence (Bada & Sasse, 2019). These tools enable practitioners to delve into complex threat investigations with greater precision and efficiency. By integrating advanced technologies into their workflows, cybersecurity professionals can engage System 2 more effectively, ensuring thorough and accurate assessments (Mäses et al., 2021).

## SYNERGIZING HUMAN AND TECHNOLOGICAL CAPABILITIES

The synergy between human cognition and technology is critical for effective cybersecurity operations. Automated systems handle routine tasks and preliminary analyses, enabling practitioners to conserve their cognitive resources for more demanding challenges. For example, while an AI tool might flag an unusual network pattern, a human analyst can apply System 2 thinking to determine whether it represents a genuine threat or a benign anomaly (Ganye & Smith, 2025; Kahneman, 2011). This partnership leverages the strengths of both systems, ensuring a balanced and adaptive approach to cybersecurity decision-making.

## EDUCATING PRACTITIONERS ON COGNITIVE BIASES

Cognitive biases, deeply ingrained in human psychology, significantly influence our decision-making processes (Berthet, 2021; Ceric & Holland, 2019; Deniz, 2020; Dror, 2020; Kahneman et al., 2019; Korteling et al., 2023). Defined succinctly, cognitive bias is a systematic pattern of deviation from norm or rationality in judgment (Dror, 2020). These biases often divert individuals from logical or normative reasoning, leading them to make judgments that may not always align with objective reality. Pioneers in the study of these biases, Amos Tversky and Daniel Kahneman made groundbreaking contributions to the understanding of this phenomenon. Their seminal work highlighted humans' frequent deviations from statistical reasoning when faced with decisions (1974). Through a series of innovative experiments, they demonstrated that individuals often resort to heuristics or mental shortcuts. While these heuristics can be efficient, they can also result in systematic errors or biases.

The availability bias is one of the most notable biases they identified (Tversky & Kahneman, 1974). Availability bias causes individuals to estimate the likelihood of an event based on how easily examples come to mind (Korteling & Toet, 2022). However, this often leads to miscalculations of actual probabilities, as the most memorable events are not always the most common. Tversky and Kahneman's research illuminated various cognitive biases, such as anchoring, which is influenced by initial information when making subsequent judgments (Tversky & Kahneman, 1974). Another bias they identified is confirmation bias, where individuals tend to favor information that aligns with their preexisting beliefs (Korteling & Toet, 2022). They also highlighted the representativeness heuristic, where people assess probabilities by comparing events to known prototypes (Tversky & Kahneman, 1974).

While Tversky and Kahneman laid the foundation for understanding these biases, exploring this subject did not end with them. The works of Berthet, Ceric, Deniz, Dror, Ganin, and many others have expanded on this foundational knowledge, each contributing unique insights and perspectives

(Berthet, 2021; Ceric & Holland, 2019; Deniz, 2020; Dror, 2020; Ganin et al., 2020). Their pioneering work acted as a catalyst, inspiring much subsequent research. Scholars and researchers delved deeper into the intricate manifestations of cognitive biases, seeking to understand their origins, impacts, and potential strategies for mitigation.

In recent years, the study of cognitive biases has taken a new turn with the integration of emerging technologies and the rise of big data (Alghamdi & Al-Baity, 2022; Belhadi et al., 2021; Booch et al., 2021; Lee & Mangalaraj, 2022; Maheshwari et al., 2020; Naik et al., 2021; Toorajipour et al., 2021). These advancements offer fresh avenues to dissect and comprehend the intricate interplay of cognitive biases in human decision-making. Researchers like Balayn, Cox, Jarjoui, Lee, and Mitchell have explored how technology can both exacerbate and mitigate the effects of these biases (Balayn et al., 2021; Cox, 2023; Jarjoui & Murimi, 2021; Lee & Mangalaraj, 2022; Mitchell, 2022). For instance, while algorithms can perpetuate biases present in their training data, they can also be designed to identify and correct for these biases, offering a more objective perspective (Baer, 2019; Binns, 2022; Burton et al., 2019; Creel & Hellman, 2022; Miles, 2021).

Anchoring bias is a particularly intriguing cognitive pitfall where individuals heavily rely on the first piece of information they encounter (the "anchor") when making decisions (Johnson et al., 2020). For instance, when negotiating a price, the first number mentioned often becomes the reference point, influencing subsequent discussions regardless of its relevance. Pricing bias can lead to suboptimal decisions, as individuals may not adjust sufficiently away from this anchor, even when presented with more accurate or relevant information.

Availability bias and confirmation bias often work hand in hand. The former refers to the tendency of individuals to base their judgments on readily available or recent information, often overlooking comprehensive data (Johnson et al., 2020). The first biases can lead to skewed perceptions, especially in a world saturated with information where the most dramatic or sensational events are remembered. On the other hand, confirmation bias is the inclination to seek, interpret, and remember information in a way that confirms one's preexisting beliefs (Johnson et al., 2020). The second bias can create a feedback loop, where individuals become more entrenched in their views, disregarding evidence to the contrary. The sunk cost bias further complicates decision-making, as individuals continue a behavior or endeavor based on previously invested resources (time, money, or effort), even if it is no longer beneficial (Johnson et al., 2020). Sunk cost bias can lead to irrational decisions, as past investments should not influence current choices.

Several other biases also play pivotal roles in shaping human judgment. The Peltzman Effect describes where people might take more significant risks when they perceive increased safety measures (White, 2023). Anecdotal evidence bias makes individuals prioritize personal experiences or isolated examples over extensive data or statistical evidence (Fleischman et al., 2023).

Omission bias judges harmful actions worse than equally harmful inactions (Berthet, 2021). Overconfidence bias makes individuals overestimate their knowledge or abilities, while framing bias refers to being influenced by the way information is presented rather than the information itself (Berthet, 2021; Zhang et al., 2022). Optimism bias leads people to believe they are less likely to experience adverse events compared to others (Alnifie & Kim, 2023). Lastly, the self-serving bias is the habit of attributing positive events to one's character but attributing adverse events to external factors (Carmichael, 2020). These biases paint a picture of the intricate web of cognitive shortcuts and pitfalls that influence human decision-making, emphasizing the importance of awareness and critical thinking in our daily choices.

## HEURISTICS

Heuristics, often called mental shortcuts, are innate cognitive tools humans use to simplify daily decisions (Andrade et al., 2022; Simon, 1955). These strategies have evolved, allowing our ancestors to make quick judgments in environments where rapid decision-making was crucial for survival (Fischhoff & Broomell, 2020). In the modern world, heuristics help individuals cut through the overwhelming influx of information, enabling them to process and react without being paralyzed by analysis. By reducing the cognitive load, heuristics allow the brain to function more efficiently, reserving its resources for other essential tasks.

However, the use of heuristics is not without its pitfalls. While they expedite decision-making, they can also introduce cognitive biases, leading individuals astray from objective or rational choices (Fischhoff, 2003). A classic example is the representativeness heuristic, where individuals assess probabilities based on how much a situation resembles a prototype in their minds (White, 2023). While this can be useful in some scenarios, it often results in overconfidence, causing individuals to overlook other crucial factors. Another heuristic, the availability heuristic, influences judgments based on the ease with which examples or memories can be recalled (White, 2023). Availability bias can lead to skewed perceptions, especially in a media-saturated world where dramatic or recent events are more easily remembered than statistical norms.

The intricate relationship between heuristics and biases underscores a fundamental aspect of human cognition: the trade-off between efficiency and accuracy (M'Manga, 2020). On the one hand, heuristics enable the brain to process information swiftly, ensuring timely reactions. On the other hand, this speed can come at the cost of precision, leading to potential errors in judgment. Recognizing this delicate balance is essential, as it shapes the foundation of human cognitive architecture (M'Manga, 2020).

Understanding the dynamics of heuristics and cognitive biases has practical implications. By delving deeper into these cognitive processes, individuals and institutions can strategize to harness the benefits of heuristics while minimizing the pitfalls of biases (Adebayo, 2022; Dror, 2020). Creating a decision-making strategy involves cultivating an environment where intuitive, heuristic-driven thinking coexists harmoniously with analytical and deliberate reasoning. By achieving this equilibrium, organizations can foster a culture of informed decision-making, ensuring they are better equipped to navigate the complexities of our information-dense world (Arellano et al., 2023). The journey to understand and leverage heuristics while being wary of biases is a testament to the human endeavor to optimize cognition in an ever-evolving landscape.

## RAISING AWARENESS OF COGNITIVE PROCESSES

Educating cybersecurity practitioners about dual-process theory can improve their decision-making capabilities. Understanding the strengths and limitations of System 1 and System 2 helps practitioners recognize when they are relying on intuition and when deliberate analysis is required (Kahneman, 2011). For example, a practitioner might learn to identify situations where cognitive shortcuts, such as assuming an alert is a false positive, could lead to critical oversights. Awareness of these dynamics empowers professionals to adjust their thinking and approach tasks more strategically.

## ADDRESSING BIASES IN CYBERSECURITY DECISION-MAKING

Cognitive biases, such as confirmation bias or the availability heuristic, can significantly impact cybersecurity decisions (Tversky & Kahneman, 1974). For instance, an analyst who recently encountered a specific type of malware may overestimate its likelihood in unrelated incidents. Training programs that highlight these biases and provide strategies to counteract them can enhance practitioners' analytical rigor. By teaching professionals to question their assumptions and consider alternative explanations, organizations can reduce the influence of biases on decision-making (Klein & O'Brien, 2018).

Encouraging cybersecurity practitioners to reflect on their decision-making processes is key to developing metacognitive awareness. For example, after completing an investigation, practitioners can review their thought processes to identify areas where they relied too heavily on intuition or missed opportunities to engage in deeper analysis. Regular reflection not only enhances individual performance but also contributes to a culture of continuous improvement within cybersecurity teams (Endsley & Kiris, 1995). This focus on self-awareness and adaptability ensures that practitioners are better equipped to handle the complexities of modern cyber threats.

## STRESS AND PERFORMANCE IN CYBERSECURITY

In high-stakes environments, the interplay between stress and performance is a critical factor in determining success. One of the most widely recognized frameworks for understanding this relationship is the Yerkes-Dodson law, introduced in 1908. This principle describes a bell-shaped curve where performance improves under moderate levels of stress, commonly referred to as eustress, but deteriorates rapidly when stress becomes excessive (Yerkes & Dodson, 1908). This relationship has been studied extensively across various disciplines, but its relevance is especially pronounced in cybersecurity, where professionals must operate under immense pressure in the face of evolving threats and tight timelines.

The cybersecurity landscape is inherently stressful, demanding quick decision-making, unwavering focus, and precise execution. Moderate stress levels can act as a catalyst, enhancing cognitive abilities, sharpening attention, and motivating teams to act decisively (Matthews & Capmbell, 1998). For instance, during a phishing incident, a controlled level of urgency can drive a cybersecurity team to quickly identify compromised accounts, isolate affected systems, and mitigate risks. However, when stress crosses an optimal threshold, it becomes detrimental. Cognitive functions such as memory recall, logical reasoning, and situational awareness begin to falter, increasing the likelihood of errors (Selye, 1976). Excessive stress not only impacts immediate performance but can also have long-term consequences, such as burnout, anxiety, and reduced team effectiveness (Maslach & Leiter, 2016).

In practice, the effects of stress often manifest in two critical ways. First, excessive stress can lead to panic-driven errors, where instinctual responses, such as shutting down entire networks during a ransomware attack, inadvertently cause further complications. Second, heightened stress can induce tunnel vision, narrowing the scope of attention and causing cybersecurity professionals to overlook critical evidence or broader vulnerabilities (Davies et al., 2000). These challenges underscore the need for structured stress management strategies tailored to the unique demands of cybersecurity roles.

Organizations must proactively address the relationship between stress and performance to ensure both immediate operational effectiveness and long-term team resilience. Simulation exercises, well-defined response playbooks, and structured debriefing sessions can prepare teams for high-pressure scenarios and provide opportunities for reflection and recovery (Younas & Khanum, 2024). Additionally, leaders play a pivotal role in fostering psychological safety, promoting clear communication, and modeling calm, decisive behavior during crises. Finally, advanced technologies, such as automated threat detection systems and user-friendly interfaces, can alleviate cognitive burdens, allowing professionals to focus on critical tasks. By understanding and applying the principles of the Yerkes-Dodson law, organizations can optimize performance under pressure, creating a more adaptive and resilient cybersecurity workforce.

## The Yerkes-Dodson Law

The Yerkes-Dodson law, introduced in 1908, is a foundational psychological theory explaining the relationship between stress and performance. It describes a bell-shaped curve where performance improves with moderate stress levels, known as eustress, but deteriorates under excessive stress (Chajut & Algom, 2003). This principle has particular relevance in cybersecurity, a field characterized by high-pressure environments. During cyberattacks, professionals must navigate tight timelines, evolving threats, and the significant consequences of failure, often leading to cognitive and emotional overload (Raywood-Burke, 2023). Moderate stress can enhance performance by improving focus and decision-making speed, motivating teams to act efficiently. However, when stress exceeds optimal levels, it becomes debilitating, impairing memory recall, pattern recognition, and logical reasoning (Otegui, 2024).

## Panic-Driven Errors

Excessive stress often triggers panic, leading cybersecurity professionals to make rash, uncalculated decisions. For instance, during a ransomware attack, a team might hastily shut down entire networks to contain the breach, inadvertently disrupting operations and complicating recovery. These actions result from the fight-or-flight response, where heightened stress drives immediate but poorly considered actions (Maslach & Leiter, 2016). Such reactive decisions frequently exacerbate problems rather than resolve them. When panic takes over, teams lose the ability to think critically or evaluate long-term consequences. This highlights the need for robust training and decision-making frameworks to counteract stress-induced errors.

## Tunnel Vision

High levels of stress can also narrow cognitive focus, a phenomenon often referred to as tunnel vision. This occurs when professionals fixate on one aspect of a problem, neglecting peripheral but critical information. In cybersecurity, this can manifest during a data breach when investigators focus solely on the immediate point of entry and overlook lateral movements by attackers within the network (Knauft et al., 2021). Tunnel vision compromises an organization's ability to understand and mitigate broader threats. By failing to account for interconnected vulnerabilities, stress-induced tunnel vision increases the risk of oversight and escalation. Strategies to manage stress are vital to maintaining situational awareness and ensuring a comprehensive response.

### Long-Term Implications

Chronic stress in cybersecurity roles has far-reaching effects on both individual and organizational performance. While acute stress impacts decision-making, prolonged exposure leads to burnout, anxiety, and increased attrition rates (Maslach & Leiter, 2016). Teams operating under consistent high pressure often struggle with reduced resilience, lowering their capacity to respond to future incidents effectively (Nobles, 2022). Over time, the mental and emotional toll diminishes overall productivity and organizational stability. Cybersecurity professionals must have access to stress management resources tailored to their unique challenges. Without proactive intervention, the long-term costs of stress extend beyond individuals, weakening the organization's entire security posture.

### Stress Management Strategies

Organizations can mitigate the adverse effects of stress by adopting structured and proactive measures. Regular simulation exercises, for example, prepare teams for high-stress scenarios by reducing uncertainty and building confidence through practice (Raywood-Burke, 2023). Similarly, clear and detailed response playbooks can minimize cognitive load during crises, allowing teams to focus on execution rather than decision-making (Otegui, 2024). Debriefing sessions after incidents are equally important, offering opportunities for teams to recover emotionally and reflect on lessons learned (Knauft et al., 2021). Providing downtime and support after high-stress events is essential for long-term performance. Such strategies enable cybersecurity teams to operate efficiently under pressure while minimizing the risks of burnout.

### Leadership's Role

Leadership plays a pivotal role in managing stress within cybersecurity teams. Transparent communication, coupled with reassurance during crises, helps foster a culture of psychological safety (Edmondson, 2019). Leaders who model calm, decisive behavior can influence the emotional states of their teams, promoting resilience even in high-pressure situations. Encouraging open dialogue about challenges enables team members to feel supported and less isolated during stressful incidents. Leadership should also prioritize the well-being of their teams by ensuring access to resources and implementing practices that alleviate stress. Effective leadership creates an environment where teams can thrive under pressure without compromising their mental health.

## TECHNOLOGY AND STRESS MITIGATION

Technological tools play a critical role in reducing stress by alleviating the cognitive burden on human operators. Automated threat detection systems and real-time analytics filter out unnecessary noise, allowing teams to focus on actionable insights (Patel et al., 2024). For instance, prioritization of critical alerts ensures that professionals direct their attention to the most pressing issues rather than being overwhelmed by minor notifications. Modern tools also provide dashboards that simplify complex data, reducing time spent interpreting information. By streamlining workflows and removing redundant tasks, technology ensures a calmer and more organized response to cyber incidents. This combination of automation and usability can significantly reduce the chaos typically associated with high-stakes operations.

## IMPACT OF COGNITIVE OVERLOAD

Cybersecurity professionals often face environments where split-second decisions are required amidst a flood of data. Excessive alerts, dense dashboards, and overly technical reports can quickly overwhelm cognitive capacity. This overload results in outcomes such as alert fatigue, where frequent notifications cause critical alerts to be ignored (Otegui, 2024). Additionally, complex interfaces delay responses by requiring extra time for interpretation, which can be costly during an attack (Raywood-Burke, 2023). Overwhelmed professionals are also more prone to errors, such as misinterpreting data or overlooking key details (Nobles, 2022). Addressing cognitive overload is essential to maintaining accuracy and effectiveness during high-pressure situations.

### Design Principles for Reducing Cognitive Load

User interface design in cybersecurity tools can help mitigate cognitive load by adhering to core principles of simplicity and prioritization. For example, systems that emphasize critical alerts using visual hierarchy, such as color coding or sizing, allow users to focus on the most important threats (Patel et al., 2024). Simplifying layouts by grouping related functions together reduces the cognitive effort required to locate information and make decisions. Automation also plays a key role by filtering out low-priority alerts, enabling professionals to concentrate on the most pressing issues without distraction (Otegui, 2024). These design principles ensure that cybersecurity teams operate efficiently, even in high-stakes situations.

### Application in Cybersecurity Tools

Modern SIEM systems exemplify the principles of effective interface design and cognitive load reduction. These tools dynamically filter threats based on severity, categorizing and prioritizing alerts for ease of action. Contextual dashboards display only the information relevant to the user's role or task at hand, simplifying workflows and reducing mental clutter. Visual aids like graphs and heatmaps further enhance data interpretation, enabling teams to assess threats quickly and accurately (Patel et al., 2024). By integrating these features, SIEM systems ensure that cybersecurity professionals can maintain focus and efficiency during critical incidents.

## COM-B MODEL

The COM-B (Capability, Opportunity, Motivation—Behavior) model, developed by Michie et al. (2011), provides a comprehensive framework for understanding and influencing behavior change. In cybersecurity, this model offers actionable insights into how organizations can shape secure practices among employees and teams (Figure 2.1).

### Capability

Capability refers to an individual's psychological and physical ability to perform a behavior. In cybersecurity:

- **Psychological Capability**: Employees must understand the threats they face and the actions required to mitigate them. This involves comprehensive training on topics like phishing, password hygiene, and device security (Michie et al., 2011).
- **Physical Capability**: Adequate tools and infrastructure, such as password managers or secure remote access systems, ensure employees can apply their training effectively (Michie et al., 2011).

### Opportunity

Opportunity encompasses external factors that enable or hinder behavior. Secure practices are more likely when systems are designed to align with human behavior:

- **Accessible Systems**: User-friendly tools reduce barriers to compliance. For instance, making multifactor authentication the default simplifies adoption (Michie et al., 2011).
- **Supportive Environments**: A culture that values security, coupled with leadership support, creates an environment where employees feel motivated to act securely (Michie et al., 2011).

### Motivation

Motivation involves the internal processes, both conscious and subconscious, that drive behavior:

- **Intrinsic Motivation**: Employees adopt secure behaviors because they align with personal values or the desire to protect their organization (Michie et al., 2011).

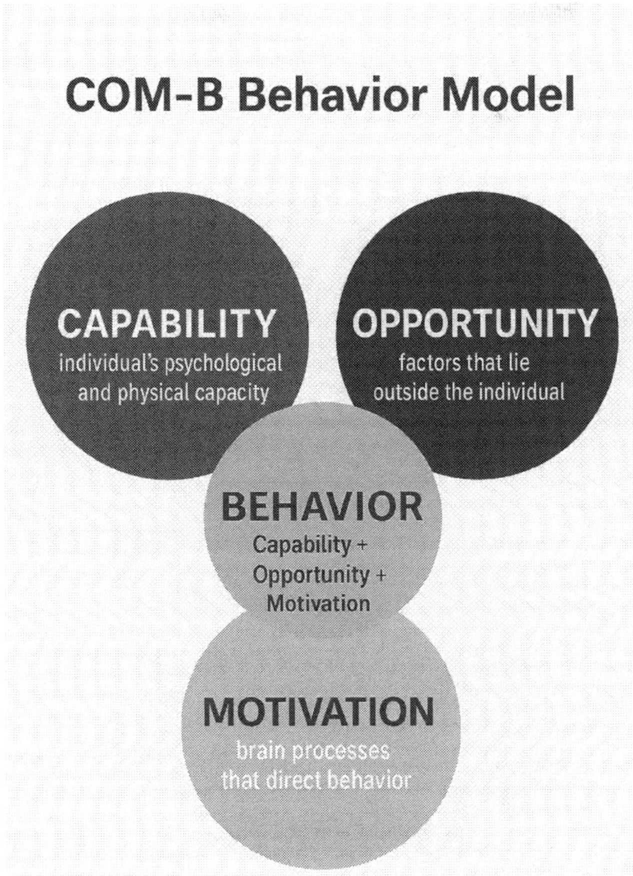


*Figure 2.1* COM-B: Capability, Opportunity, Motivation

- **Extrinsic Motivation**: Incentives, such as rewards for completing security training, reinforce positive behaviors (Michie et al., 2011).

## APPLYING THE COM-B MODEL

- **Training Programs**: Capability is addressed through structured, interactive training that builds knowledge and skills.
- **System Design**: Opportunity is enhanced by designing workflows that seamlessly integrate security measures, such as single sign-on (SSO) systems.
- **Recognition**: Motivation is fostered through positive reinforcement, such as public acknowledgment of employees who report vulnerabilities.

### Case Study: Phishing Awareness

A financial institution used the COM-B model to reduce phishing susceptibility:

- **Capability**: Training sessions improved employees' ability to identify phishing attempts.
- **Opportunity**: Default spam filters flagged suspicious emails, reducing exposure.
- **Motivation**: Gamified leaderboards rewarded teams with the highest phishing detection rates (Michie et al., 2011).

## FOGG BEHAVIOR MODEL

The Fogg Behavior Model, developed by BJ Fogg (2009), simplifies behavior change into three essential components: Motivation, Ability, and Trigger. For behavior to occur, all three must converge (Figure 2.2).

### Motivation

Motivation drives the desire to act:

- **High Motivation**: Users are more likely to engage in secure behaviors when they perceive an immediate threat, such as after a phishing attempt (Fogg, 2009).
- **Low Motivation**: If users don't understand the risks, they may ignore security protocols (Fogg, 2009).

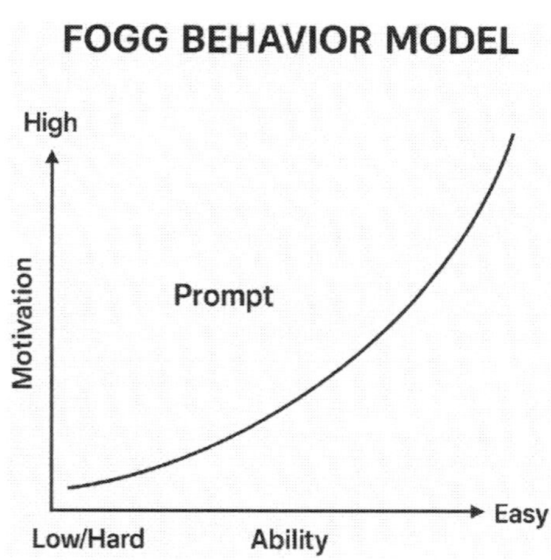


*Figure 2.2* Fogg Behavioral Model: Motivation, Ability, Prompt

### Ability

Ability refers to how easy or difficult it is to perform a behavior:

- **Low Complexity**: Simplified systems reduce the effort required to act securely.
  - **Example**: Password managers allow users to create and store strong passwords effortlessly (Fogg, 2009).

### Trigger

A trigger initiates the behavior:

- **Effective Triggers**: Notifications, pop-ups, or reminders prompt users to act.
  - **Example**: A real-time warning, such as "Your password is about to expire, click here to update," leverages timing to ensure compliance (Fogg, 2009).

### Application in Cybersecurity

Organizations can design interventions by ensuring that:

- **Motivation is high**: Communicate the risks and benefits of secure behavior (Fogg, 2009).
- **Ability is maximized**: Provide user-friendly tools (Fogg, 2009).
- **Triggers are timely**: Send reminders or alerts when action is required (Fogg, 2009).

### Case Study: Security Patch Compliance

A manufacturing firm improved patch compliance by applying the Fogg Behavior Model:

- **Motivation**: Employees were shown the financial and operational risks of outdated software.
- **Ability**: Automated systems installed patches with minimal user input.
- **Trigger**: Notifications prompted users to approve updates (Fogg, 2009).

## CHAPTER SUMMARY

This chapter provides a comprehensive examination of the interplay between behavioral science theories and decision-making processes, with a focus on cybersecurity applications. It begins by outlining foundational theories such as bounded rationality and dual-process theory, which highlight the cognitive limitations and modes of thinking that influence human behavior. These concepts are directly linked to cybersecurity challenges, such as user tendencies to rely on intuitive decision-making (System 1) or the need for deliberate analysis (System 2) in complex scenarios. By understanding these theories, cybersecurity professionals can design systems and training programs that align with natural decision-making patterns to mitigate risks effectively.

This section explores key cognitive biases, loss aversion, social proof, and the availability heuristic, and their impact on secure behavior. To counter these biases, strategies such as promoting a strong security culture, simplifying processes, and framing actions in terms of loss prevention are recommended. The discussion also incorporates findings from cognitive neuroscience and decision theory. These insights highlight how psychological and neural mechanisms influence decision-making under pressure.

Finally, practical frameworks like the COM-B and Fogg Behavior Models are presented as tools to drive behavioral change in cybersecurity settings. These models emphasize the importance of capability, opportunity, and motivation in fostering secure practices, alongside actionable strategies such as user-friendly system designs, timely triggers, and gamified incentives. This chapter concludes with a call to bridge the gap between theoretical insights and practical implementation, advocating holistic approaches that integrate human-centric design with robust technical solutions to enhance organizational resilience.

## REFERENCES


Acquisti, A., Adjerid, I., & Grossklags, J. (2017). Nudges for privacy and security: Understanding and assisting users' choices online. *ACM Computing Surveys, 50*(3), Article 44. https://doi.org/10.1145/3054926

Adebayo, A. (2022). *Contextualizing influence of organizational governance on information security risk management efficacy* (Publication Number 30243867) [D.I.T., Capella University]. ProQuest One Academic. United States.

Ajzen, I. (1991). The theory of planned behavior. *Organizational Behavior and Human Decision Processes, 50*(2), 179–211. https://doi.org/10.1016/0749-5978(91)90020-T

Alecse, C. (2022). The impact of choice overload on decision deferral in cybersecurity. *SAIS 2022 Proceedings.*

Alghamdi, N. A., & Al-Baity, H. H. (2022). Augmented analytics driven by AI: A digital transformation beyond business intelligence. *Sensors, 22*(20), 8071. https://doi.org/10.3390/s22208071

Allais, M. (1979). The foundations of a positive theory of choice involving risk and a criticism of the postulates and axioms of the American school (1952). In M. Allais & O. Hagen (Eds.), *Expected utility hypotheses and the Allais paradox* (pp. 27–145). Springer Netherlands. https://doi.org/10.1007/978-94-015-7629-1_2

Alnifie, K. M., & Kim, C. (2023). Appraising the manifestation of optimism bias and its impact on human perception of cyber security: A meta analysis. *Journal of Information Security, 14*(02), 93–110. https://doi.org/10.4236/jis.2023.142007

Andrade, R. O., Fuertes, W., Cazares, M., Ortiz-Garcés, I., & Navas, G. (2022). An exploratory study of cognitive sciences applied to cybersecurity. *Electronics*, *11*(11), 1692. https://doi.org/10.3390/electronics11111692

Arellano, J., Coello, P., Fucci, E., & Uliana, E. (2023). A better way: How to reduce bias and improve decision-making in multidisciplinary teams. In A. Samson (Ed.), *Behavioral economics guide 2023* (pp. 26–35). Behavioral Science Solutions Ltd.

Aurelien, J. (2021). Exploring effective defensive cybersecurity strategies for small businesses (Publication Number 28968351) [D.C.S., Colorado Technical University]. ProQuest dissertations & theses Global. Ann Arbor.

Bada, M., Sasse, A. M., & Nurse, J. R. C. (2019). *Cyber security awareness campaigns: Why do they fail to change behaviour?* arXiv. https://arxiv.org/abs/1901.02672

Baer, T. (2019). *Understand, manage, and prevent algorithmic bias: A guide for business users and data scientists*. Springer.

Balayn, A., Lofi, C., & Houben, G.-J. (2021). Managing bias and unfairness in data for decision support: a survey of machine learning and data engineering approaches to identify and mitigate bias and unfairness within data management and analytics systems. *The VLDB Journal, 30*(5), 739–768. https://doi.org/10.1007/s00778-021-00671-8

Belhadi, A., Kamble, S., Fosso Wamba, S., & Queiroz, M. M. (2021). Building supply-chain resilience: An artificial intelligence-based technique and decision-making framework. *International Journal of Production Research, 60*(14), 4487–4507. https://doi.org/10.1080/00207543.2021.1950935

Berthet, V. (2021). The impact of cognitive biases on professionals' decision-making: A review of four occupational areas. *Frontiers in Psychology, 12,* 802439. https://doi.org/10.3389/fpsyg.2021.802439

Binns, R. (2022). Human judgment in algorithmic loops: Individual justice and automated decision-making. *Regulation & Governance, 16*(1), 197–211. https://doi.org/10.1111/rego.12358

Bonneau, J., Herley, C., Van Oorschot, P. C., & Stajano, F. (2012). The quest to replace passwords: A framework for comparative evaluation of web authentication schemes. In *2012 IEEE Symposium on Security and Privacy* (pp. 553–567). IEEE. https://doi.org/10.1109/SP.2012.44

Booch, G., Fabiano, F., Horesh, L., Kate, K., Lenchner, J., Linck, N., Loreggia, A., Murgesan, K., Mattei, N., Rossi, F., & Srivastava, B. (2021). Thinking fast and slow in AI. *Proceedings of the AAAI Conference on Artificial Intelligence, 35*(17), 15042–15046. https://doi.org/10.1609/aaai.v35i17.17765

Brandtner, P. (2023). Predictive analytics and intelligent decision support systems in supply chain risk management, research directions for future studies. In *Proceedings of Seventh International Congress on Information and Communication Technology* (pp. 549–558). London. https://doi.org/10.1007/978-981-19-2394-4_50

Burton, J. W., Stein, M. K., & Jensen, T. B. (2019). A systematic review of algorithm aversion in augmented decision making. *Journal of Behavioral Decision Making, 33*(2), 220–239. https://doi.org/10.1002/bdm.2155

Cains, M. G., Flora, L., Taber, D., King, Z., & Henshel, D. S. (2022). Defining cyber security and cyber security risk within a multidisciplinary context using expert elicitation. *Risk Analysis, 42*(8), 1643–1669. https://doi.org/10.1111/risa.13687

Carmichael, D. G. (2020). Bias and decision making – An overview systems explanation. *Civil Engineering and Environmental Systems, 37*(1–2), 48–61. https://doi.org/10.1080/10286608.2020.1744133

Ceric, A., & Holland, P. (2019). The role of cognitive biases in anticipating and responding to cyberattacks. *Information Technology & People, 32*(1), 171–188. https://doi.org/10.1108/itp-11-2017-0390

Chajut, E., & Algom, D. (2003). Selective attention improves under stress: Implications for theories of social cognition. *Journal of Personality and Social Psychology, 85*(2), 231–248. https://doi.org/10.1037/0022-3514.85.2.231

Chambers, M. D. (2022). Exploring the standards cybersecurity practitioners need to comply with multinational cybersecurity requirements (Publication Number 29324922) [D.C.S., Colorado Technical University]. ProQuest dissertations & theses Global. United States, Colorado.

Chowdhury, N. H., Adam, M. T. P., & Skinner, G. (2019). The impact of time pressure on cybersecurity behaviour: A systematic literature review. *Behaviour & Information Technology, 38*(12), 1290–1308. https://doi.org/10.1080/0144929x.2019.1583769

Cialdini, R. B. (2009). *Influence: Science and practice* (Vol. 4, pp. 51–96). Pearson Education.

Cox, L. A. (2023). Natural, artificial, and social intelligence for decision-making. In *AI-ML for decision and risk analysis* (pp. 65–101). https://doi.org/10.1007/978-3-031-32013-2_3

Creel, K., & Hellman, D. (2022). The algorithmic leviathan: Arbitrariness, fairness, and opportunity in algorithmic decision-making systems. *Canadian Journal of Philosophy, 52*(1), 26–43. https://doi.org/10.1017/can.2022.3

Davies, D. R., Matthews, G., Stammers, R. B., & Westerman, S. J. (2000). *Human performance: Cognition, stress and individual differences* (1st ed.). Psychology Press. https://doi.org/10.4324/9781315812809

Dekker, S. (2014). *The field guide to understanding 'human error'* (3rd ed.). CRC Press. https://doi.org/10.1201/9781317031833

Deniz, N. (2020). Cognitive biases in MCDM methods: An embedded filter proposal through sustainable supplier selection problem. *Journal of Enterprise Information Management, 33*(5), 947–963. https://doi.org/10.1108/jeim-09-2019-0285

Dror, I. E. (2020). Cognitive and human factors in expert decision making: Six fallacies and the eight sources of bias. *Analytical Chemistry, 92*(12), 7998–8004. https://doi.org/10.1021/acs.analchem.0c00704

Edmondson, A. C. (2019). *The fearless organization: Creating psychological safety in the workplace for learning, innovation, and growth*. Wiley.

Ellsberg, D. (1961). Risk, ambiguity, and the savage axioms. *The Quarterly Journal of Economics, 75*(4), 643–669. https://doi.org/10.2307/1884324

Endsley, M. R., & Kiris, E. O. (1995). The out-of-the-loop performance problem and level of control in automation. *Human Factors, 37*(2), 381–394. https://doi.org/10.1518/001872095779064555

Evans, J. S. B. T., & Stanovich, K. E. (2013). Dual-process theories of higher cognition: Advancing the debate. *Perspectives on Psychological Science, 8*(3), 223–241. https://doi.org/10.1177/1745691612460685

Fischhoff, B. (2003). Hindsight ≠ foresight: The effect of outcome knowledge on judgment under uncertainty. *Quality & Safety in Health Care, 12*(4), 304–311. https://doi.org/10.1136/qhc.12.4.304

Fischhoff, B., & Broomell, S. B. (2020). Judgment and decision making. *Annual Review of Psychology, 71*, 331–355. https://doi.org/10.1146/annurev-psych-010419-050747

Fleischman, G. M., Valentine, S. R., Curtis, M. B., & Mohapatra, P. S. (2023). The influence of ethical beliefs and attitudes, norms, and prior outcomes on cybersecurity investment decisions. *Business & Society, 62*(3), 488–529. https://doi.org/10.1177/00076503221110156

Fogg, B. J. (2009). A behavior model for persuasive design. In *Proceedings of the 4th International Conference on Persuasive Technology* (pp. 1–7). ACM. https://doi.org/10.1145/1541948.1541999

Ganin, A. A., Quach, P., Panwar, M., Collier, Z. A., Keisler, J. M., Marchese, D., & Linkov, I. (2020). Multicriteria decision framework for cybersecurity risk assessment and management. *Risk Analysis, 40*(1), 183–199. https://doi.org/10.1111/risa.12891

Ganye, D., & Smith, K. (2025). Examining the effects of cognitive load on information systems security policy compliance. *Internet Research, 35*(1), 380–418. https://doi.org/10.1108/INTR-04-2023-0329

Giudici, P., & Raffinetti, E. (2021). Explainable AI methods in cyber risk management. *Quality and Reliability Engineering International, 38*(3), 1318–1326. https://doi.org/10.1002/qre.2939

Goel, R., Kumar, A., & Haddow, J. (2020). PRISM: A strategic decision framework for cybersecurity risk assessment. *Information & Computer Security, 28*(4), 591–625. https://doi.org/10.1108/ics-11-2018-0131

Greene, J. D., & Paxton, J. M. (2009). Patterns of neural activity associated with honest and dishonest moral decisions. *Proceedings of the National Academy of Sciences, 106*(30), 12506–12511. https://doi.org/10.1073/pnas.0900152106

Groenendaal, J., Helsloot, I., & Reuter, C. (2022). Towards more insight into cyber incident response decision making and its implications for cyber crisis management. In R. Grace & H. Baharmand (Eds.), *ISCRAM 2022 Conference Proceedings – 19th International Conference on Information Systems for Crisis Response and Management* (pp. 1025–1036). ISCRAM Association.

Herath, T., & Rao, H. R. (2009). Encouraging information security behaviors in organizations: Role of penalties, pressures and perceived effectiveness. *Decision Support Systems, 47*(2), 154–165. https://doi.org/10.1016/j.dss.2009.02.005

Herley, C. (2009). So long, and no thanks for the externalities: The rational rejection of security advice by users. In *Proceedings of the 2009 Workshop on New Security Paradigms* (pp. 133–144). ACM. https://doi.org/10.1145/1719030.1719050

Hiruta, S., Ikeda, S., Shima, S., & Takakura, H. (2019). IDS alert priority determination based on traffic behavior. In N. Attrapadung & T. Yagi (Eds.), *Advances in Information and Computer Security. IWSEC 2019. Lecture Notes in Computer Science* (Vol. 11689, pp. 189–206). Springer, Cham. https://doi.org/10.1007/978-3-030-26834-3_11

Hofmann, A. (2022). Expected utility, prospect theory, and the Allais paradox: Why reference points are important. In *The ten commandments of risk leadership: A behavioral guide on strategic risk management* (pp. 23–38). Springer International Publishing. https://doi.org/10.1007/978-3-030-88797-1_3

Hutchins, E. M., Cloppert, M. J., & Amin, R. M. (2011). Intelligence-driven computer network defense informed by analysis of adversary campaigns and intrusion kill chains. *Leading Issues in Information Warfare & Security Research, 1*(1), 80–106.

Ifinedo, P. (2012). Understanding information systems security policy compliance: An integration of the theory of planned behavior and the protection motivation theory. *Computers & Security, 31*(1), 83–95. https://doi.org/10.1016/j.cose.2011.10.007

Jalali, M. S., Siegel, M., & Madnick, S. (2019). Decision-making and biases in cybersecurity capability development: Evidence from a simulation game experiment. *The Journal of Strategic Information Systems, 28*(1), 66–82. https://doi.org/10.1016/j.jsis.2018.09.003

Jarjoui, S., & Murimi, R. (2021). A framework for enterprise cybersecurity risk management. In K. Daimi & C. Peoples (Eds.), *Advances in cybersecurity management* (pp. 139–161). Springer, Cham. https://doi.org/10.1007/978-3-030-71381-2_8

Johnson, C., Gutzwiller, R., Ferguson-Walter, K., & Fugate, S. (2020). A cyber-relevant table of decision-making biases and their definitions. In *Proceedings of the Human Factors and Ergonomics Society Annual Meeting.*

Kahneman, D. (2011). *Thinking, fast and slow*. Farrar, Straus and Giroux.

Kahneman, D., & Frederick, S. (2005). A model of heuristic judgment. In K. Holyoak & B. Morrison (Eds.), *The Cambridge handbook of thinking and reasoning* (pp. 267–293). Cambridge University Press.

Kahneman, D., Lovallo, D., & Sibony, O. (2019). A structured approach to strategic decisions. *MIT Sloan Management Review, 60*(3), 67–73.

Kahneman, D., Sibony, O., & Sunstein, C. R. (2021). *Noise: A flaw in human judgment*. Little, Brown.

Ketchen, D. J., & Craighead, C. W. (2024). Cognitive biases as impediments to enhancing supply chain entrepreneurial embeddedness. *Journal of Business Logistics, 45*, e12307. https://doi.org/10.1111/jbl.12307

Khrennikov, A. Y. (2023). Classical expected utility theory and its paradoxes. In *Open quantum systems in biology, cognitive and social sciences* (pp. 319–325). Springer International Publishing. https://doi.org/10.1007/978-3-031-29024-4_19

Khusainov, P., Toliupa, S., Bakanov, V., & Shtanenko, S. (2022). Substantial formulation of the task of improving the information model of decision-making in the prompt (crisis) response to cyber incidents. In *2022 IEEE 16th International Conference on Advanced Trends in Radioelectronics, Telecommunications and Computer Engineering (TCSET)* (pp. 287–290). IEEE. https://doi.org/10.1109/TCSET55632.2022.9766994

Klein, N., & O'Brien, E. (2018). People use less information than they think to make up their minds. *Proceedings of the National Academy of Sciences, 115*(52), 13222–13227. https://doi.org/10.1073/pnas.1805327115

Knauft, K., Waldron, A., Mathur, M., Deldin, P., & Turel, O. (2021). Perceived chronic stress influences the effect of acute stress on cognitive flexibility. *Scientific Reports, 11*, Article 23629. https://doi.org/10.1038/s41598-021-03101-5

Korteling, J. E., & Toet, A. (2022). Cognitive biases. In S. Della Sala (Ed.), *Encyclopedia of behavioral neuroscience, 2nd edition* (Second Edition) (pp. 610–619). Elsevier. https://doi.org/10.1016/B978-0-12-809324-5.24105-9

Korteling, J. E. H., Paradies, G. L., & Sassen-van Meer, J. P. (2023). Cognitive bias and how to improve sustainable decision-making. *Frontiers in Psychology, 14*, 1129835. https://doi.org/10.3389/fpsyg.2023.1129835

**APA Style**

Lee, I., & Mangalaraj, G. (2022). Big data analytics in supply chain management: A systematic literature review and research directions. *Big Data and Cognitive Computing*, 6(1), 17. https://doi.org/10.3390/bdcc6010017

Levy, M. (2022). An evolutionary explanation of the Allais paradox. *Journal of Evolutionary Economics, 32*(5), 1545–1574. https://doi.org/10.1007/s00191-022-00783-6

Li, X. (2023). New advances in social cognitive neuroscience. *Scientific and Social Research, 5*(8), 19–24. https://doi.org/10.26689/ssr.v5i8.5279

Lundberg, J. (2015). Situation awareness systems, states and processes: A holistic framework. *Theoretical Issues in Ergonomics Science*, 16(5), 447–473. https://doi.org/10.1080/1463922X.2015.1008601

Maalem Lahcen, R. A., Caulkins, B., Mohapatra, R., & Kumar, M. (2020). Review and insight on the behavioral aspects of cybersecurity. *Cybersecurity, 3*(1). https://doi.org/10.1186/s42400-020-00050-w

Maheshwari, S., Gautam, P., & Jaggi, C. K. (2020). Role of big data analytics in supply chain management: Current trends and future perspectives. *International Journal of Production Research, 59*(6), 1875–1900. https://doi.org/10.1080/00207543.2020.1793011

Marchewka, E. J., Jr. (2022). Reducing cybersecurity risk information asymmetry phenomenon: A prescriptive approach to improving cybersecurity risk perception (Publication Number 28971250) [D.B.A., California Southern University]. ProQuest One Academic. Ann Arbor.

M'Manga, A. (2020). Designing for cyber security risk-based decision making (Publication Number Dissertation/Thesis). ProQuest dissertations publishing.

Mäses, S., Maennel, K., Toussaint, M., & Rosa, V. (2021). Success factors for designing a cybersecurity exercise on the example of incident response. *2021 IEEE European symposium on security and privacy workshops (EuroS&PW)* (pp. 259–268). IEEE. https://doi.org/10.1109/EuroSPW54576.2021.00033

Maslach, C., & Leiter, M. P. (2016). Understanding the burnout experience: Recent research and its implications for psychiatry. *World Psychiatry*, 15, 103–111. https://doi.org/10.1002/wps.20311

Matthews, G., & Campbell, S. E. (1998). Task-induced stress and individual differences in coping. *Proceedings of the Human Factors and Ergonomics Society Annual Meeting*, 42(11), 821–825. https://doi.org/10.1177/154193129804201111

McNeese, M. D., & Hall, D. L. (2017). The cognitive sciences of cyber-security: A framework for advancing socio-cyber systems. In P. Liu, S. Jajodia & C. Wang (Eds.), *Theory and models for cyber situation awareness* (Vol. 10030, pp. 127–145). Springer. https://doi.org/10.1007/978-3-319-61152-5_7

Michie, S., van Stralen, M. M., & West, R. (2011). The behaviour change wheel: A new method for characterising and designing behaviour change interventions. *Implementation Science*, 6(1), Article 42. https://doi.org/10.1186/1748-5908-6-42

Miles, L. A. (2021). An analysis of the combined effects of advanced information technologies and enterprise risk management on organizational performance (Publication Number 28549351) [D.B.A., Drexel University]. ProQuest One Academic. Ann Arbor.

Milkman, K. L., Chugh, D., & Bazerman, M. H. (2009). How can decision making be improved? *Perspectives on Psychological Science*, 4(4), 379–383. https://doi.org/10.1111/j.1745-6924.2009.01142.x

Mitchell, J. D. (2022). Behavioral supply chain management: Exploring interventions for supply chain managers (Publication Number 29998036) [D.M., Colorado Technical University]. ProQuest One Academic. United States.

Moustafa, A. A., Bello, A., & Maurushat, A. (2021). The role of user behaviour in improving cyber security management. *Frontiers in Psychology, 12,* 561011. https://doi.org/10.3389/fpsyg.2021.561011

Naik, B., Mehta, A., Yagnik, H., & Shah, M. (2021). The impacts of artificial intelligence techniques in augmentation of cybersecurity: A comprehensive review. *Complex & Intelligent Systems, 8*(2), 1763–1780. https://doi.org/10.1007/s40747-021-00494-8

Nobles, C. (2022). Stress, burnout, and security fatigue in cybersecurity: A human factors problem. *HOLISTICA – Journal of Business and Public Administration, 13*(1), 49–72. https://doi.org/10.2478/hjbpa-2022-0003

Otegui, D. (2024). Understanding cognitive processes in high-stakes environments. In *Business growth in times of instability: Empowering private companies through disaster risk reduction* (pp. 43–63). Springer. https://doi.org/10.1007/978-3-031-69370-0_3

Panda, S. (2022). Optimal strategies for cyber security decision-making [Doctoral Dissertation, University of Surrey]. https://openresearch.surrey.ac.uk/esploro/outputs/doctoral/Optimal-Strategies-for-Cyber-Security-Decision-Making/99641066402346

Panigutti, C., Beretta, A., Giannotti, F., & Pedreschi, D. (2022). Understanding the impact of explanations on advice-taking: A user study for AI-based clinical decision support systems. In *Proceedings of the 2022 CHI Conference on Human Factors in Computing Systems*, New Orleans, LA, USA. https://doi.org/10.1145/3491102.3502104

Patel, B., Bhagavanbhai, P. K., & Dhameliya, N. (2024). Revolutionizing cybersecurity with AI: Predictive threat intelligence and automated response systems. *Darpan International Research Analysis, 12*(4), 1–5. https://doi.org/10.36676/dira.v12.i4.126

Perry, O., Jaffe, E., Goldberg, A., & Bitan, Y. (2024). Incident commander decision making: Quantitative evaluation of instantaneous and considered decisions. *Applied Ergonomics, 114*, 104139. https://doi.org/10.1016/j.apergo.2023.104139

Pignatiello, G. A., Martin, R. J., & Hickman Jr, R. L. (2020). Decision fatigue: A conceptual analysis. *Journal of Health Psychology, 25*(1), 123–135.

Ramakrishnan, S., & Chittibala, D. R. (2024). Enhancing cyber resilience: Convergence of SIEM, SOAR, and AI in 2024. *International Journal of Computing and Engineering*, *5*(2), 36–44. https://doi.org/10.47941/ijce.1754

Raywood-Burke, G. (2023). *Cognitive load and subjective time pressure: How contextual factors impact the quality of cyber-security decision making* (Doctoral dissertation, Cardiff University).

Rios Insua, D., Couce-Vieira, A., Rubio, J. A., Pieters, W., Labunets, K., & D, G. R. (2021). An adversarial risk analysis framework for cybersecurity. *Risk Analysis, 41*(1), 16–36. https://doi.org/10.1111/risa.13331

Selye, H. (1976). *The stress of life* (Revised ed.). McGraw-Hill.

Serra, D. (2021). Decision-making: From neuroscience to neuroeconomics, an overview. *Theory and Decision, 91*(1), 1–80. https://doi.org/10.1007/s11238-021-09830-3

Sharp, P. B., Fradkin, I., & Eldar, E. (2022). Hierarchical inference as a source of human biases. *Cognitive, Affective, & Behavioral Neuroscience*, *23*, 476–490. https://doi.org/10.3758/s13415-022-01020-0

Simon, H. A. (1955). A behavioral model of rational choice. *The Quarterly Journal of Economics, 69*(1), 99–118. https://doi.org/10.2307/1884852

Singh, T., Johnston, A. C., D'Arcy, J., & Harms, P. D. (2023). Stress in the cybersecurity profession: A systematic review of related literature and opportunities for future research. *Organizational Cybersecurity Journal: Practice, Process and People*, *3*(2), 100–126. https://doi.org/10.1108/ocj-06-2022-0012

Thaler, R. H., & Sunstein, C. R. (2008). *Nudge: Improving decisions about health, wealth, and happiness*. Yale University Press.

Toorajipour, R., Sohrabpour, V., Nazarpour, A., Oghazi, P., & Fischl, M. (2021). Artificial intelligence in supply chain management: A systematic literature review. *Journal of Business Research, 122,* 502–517. https://doi.org/10.1016/j.jbusres.2020.09.009

Tversky, A., & Kahneman, D. (1974). Judgment under uncertainty: Heuristics and biases. *Science, 185*(4157), 1124–1131. https://doi.org/10.1126/science.185.4157.1124

Tversky, A., & Kahneman, D. (1991). Loss aversion in riskless choice: A reference-dependent model. *The Quarterly Journal of Economics, 106*(4), 1039–1061. https://doi.org/10.2307/2937956

von Neumann, J., & Morgenstern, O. (1944). *Theory of games and economic behavior: 60th anniversary commemorative edition*. Princeton University Press. https://books.google.com/books?id=jCN5aNJ-n-0C

Wash, R. (2010). Folk models of home computer security. In *Proceedings of the Sixth Symposium on Usable Privacy and Security (SOUPS)* (pp. 1–16). ACM. https://doi.org/10.1145/1837110.1837125

West, R. (2008). The psychology of security. *Communications of the ACM, 51*(4), 34–40. https://doi.org/10.1145/1330311.1330320

White, C. A. (2023). Mixed method exploration of cybersecurity executive decisions and cognitive bias (Publication Number Dissertation/Thesis). ProQuest dissertations publishing.

Yerkes, R. M., & Dodson, J. D. (1908). The relation of strength of stimulus to rapidity of habit-formation. *Journal of Comparative Neurology and Psychology, 18*(5), 459–482. https://doi.org/10.1002/cne.920180503

Yoon, H., Scopelliti, I., & Morewedge, C. K. (2021). Decision making can be improved through observational learning. *Organizational Behavior and Human Decision Processes, 162,* 155–188. https://doi.org/10.1016/j.obhdp.2020.10.011

Younas, S., & Khanum, S. (2024). Examining the role of stress and team support in decision making under uncertainty and time pressure. *MDM Policy & Practice, 9*(2). https://doi.org/10.1177/23814683241273575

Zhang, M., Nazir, M. S., Farooqi, R., & Ishfaq, M. (2022). Moderating role of information asymmetry between cognitive biases and investment decisions: A mediating effect of risk perception. *Frontiers in Psychology, 13,* 828956. https://doi.org/10.3389/fpsyg.2022.828956

Chapter 3

# Human Factors in Cybersecurity

## LEARNING OBJECTIVES

- Understand the role human behavior plays in creating cybersecurity risks, including how psychological tendencies, habits, and errors make individuals and organizations susceptible to attacks.
- Gain insights into how attackers manipulate human trust, biases, and emotions through various social engineering tactics and explore effective strategies to defend against such threats.
- Utilize behavioral analysis techniques to identify patterns of risky behavior among users and leverage this information to design more effective and adaptive security protocols.

## DEFINITION OF HUMAN FACTORS

Human factors in cybersecurity refer to the psychological, social, and behavioral elements that influence how cybersecurity professionals design, implement, and manage security systems (Hakimi et al., 2024). Unlike end-user vulnerabilities, this concept focuses on the cognitive and organizational behaviors of professionals tasked with securing systems. These factors encompass decision-making under stress, cognitive biases in risk assessments, teamwork dynamics, and how professionals interact with technology and processes in high-stakes environments.

Human factors in cybersecurity represent a critical lens for understanding how the behaviors, psychology, and social dynamics of cybersecurity professionals shape the security landscape (Pollini et al., 2022). Unlike the vulnerabilities often discussed in the context of end users, human factors for cybersecurity professionals focus on the internal processes that influence how systems are secured, managed, and defended. This perspective acknowledges that even highly skilled experts are not immune to the limitations and challenges of human cognition, decision-making, and collaboration, particularly in high-pressure scenarios.

 DOI: 10.1201/9781003606345-3

One of the most significant human factors is decision-making under stress. Cybersecurity professionals often operate in environments where rapid responses are necessary to mitigate threats, such as during a ransomware attack or a data breach. Stress can impair cognitive function, leading to errors in judgment, overlooked vulnerabilities, or the failure to implement an appropriate incident response strategy (Montañez et al., 2020). Understanding how professionals react under pressure can guide the development of training programs and processes that enhance decision-making during critical moments.

Cognitive biases also play a prominent role in shaping the work of cybersecurity professionals. Biases such as overconfidence, confirmation bias, and anchoring can lead to flawed risk assessments or the misprioritization of threats (Darley, 2023). For example, overconfidence in a particular technology or strategy may result in a false sense of security, leaving certain vulnerabilities unaddressed. Addressing these biases through structured frameworks, continuous education, and diverse team perspectives can improve the accuracy of risk assessments and strategic planning.

Teamwork dynamics are another essential element of human factors in cybersecurity. Effective cybersecurity is rarely a solo endeavor and often requires collaboration across multidisciplinary teams. Poor communication, lack of trust, or conflicting priorities within a team can undermine security efforts (Rohan et al., 2021). Emphasizing strong interpersonal skills, fostering a culture of collaboration, and implementing clear communication protocols are critical to ensuring teams work cohesively, particularly in incident response scenarios where time and coordination are paramount.

The interaction between cybersecurity professionals and technology is a key area where human factors come into play. While technical skills are essential, how professionals perceive, understand, and utilize tools and systems can significantly impact their effectiveness (Axon et al., 2021). Complex or poorly designed interfaces may lead to misconfigurations or missed alerts, while streamlined, intuitive technologies can enhance efficiency and reduce the likelihood of human error. Human-centric design principles should therefore be a cornerstone of technology development in cybersecurity.

Organizational culture also exerts a profound influence on human factors in cybersecurity. A culture that prioritizes innovation and open dialogue can encourage professionals to identify and address weaknesses proactively (Georgiadou et al., 2020). Conversely, a blame-oriented culture may stifle reporting of mistakes or vulnerabilities, allowing risks to persist (Renaud et al., 2021). Training and professional development further intersect with human factors. The rapidly evolving threat landscape requires cybersecurity professionals to constantly update their knowledge and skills (Kumar, 2023). However, training programs that fail to address the psychological and behavioral aspects of cybersecurity work, such as stress management or decision-making under uncertainty, may not fully equip professionals to handle real-world challenges (Singh & Cheema, 2024). Effective training should incorporate both technical and human elements to build resilience and adaptability.

Lastly, the ethical dimensions of human factors should not be overlooked. Cybersecurity professionals frequently face ethical dilemmas, such as balancing privacy with security or deciding how much information to share during a breach (Fenech et al., 2024). How these decisions are approached is influenced by personal values, organizational pressures, and societal expectations. Encouraging ethical decision-making through robust policies, clear guidelines, and open discussions can help professionals navigate these challenges effectively (Pollini et al., 2022).

## HUMAN BEHAVIOR AS A VULNERABILITY

Human behavior remains one of the most significant yet underestimated vulnerabilities in cybersecurity. While organizations invest heavily in advanced technologies and fortified systems, the human element often becomes the weak link that adversaries exploit (Pollini et al., 2022). Cybersecurity professionals, like end users, are not immune to the same behavioral tendencies that lead to mistakes, gaps in judgment, or inadvertent risks. Traits such as forgetfulness, overconfidence, complacency, and lack of cybersecurity awareness among professionals can amplify these vulnerabilities, even in environments designed with security as a top priority.

Human errors are among the most common ways vulnerabilities manifest in organizational security (Mimecast, 2024). Even experienced cybersecurity professionals can unintentionally make errors such as misconfiguring firewalls, leaving critical systems exposed, or overlooking essential updates. Phishing emails, for example, are not just an issue for end users; sophisticated spear-phishing attacks target cybersecurity professionals by mimicking trusted partners or urgent scenarios, leading to inadvertent credential sharing or malware introduction. Weak or reused passwords, a frequent oversight even among professionals, can further exacerbate risks, especially when critical systems are involved. Such errors, though often small, can have cascading effects on organizational security.

Cognitive biases play a pivotal role in creating vulnerabilities among cybersecurity professionals, often leading to misjudgments that increase an organization's exposure to risk (Maalem Lahcen et al., 2020). These biases influence decision-making, risk perception, and overall security posture, sometimes in ways that are difficult to recognize. When left unchecked, they can result in overconfidence, blind spots, and a failure to anticipate or respond effectively to evolving threats. Understanding these biases is essential for cybersecurity professionals to make more informed and balanced decisions in an increasingly complex threat landscape.

One such bias is overreliance on technology, where professionals assume that automated systems, artificial intelligence (AI), or security tools will catch every anomaly or threat (Papatsaroucha et al., 2021). This misplaced trust can result in complacency, reducing proactive threat-hunting efforts or human oversight that might detect sophisticated attacks designed to bypass automated defenses. While security technologies are essential, they are not infallible, and cybercriminals constantly develop methods to evade detection. Without human vigilance and critical analysis, organizations risk assuming that security tools alone are sufficient to protect against cyber threats.

A related cognitive bias, optimism bias, fosters the belief that "it won't happen to us," leading professionals to underestimate risks or dismiss early warning signs of potential breaches (Papatsaroucha et al., 2021). This mindset can cause organizations to deprioritize cybersecurity investments, leaving them vulnerable to threats they assumed were unlikely to materialize. It also contributes to a reactive rather than proactive security posture, where action is taken only after an incident has occurred. Overcoming optimism bias requires shifting to a mindset that acknowledges potential risks and implements preventive measures before an attack takes place.

Additionally, groupthink and confirmation bias can severely hinder cybersecurity teams by reinforcing existing assumptions without critically examining alternative perspectives or emerging threats (Papatsaroucha et al., 2021). When teams operate in echo chambers, dissenting viewpoints are often overlooked, and potential vulnerabilities may go unaddressed. This dynamic can lead to flawed risk assessments, where teams only seek out evidence that supports their current security strategies while ignoring potential weaknesses. Encouraging open discussions, fostering diverse perspectives, and challenging assumptions are crucial in mitigating these biases within cybersecurity teams.

Beyond these well-known biases, several lesser-discussed cognitive distortions contribute significantly to cybersecurity vulnerabilities (Kahneman, 2011; Tversky & Kahneman, 1974). These biases often influence how professionals assess risk, respond to security measures, and interact with organizational policies (Furnell & Clarke, 2012). By understanding the psychological factors that shape decision-making, cybersecurity teams can build more resilient strategies and reduce their susceptibility to cognitive distortions (Burda et al., 2024).

Below are three additional biases that have profound implications for cybersecurity practices.

1. **The Peltzman Effect**—This bias suggests that individuals and organizations may engage in riskier behavior when they believe protective measures are in place (Peltzman, 1975). In cybersecurity, the Peltzman Effect manifests when professionals assume that having robust security frameworks, such as firewalls, endpoint detection, or multifactor

authentication (MFA), means they can afford to relax other security practices (West, 2008). For example, employees might engage in riskier behaviors, such as using weak passwords or clicking on suspicious links, because they assume security tools will mitigate any negative consequences (Beautement et al., 2016). This overconfidence in protective mechanisms can paradoxically increase risk rather than reduce it, as attackers exploit weaknesses that arise from human complacency (Hadlington, 2017). Cybersecurity leaders must counteract this effect by reinforcing that security tools are only part of a layered defense strategy, and individual vigilance remains essential (Herley, 2009).

2. **Consensus Bias**—Also known as the false consensus effect, this bias leads individuals to believe that others share their thoughts, beliefs, or behaviors more than they actually do (Ross et al., 1977). In a cybersecurity context, professionals may assume that their colleagues, employees, or third-party vendors possess the same level of security awareness and diligence (Workman et al., 2008). This false assumption can lead to critical gaps in security policies, such as failing to enforce stringent access controls, assuming everyone understands phishing threats, or neglecting proper cybersecurity training for non-technical staff (Alsharif et al., 2022). The result is an uneven security culture where assumptions about shared responsibility create vulnerabilities (Parsons et al., 2014). Organizations must address this bias by implementing consistent training programs, conducting periodic security awareness assessments, and fostering a culture of accountability in cybersecurity practices (Siponen et al., 2014).
3. **The Ostrich Effect**—This cognitive bias refers to the tendency to avoid negative information, particularly when it relates to potential threats or challenges (Karlsson et al., 2009). Cybersecurity professionals may subconsciously ignore or downplay warning signs of a breach, misconfigurations, or compliance violations because acknowledging them would require additional effort, resources, or difficult conversations (D'Arcy et al., 2014). This effect can be particularly dangerous when organizations deprioritize risk assessments or delay addressing security gaps due to budget constraints, fear of reputational damage, or the complexity of remediation (Anderson & Agarwal, 2010). Attackers exploit such avoidance behaviors, knowing that security flaws often persist when organizations hesitate to confront them head-on (Pfleeger & Caputo, 2012). To counteract the Ostrich Effect, organizations must establish clear escalation processes, encourage proactive risk reporting, and cultivate a culture where identifying and addressing security issues is rewarded rather than avoided.

These cognitive biases, individually and collectively, can cloud judgment, impair situational awareness, and hinder effective decision-making in cybersecurity (Burda et al., 2024). Their impact is often subtle, making it difficult for professionals to recognize when they are falling victim to biased thinking (Kahneman, 2011). However, by fostering awareness, promoting critical thinking, and integrating structured decision-making frameworks, cybersecurity teams can reduce the influence of these biases (Beautement et al., 2016). Encouraging dissenting viewpoints, implementing rigorous security protocols, and promoting transparency in security discussions can help counteract these biases, ultimately strengthening an organization's resilience against emerging threats (Herley, 2009).

Professionals' habits and inconsistencies in their workflows often contribute to security gaps, largely due to the influence of cognitive heuristics and System 1 thinking (Kahneman, 2011). Heuristics, mental shortcuts that help individuals make quick decisions, are essential for efficiency but can lead to oversights when applied to security processes (Tversky & Kahneman, 1974). System 1 thinking, which operates automatically and intuitively, often drives professionals to default to past behaviors without deliberate analysis (West, 2008). This fast, effortless thinking can cause individuals to overlook critical security steps, assuming that what has worked before will continue to be safe, even when circumstances have changed (Beautement et al., 2016).

Repetitive tasks can lead to complacency, reinforcing behaviors that prioritize convenience over security, as System 1 thinking encourages reliance on patterns and habits rather than critical evaluation (Workman et al., 2008). For example, if an employee frequently encounters MFA prompts and has never experienced an account compromise, they may develop an availability heuristic, believing that skipping MFA does not result in harm because they have never personally observed a breach (Parsons et al., 2014). This type of cognitive bias can lead to a false sense of security, where employees view protective measures as unnecessary hindrances rather than essential safeguards (Hadlington, 2017). Over time, this habitual bypassing of security controls can normalize risky behavior across the organization, creating a culture where convenience takes precedence over security (D'Arcy et al., 2014).

Similarly, reliance on "workarounds" to circumvent cumbersome security protocols is often driven by cognitive ease, a principle of System 1 thinking where individuals favor actions that require less effort (Kahneman, 2011). When employees face complex or inconvenient security measures, they may unconsciously search for a more efficient alternative, even if it compromises security (Beautement et al., 2016). For instance, if a secure file transfer process is slow or difficult to navigate, users might opt to email sensitive documents to personal accounts, unknowingly exposing data to potential leaks (Herley, 2009). These quick, instinctual decisions, shaped by heuristics such as the efficiency bias or status quo bias, make security risks more pervasive and difficult to detect (Pfleeger & Caputo, 2012).

These behaviors, while often well intentioned, ultimately undermine an organization's broader security posture by embedding insecure practices into daily routines (Chowdhury et al., 2020). Once security shortcuts become habitual, System 1 thinking reinforces their use, reducing the likelihood of critical reflection on potential risks (Kahneman, 2011). Additionally, confirmation bias may lead professionals to disregard warnings about security gaps, as they rely on past experiences where breaches did not occur despite risky behavior (Tversky & Kahneman, 1974). To counteract these tendencies, organizations must implement strategies that engage System 2 thinking, the slower, more analytical mode of decision-making, by fostering awareness, promoting security-conscious habits, and designing policies that align security with efficiency rather than opposition (West, 2008).

## SOCIAL ENGINEERING EXPLAINED

World renown social engineer famously began his book *The Art of Deception* with the statement that

> Social Engineering uses influence and persuasion to deceive people by convincing them that the social engineer is someone he is not, or by manipulation. As a result, the social engineer is able to take advantage of people to obtain information with or without the use of technology.
>
> *(Mitnick & Simon, 2011)*

Social engineering remains one of the most effective tools for cybercriminals, as it exploits psychological manipulation rather than technical vulnerabilities (Burda et al., 2024). These attacks capitalize on the human inclination to trust, obey authority, and act quickly in response to perceived urgency. Unlike technical exploits that require breaching firewalls or bypassing encryption, social engineering preys on the human element, often bypassing robust technical defenses.

A key psychological factor that makes social engineering so effective is the illusion of experience, also known as experience bias (Montañez et al., 2020). This cognitive bias leads individuals to overestimate their ability to detect deception based on past experiences, creating a false sense of security. Many professionals believe that their familiarity with phishing attempts, fraudulent calls, or other manipulative tactics makes them less susceptible to future attacks (Wang et al., 2016). However, attackers continuously refine their methods, leveraging evolving tactics that exploit assumptions and blind spots (Bundala, 2024). This overconfidence can lead to critical lapses in judgment, making even seasoned cybersecurity professionals vulnerable.

To combat social engineering threats and mitigate the risks associated with experience bias, cybersecurity professionals must adopt a mindset of continuous skepticism and adaptive learning. Organizations should implement ongoing security awareness training, simulated social engineering exercises, and behavioral reinforcement techniques to counteract overconfidence and maintain vigilance. Additionally, fostering a culture of zero trust verification, where employees routinely question unexpected requests and validate identities, can significantly reduce the success rate of social engineering attacks.

One of the most common social engineering tactics is phishing, where attackers send fraudulent communications designed to trick recipients into revealing sensitive information or installing malware (Pollini et al., 2022). Variants such as spear phishing target specific individuals or organizations using personalized details to increase credibility, while whaling specifically focuses on high-ranking executives with access to critical information. Other methods, like pretexting, involve creating a believable backstory to obtain sensitive data, while baiting tempts victims with something appealing, such as a free download or physical media like universal serial bus (USB) drives. Quid pro quo attacks offer a service in exchange for information, often under the guise of IT support. Physical tactics such as tailgating, where attackers follow authorized personnel into secure areas, also highlight the multifaceted nature of social engineering (Chinta et al., 2016).

The success of these tactics lies in their ability to exploit core psychological principles. Social engineers leverage trust by appearing authoritative or familiar, creating a sense of security in the victim (Papatsaroucha et al., 2021). Fear and urgency are also powerful motivators; attackers often pressure their targets into making quick decisions by suggesting dire consequences if they fail to act, such as account suspension or data loss. Authority bias, where individuals are more likely to comply with perceived authority figures, is frequently used, particularly in whaling attacks. Reciprocity, the human tendency to return favors, is also manipulated, such as when attackers pose as helpful IT personnel (Wantenaar, 2022).

Mitigating social engineering risks requires a proactive, multilayered approach (Ayoola et al., 2024; Rys et al., 2025; Tsanov, 2024). Training and awareness programs are foundational, helping employees recognize and respond to manipulative tactics (Ayoola et al., 2024). These programs should include real-world examples of phishing attempts and strategies for verifying requests. Role-playing exercises, tabletops that include not just executives, and phishing simulations allow cybersecurity teams to practice identifying and neutralizing social engineering threats in a controlled environment, reinforcing training through hands-on experience. By repeatedly exposing professionals to potential attack scenarios, these exercises foster a culture of skepticism and vigilance.

The service desk plays a critical role in enforcing cybersecurity policies designed to combat social engineering. As the front line for IT support, service desk personnel are often prime targets for attackers seeking unauthorized access, password resets, or other privileged actions (La Fleur et al., 2021). Strengthening verification processes, such as mandatory identity confirmation for sensitive requests, helps mitigate these risks. However, these additional steps can create friction, as employees accustomed to quick resolutions may resist them. Service desk teams must be trained to communicate the importance of these security measures, reinforcing that strict verification protects both the organization and its employees. Additionally, experience bias can lead agents to trust familiar requesters, making them more susceptible to deception (La Fleur et al., 2021). A zero trust approach, where every request is verified regardless of perceived authority, is essential to counteract this risk.

Implementing dual-approval mechanisms for high-risk actions, such as privilege escalations or financial transactions, further strengthens security by requiring multiple layers of authorization (Rys et al., 2025). While these measures may slow down service desk response times, they significantly reduce the likelihood of a single point of failure. Attackers often apply psychological pressure, using urgency or impersonating executives to manipulate service desk agents into bypassing security protocols (Rys et al., 2025). By requiring secondary approvals, the burden of decision-making is distributed, ensuring that no single employee is pressured into granting unauthorized access. Automated ticketing systems can also streamline this process, ensuring approvals are logged and auditable, providing an additional layer of security and accountability.

Beyond digital security, physical security remains a critical concern. Attackers may attempt to gain unauthorized access by impersonating contractors, vendors, or even employees seeking IT assistance in person (Choi & Rubin, 2023). Service desk teams must enforce strict identity verification before fulfilling any access-related requests, ensuring that attackers cannot manipulate human trust to bypass technical controls. Access to critical hardware and authentication devices should be strictly monitored, and any suspicious interactions should be logged and escalated to cybersecurity teams for further investigation. Ongoing training, real-world social engineering scenario drills, and adaptive learning processes help ensure that service desk personnel remain vigilant against evolving threats. By embedding these security-first practices into daily operations, organizations can significantly reduce the success rate of social engineering attacks (Wibowo, 2024).

Ultimately, combating social engineering requires collaboration across teams and departments (Wibowo, 2024). Cybersecurity professionals must work closely with leadership to foster an organizational culture that prioritizes security awareness. By addressing both technical and human vulnerabilities, organizations can significantly reduce their exposure to social engineering attacks, building resilience against one of the most pervasive and effective tactics used by adversaries.

## USER BEHAVIOR ANALYSIS

Understanding and analyzing practitioner behavior is a critical component of modern cybersecurity strategies (Mihailescu et al., 2023). By monitoring, evaluating, and interpreting actions, cybersecurity teams can identify potential vulnerabilities, mitigate risks, and design effective interventions.

Behavioral analytics not only helps organizations detect threats more efficiently but also strengthens overall security by addressing practitioner-centric risks (Mihailescu et al., 2023). This section explores the importance of practitioner behavior analysis, focusing on tools and techniques, risk identification, and the creation of targeted interventions.

Behavioral analytics in cybersecurity involves the use of advanced tools and methodologies to monitor and assess practitioner activities across systems (Ofoegbu et al., 2023). These tools leverage data such as login patterns, file access histories, and system interactions to identify anomalies or deviations from normal behavior. For example, User and Entity Behavior Analytics (UEBA) platforms use machine learning and AI to establish baselines of typical behavior for each practitioner and flag activities that fall outside these norms (Ofoegbu et al., 2023). By focusing on real-time data and contextual insights, these tools enable cybersecurity teams to detect potential indicators of concern, such as unethical actions, burnout, decision fatigue, or inefficient work habits before they escalate into significant security risks.

Risk identification is the next step in the process, where behavioral data is analyzed to pinpoint high-risk activities or trends among cybersecurity practitioners (Ben-Asher & Meyer, 2018). Indicators of concern may include unusually high-quality requests, frequent changes in security settings without proper documentation, or excessive failed login attempts. Additionally, signs of burnout and decision fatigue, such as abrupt changes in work patterns, reduced response times, or an increase in security errors, can signal the need for intervention. Identifying these behaviors enables organizations to provide necessary support, whether through workload redistribution, wellness programs, or enhanced oversight mechanisms

Once risks are identified, the focus shifts to designing targeted interventions that address specific vulnerabilities revealed by behavioral analysis (Mihailescu et al., 2023). Unlike generic security measures, targeted interventions are tailored to the unique needs of cybersecurity practitioners. For instance, if certain practitioners exhibit signs of fatigue or inefficiency, structured work breaks, automation tools, or cognitive support mechanisms can be introduced to optimize productivity. Training programs focused on ethical decision-making, stress management, and effective workload handling can also help practitioners maintain high performance levels without compromising security (Mihailescu et al., 2023).

Tailored interventions also extend to technical controls (Mihailescu et al., 2023). For example, practitioners engaging in high-risk behaviors, such as repeated unauthorized access attempts or irregular data transfers, may require additional oversight, mandatory peer reviews, or stricter privilege controls. These proactive measures not only mitigate risk but also demonstrate the organization's commitment to ethical and sustainable cybersecurity practices without alienating employees.

Behavioral analysis also has a significant role in fostering a culture of accountability and well-being within cybersecurity teams (Mihailescu et al., 2023). By engaging practitioners with personalized feedback and transparent communication about how their behaviors impact security and efficiency, organizations can build trust and cooperation. This collaborative approach ensures that cybersecurity practitioners feel supported in their roles while maintaining a high standard of security and ethical responsibility. It also increases the chances that interventions will be sticky.

## ADDRESSING INSIDER THREATS IN CYBERSECURITY

Insider threats remain one of the most challenging aspects of cybersecurity. A 2024 report from Mimecast reveals that 85% of cybersecurity leaders expected a data loss incident from an insider in the subsequent 12 months (Mimecast, 2024). These attacks are especially insidious, as they stem from individuals within an organization who have access to sensitive systems, data, or processes. These threats are not limited to malicious actions but can also arise from negligence or accidental behavior. Malicious insiders deliberately misuse their access for personal gain or to harm the organization, while negligent insiders create vulnerabilities through carelessness, such as failing to follow security protocols or clicking on phishing links. Accidental insiders, on the other hand, unintentionally cause harm due to a lack of awareness or understanding of security policies. Each type of insider threat requires a tailored approach to prevention and mitigation (Ajani et al., 2024).

Recognizing early warning signs of potential insider threats is critical to proactive mitigation. Behavioral indicators often precede malicious or negligent actions, including increased stress levels, sudden financial difficulties, unexplained changes in work patterns, or displays of dissatisfaction with management or organizational policies (Greitzer et al., 2008). Cybersecurity professionals must collaborate with human resources and leadership to create systems that identify and address these signs without stigmatizing employees. For example, monitoring tools can flag unusual behaviors, such as unauthorized access attempts or the use of personal devices for work tasks, while managers remain alert to changes in demeanor or engagement.

One of the most effective strategies for addressing insider threats is fostering a culture of trust and accountability (Greitzer et al., 2008). Organizations should aim to create an environment where employees feel valued, supported, and incentivized to act in the organization's best interest. Open communication channels, transparent policies, and recognition programs can help reduce the likelihood of malicious insider actions (Greitzer et al., 2008). Building a strong sense of organizational commitment and engagement often dissuades employees from engaging in harmful behaviors, as they are more likely to align their goals with those of the company.

Regular training on secure practices is essential to reduce accidental and negligent breaches (Greitzer et al., 2008). Cybersecurity training programs should emphasize the importance of following protocols, recognizing phishing attempts, and securely managing credentials. Role-based training can further ensure employees understand the specific security risks tied to their responsibilities. Interactive and engaging methods, such as gamified exercises and phishing simulations, can help employees retain critical security knowledge and apply it effectively in real-world situations (Greitzer et al., 2008).

To balance security and privacy, organizations can implement monitoring systems that identify potential threats without infringing on practitioner rights (Allahrakha, 2023). These systems should focus on detecting unusual or high-risk behaviors rather than scrutinizing every activity. For example, using machine learning algorithms, organizations can monitor for deviations from normal access patterns, large-scale data transfers, or sudden escalations in privilege usage by cybersecurity practitioners and leaders. Transparency about monitoring policies, combined with clear communication about how data is used, helps maintain trust among cybersecurity teams while ensuring security objectives are met (Allahrakha, 2023).

Policies that encourage whistleblowing and anonymous reporting can also play a significant role in mitigating insider threats (Pacella, 2016). Cybersecurity practitioners and leaders are often the first to notice concerning behaviors or potential vulnerabilities within their teams. Establishing clear, confidential reporting mechanisms allows individuals to flag potential risks without fear of retaliation. Organizations should also promote awareness of these mechanisms through regular communication and ensure that timely action is taken when reports are received to build confidence in the process.

Addressing insider threats requires a multifaceted approach that combines human-centric strategies with advanced technological tools (Asasfeh et al., 2024). By understanding the types of insider threats, recognizing early warning signs, and implementing strategies to foster trust, accountability, and awareness, organizations can significantly reduce the risks posed by insiders. Through continuous training, transparent policies, and a strong organizational culture, cybersecurity professionals can create an environment that minimizes vulnerabilities while empowering employees to contribute positively to the organization's security posture (Asasfeh et al., 2024). Ultimately, integrating AI-driven monitoring tools with human-centric policies ensures a more resilient defense against evolving insider threats (Thite & Iyer, 2024).

## WHY HUMAN FACTORS MATTER

Human factors are critical in cybersecurity, as decisions and actions by leaders and practitioners directly influence an organization's security posture. Leadership failures, human errors, and mismanagement have led to some of the most significant cybersecurity breaches in recent history. Incidents such as the Office of Personnel Management (OPM) data breach and the collapse of IronNet illustrate how poor decision-making and organizational culture can contribute to security failures (AP News, 2023; FedScoop, 2015). These cases emphasize the need for proactive leadership, ethical decision-making, and a strong security culture within organizations to mitigate cyber risks.

## OPM Data Breach

In 2015, the OPM experienced a massive data breach that compromised sensitive information of over 22 million individuals. Investigations revealed that the breach resulted from leadership failures and a culture that neglected cybersecurity (FedScoop, 2015). Despite warnings from the OPM Inspector General about vulnerabilities as early as 2005, the agency failed to implement essential security measures, such as MFA and regular system authorizations. This negligence allowed attackers to exploit weaknesses, leading to one of the most significant data breaches in U.S. history. The incident underscores the importance of proactive leadership and a culture that prioritizes cybersecurity.

## Collapse of IronNet

IronNet, a cybersecurity firm founded by former National Security Agency (NSA) Director Keith Alexander, aimed to revolutionize cyber defense by leveraging the expertise of former intelligence officials. Despite initial success and a valuation exceeding $3 billion after going public in 2021, the company collapsed by September 2023. The downfall was attributed to several factors:

- **Leadership Missteps**: The company's executives engaged in questionable business practices and failed to deliver on overhyped promises. Former employees likened the culture to that of the fraudulent firm Theranos, highlighting a pervasive culture of deceit (AP News, 2023).
- **Product Deficiencies**: IronNet's products did not meet industry expectations, leading to an inability to secure significant contracts and meet revenue projections. This shortfall reflects the consequences of overconfidence and inadequate quality control in product development (AP News, 2023).
- **Dubious Associations**: The company's ties with venture capital firm C5 Capital, led by Andre Pienaar, raised concerns due to Pienaar's associations with sanctioned Russian oligarchs. These connections potentially exposed the company to security risks and undermined trust with clients and investors (AP News, 2023).

The IronNet case illustrates how leadership decisions, ethical lapses, and mismanagement can precipitate the downfall of a cybersecurity firm, regardless of the founders' credentials.

These examples demonstrate that human factors, ranging from leadership decisions and ethical standards to organizational culture, are pivotal in determining the effectiveness of cybersecurity measures. Addressing these challenges requires committed leadership, continuous training, and a culture that prioritizes security at every level.

## SOCIAL ENGINEERING FROM A COGNITIVE NEUROSCIENCE STANDPOINT

Social engineering is the psychological manipulation of individuals to deceive them into divulging confidential information or performing actions that compromise security. From a cognitive neuroscience perspective, social engineering exploits emotional responses, memory processes, and trust mechanisms to bypass logical decision-making (Abdelrahman et al., 2023). Understanding how the brain perceives, processes, and reacts to different stimuli allows attackers to craft strategies that effectively manipulate their targets.

While cognitive biases, heuristics, and uncertainty-based decision-making are key factors influencing susceptibility to social engineering, this discussion will focus on emotional and social triggers, neural mechanisms of trust and deception, memory manipulation, neurobiological fear responses, and neuroscientific mitigation strategies (Montañez et al., 2020)). These interconnected processes highlight the vulnerabilities in human cognition that attackers exploit. The insights provided by neuroscience can guide organizations in developing countermeasures that reinforce rational thinking and enhance resistance to manipulation.

### Emotional and Social Triggers in Social Engineering

Humans are inherently social creatures, and emotions play a central role in decision-making (Volz & Hertwig, 2016). Social engineers manipulate emotional responses to bypass rational scrutiny and push their victims toward impulsive actions. When an individual is emotionally engaged, their ability to think critically diminishes, making them more susceptible to deception. This phenomenon is particularly evident in attacks that leverage fear, urgency, curiosity, or empathy (Volz & Hertwig, 2016).

Fear and anxiety are powerful motivators, often used in phishing scams or urgent fraud schemes (Burda et al., 2021). For instance, an email claiming that an account has been compromised triggers an immediate sense of panic, activating the brain's amygdala, which is responsible for processing fear. This heightened emotional state can override logical thinking, leading the victim to click on a malicious link or provide sensitive information without verifying the legitimacy of the request (Burda et al., 2021). Attackers craft their messages carefully to maximize emotional impact, ensuring that their target does not take the time to critically analyze the situation.

Empathy and sympathy are also exploited in social engineering attacks (Burda et al., 2021). Scammers pose as distressed individuals, charity organizations, or colleagues in need, appealing to the target's innate desire to help others. The ventromedial prefrontal cortex (vmPFC), which governs emotional decision-making, plays a role in generating feelings of moral obligation (Garr, 2023). Attackers manipulate this mechanism by constructing narratives that invoke a sense of duty or responsibility, increasing compliance with their requests. This technique is commonly used in CEO fraud, where attackers impersonate high-ranking executives and request urgent financial transactions.

Curiosity and reward anticipation further drive impulsive behaviors that benefit social engineers (Marvin et al., 2020). A well-crafted email or message offering exclusive content, insider information, or financial incentives can activate the brain's dopaminergic reward system, which fuels the urge to explore. By exploiting these neurobiological responses, attackers increase the likelihood that their target will click on a malicious link or download an infected file without evaluating the risks (Marvin et al., 2020). The interplay between these emotional and social triggers makes social engineering one of the most effective methods of cyber exploitation.

## Neural Mechanisms of Trust and Deception

Trust is an essential element of human interactions, and social engineers exploit the neural pathways responsible for trust formation to manipulate their targets (Budniok et al., 2024; Eskander et al., 2020; Petropoulou & Varouchas, 2024). The brain relies on various cognitive and emotional cues to determine whether someone is trustworthy. These cues include familiarity, perceived authority, and social validation, all of which can be fabricated or manipulated by an attacker (Eskander et al., 2020). Understanding the underlying neural mechanisms can help explain why people fall victim to social engineering techniques.

One of the key neurochemicals involved in trust is oxytocin, which enhances social bonding and reduces suspicion (Eskander et al., 2020). When individuals experience positive interactions, oxytocin levels rise, increasing their willingness to believe and comply with others. Social engineers establish rapport by mirroring speech patterns, demonstrating familiarity with their target, and displaying confidence (Eskander et al., 2020). These tactics create a false sense of trust, making the victim more likely to disclose sensitive information or follow directives without question.

Another critical factor in deception is the Theory of Mind (ToM), which allows individuals to infer others' intentions, beliefs, and emotions (Zheltyakova et al., 2020). The temporoparietal junction (TPJ) is involved in this process, helping people assess whether someone is being truthful or deceitful. However, experienced social engineers manipulate this cognitive function by employing deception techniques that align with expected social behaviors (Zheltyakova et al., 2020). By crafting convincing narratives and mimicking genuine interactions, attackers exploit the brain's trust mechanisms to gain an advantage.

Cognitive load also plays a role in susceptibility to deception (Agbangla et al., 2022). When individuals are multitasking or under pressure, the dorsolateral prefrontal cortex (dlPFC), which is responsible for analytical thinking and skepticism, becomes overwhelmed (Zheltyakova et al., 2020). This state reduces a person's ability to detect inconsistencies or question suspicious requests. Attackers take advantage of this cognitive overload by introducing urgency or complexity into their requests, ensuring that their target defaults to heuristic-based decision-making rather than careful analysis (Andrade et al., 2022).

## Memory Manipulation and False Memories

Memory is a reconstructive process, meaning that it is susceptible to manipulation and distortion (Ilangakoon & Abeywardena, 2018; Lau et al., 2020; Murphy et al., 2020). Social engineers exploit these vulnerabilities by using suggestive language, misinformation, and cognitive priming to implant false memories or distort existing ones (Ilangakoon & Abeywardena, 2018). This technique can be particularly effective in long-term social engineering campaigns, where attackers gradually influence their targets' recollection of past events or interactions.

One common memory-related exploit is the misattribution effect, where individuals mistakenly attribute familiarity to authenticity (Mitchell et al., 2006). For example, an attacker may reference a previous conversation, email, or company policy that never actually occurred, but the victim, relying on partial recollection, assumes it is legitimate. The hippocampus, responsible for memory encoding and retrieval, reconstructs information based on associations, making it vulnerable to these manipulations (Mitchell et al., 2006). Attackers use this to reinforce trust and credibility, making their requests appear reasonable and expected.

False memories can also be induced through leading questions and contextual framing. The prefrontal cortex (PFC) plays a role in reconstructing past events, but it is susceptible to suggestion (Gupta, 2024). Social engineers exploit this by subtly influencing how information is recalled. For instance, if an attacker poses as IT support and claims that an employee previously approved a security protocol, the employee may generate a false memory of the interaction and comply with the request without verification.

Cognitive fluency further amplifies memory-related deception (Gupta, 2024). When information is presented in a clear, professional, and familiar format, the brain processes it more easily and assumes it to be accurate. Well-designed phishing emails mimic legitimate communications, reducing skepticism and increasing the likelihood of compliance (Gupta, 2024). Understanding these memory vulnerabilities highlights the importance of verifying information and maintaining a critical mindset when responding to unfamiliar or unexpected requests.

### Neurobiological Responses to Fear and Urgency

Fear and urgency are among the most effective tactics used in social engineering attacks (Putnam & Chang, 2021). These emotions trigger automatic responses that override logical reasoning and encourage immediate action. The amygdala, which processes fear and threat perception, plays a central role in this response. When faced with a perceived danger, the brain prioritizes rapid action over detailed analysis, making individuals more susceptible to deception (Ilangakoon & Abeywardena, 2018).

One-way attackers exploit this response is through fear appeals, such as messages warning that an account has been compromised or that legal action is imminent (Putnam & Chang, 2021). These threats create an emotional reaction that suppresses activity in the PFC, reducing the ability to evaluate the credibility of the message. Victims in a heightened state of fear often act impulsively, following the attacker's instructions without seeking confirmation from official sources (Putnam & Chang, 2021). This manipulation of fear and urgency is a cornerstone of social engineering tactics, effectively overriding rational decision-making processes and increasing susceptibility to cyber threats.

Urgency further amplifies this effect by limiting the time available for rational decision-making (Putnam & Chang, 2021). Attackers impose strict deadlines or immediate consequences to force hasty responses. Under time pressure, the brain engages the hypothalamic-pituitary-adrenal (HPA) axis, which releases cortisol, increasing stress levels and impairing cognitive control (Putnam & Chang, 2021). This state makes individuals more prone to compliance, as they prioritize risk avoidance over careful analysis.

The concept of loss aversion also plays a role in urgency-based attacks (Putnam & Chang, 2021). People have a stronger emotional reaction to potential losses than to equivalent gains, making them more likely to act when faced with the risk of losing access, money, or status. Attackers exploit this bias by framing their requests in terms of avoiding negative consequences, ensuring a higher rate of compliance. Understanding these neural mechanisms is crucial in developing effective cybersecurity awareness programs and defensive strategies to mitigate the impact of social engineering attacks.

## UNDERSTANDING NOISE IN DECISION-MAKING

"Noise" in decision-making refers to unwanted variability in judgments that should be consistent (Kahneman et al., 2021). Unlike bias, which is a systematic deviation, noise is randomness in decision-making, leading to unpredictable inconsistencies. This means that two individuals, or even the same person at different times, might reach different conclusions despite evaluating the same situation. Noise affects various fields, including legal judgments, medical diagnoses, employee evaluations, and financial decisions (Kahneman et al., 2021). In cybersecurity, noise can lead to inconsistent risk assessments, fluctuating security responses, and unpredictable decision-making in incident response scenarios (Sachs, 2024). Addressing noise is critical to improving decision quality, reducing errors, and ensuring consistency in both everyday and high-stakes choices (Kahneman et al., 2021).

## Three Types of Noise in Decision-Making

1. **Level Noise** (Kahneman et al., 2021)
   - This occurs when different decision-makers (or even the same person at different times) produce systematically different outcomes despite identical inputs. It reflects inconsistencies between individuals who are expected to evaluate situations similarly but show substantial variation. For instance, two grocery store managers might evaluate employees' performances differently: one is consistently lenient, while the other is harsh, even if the employees' behaviors are the same. Similarly, a grocery store customer who always prioritizes price over quality may consistently make different purchasing choices than someone who always opts for organic products. In cybersecurity, level noise appears when different security analysts assess the same vulnerability but assign vastly different risk ratings. One analyst may view a vulnerability as critical, while another deems it moderate, leading to inconsistent security policies and prioritization of threats.

2. **Pattern Noise** (Kahneman et al., 2021)
   - This is caused by individual tendencies or idiosyncrasies that create variation in decisions. Even when two people face the same scenario, their unique perspectives cause different conclusions, driven by personal habits, training, or even subconscious biases. A customer's grocery shopping behavior may vary depending on personal habits: one might always prioritize organic produce, while another focuses on price. This can result in different shopping experiences even when both individuals are exposed to the same store layout, promotions, and product availability. In cybersecurity, pattern noise occurs when security analysts have different levels of risk tolerance based on their experience or training. For example, one security team might aggressively patch every software update immediately, while another may delay patches due to

concerns about system stability. These inconsistent decisions can lead to security gaps or unnecessary delays in risk mitigation.

3. **Occasion Noise** (Kahneman et al., 2021)
   - This occurs when a decision is influenced by temporary external factors such as mood, time of day, hunger, fatigue, or upcoming events. People may not realize how these factors impact their choices, leading to inconsistencies in judgment. For example, a grocery shopper might make healthier choices in the morning when they are more disciplined but buy more impulsively when tired in the evening. Likewise, a person shopping after work might be more likely to pick up ready-to-eat meals rather than fresh ingredients for cooking due to fatigue. In cybersecurity, occasion noise can impact how an organization responds to a security threat. A security analyst investigating an incident early in the morning might take a methodical, thorough approach, while the same analyst handling a similar incident late at night, when exhausted, might rush the investigation or overlook key details. This variability can affect the overall security posture and incident response effectiveness.

## How Noise Unconsciously Impacts Decision-Making

Noise affects decisions without people realizing it, leading to inconsistent and suboptimal choices (Kahneman et al., 2021; Sachs, 2024). This variability can be driven by hunger, fatigue, stress, and social influences, which subtly alter judgment (Kahneman et al., 2021). Even though individuals believe they are making rational choices, external factors introduce unpredictability, making their decisions inconsistent. Below are key scenarios where noise affects decision-making and leads to unconscious errors. Recognizing these influences can help in making more deliberate, well-thought-out choices.

1. **Grocery Shopping When Hungry**
   - **Occasion Noise Effect:** Hunger affects decision-making by making high-calorie and unhealthy foods more attractive. When the body signals a need for energy, the brain prioritizes immediate satisfaction over long-term health or financial considerations. This impulse-driven shopping can lead to excessive spending and poor dietary choices. A shopper who enters the grocery store while hungry is more likely to buy snacks, processed foods, or fast-food items rather than sticking to a planned shopping list. Their physiological state influences their perception of food value, leading to impulse purchases they might later regret. Similarly, in cybersecurity, professionals who are under stress, such as when dealing with an active cyberattack, may

make impulsive decisions rather than following protocol. If a team is exhausted and overwhelmed, they may rush to remediate a perceived issue without fully assessing its impact, potentially causing system failures or overlooking a deeper security breach.

2. **Decision-Making in the Afternoon**
   - **Cognitive Fatigue and Noise**: Mental energy depletes over the day, causing lower-quality decisions. As cognitive resources diminish, individuals rely more on heuristics (mental shortcuts) rather than deliberate thinking, leading to inconsistent choices. This phenomenon affects consumers, professionals, and decision-makers across industries. A manager reviewing vendor proposals may be more meticulous in the morning but make rushed decisions in the afternoon due to fatigue. Similarly, a shopper visiting the store in the afternoon after work may buy prepackaged meals or convenience foods because they are too tired to plan for a balanced meal. In cybersecurity, fatigue affects security analysts as well. Security professionals working long hours may be less likely to detect sophisticated phishing attacks late in the day compared to earlier when they are more alert. This cognitive depletion can lead to misjudgments in security assessments, making an organization more vulnerable to cyber threats.

3. **Decision-Making Right Before the Weekend**
   - **Pattern and Occasion Noise due to Anticipation**: People behave differently when anticipating a break or event. Psychological anticipation of leisure time can impact decision-making, leading to choices that prioritize short-term rewards over long-term benefits. A shopper on a Friday evening might buy more indulgent foods (e.g., snacks, desserts, alcohol) than if they shopped on a Monday because they unconsciously associate the weekend with relaxation. Their purchasing behavior reflects a shift in priorities influenced by external circumstances. In cybersecurity, decision-making before a weekend or holiday can lead to rushed approvals or overlooked security measures. Employees preparing for a break may cut corners in reviewing security alerts, leaving vulnerabilities unaddressed. Additionally, cybercriminals often time attacks for weekends or holidays, knowing that security teams may be understaffed or less vigilant, increasing the likelihood of a successful breach.

## How Understanding Noise Can Improve Cybersecurity

Recognizing the role of noise in decision-making can help organizations develop strategies to minimize inconsistencies. Just as structured shopping habits (e.g., making a list, shopping at set times) can reduce impulse buying, structured decision-making frameworks can improve cybersecurity outcomes. Implementing standardized risk assessment protocols, checklists for incident response, and automated security controls can mitigate the impact of noise on cybersecurity operations (Bollarino et al., 2023). For example, structured cybersecurity workflows can ensure that risk assessments are consistent regardless of analyst fatigue or external factors. Automation in security monitoring can reduce reliance on human decision-making, which is prone to variability (Chamberlain et al., 2020). Additionally, regular training and awareness programs can help cybersecurity professionals recognize how fatigue, stress, or other external factors might unconsciously influence their decisions (Reeves et al., 2021). By addressing noise, organizations can improve security outcomes, reduce vulnerabilities, and enhance decision-making consistency across all levels of cybersecurity operations. Just as understanding noise helps consumers make better shopping choices, it enables cybersecurity teams to make more rational, strategic, and effective security decisions.

## EMOTIONAL AND PSYCHOLOGICAL STATES

The emotional and psychological states of cybersecurity professionals have a direct impact on their ability to perform effectively (Nobles, 2022). Stress is one of the most common challenges in cybersecurity, often caused by high workloads, long hours, and the high stakes of incident response. Prolonged stress can impair cognitive functions such as problem-solving and attention to detail, increasing the likelihood of errors (Nobles, 2022). Providing resources such as employee assistance programs, mental health support, and stress management workshops helps professionals manage the pressures of their roles. Organizations that actively address stress foster a healthier and more productive workforce (Nobles, 2022).

Fear and anxiety can also influence decision-making in cybersecurity environments (Nobles, 2022). Professionals worried about the consequences of mistakes, such as reputational damage or disciplinary actions, may hesitate to report errors or vulnerabilities. This reluctance can allow minor issues to escalate into significant breaches. Creating a nonpunitive reporting culture, where the focus is on resolving issues rather than assigning blame, encourages transparency and quicker responses (Nobles, 2022). For example, incident reporting platforms that allow anonymity can further reduce barriers to open communication.

Motivation and engagement are critical for maintaining high levels of performance among cybersecurity teams (Donovan, 2022). Professionals who feel valued, supported, and recognized for their contributions are more likely to stay committed to their roles. Offering opportunities for career advancement, certifications, or participation in industry events demonstrates an organization's investment in its employees (Donovan, 2022). For instance, sponsoring professionals to attend cybersecurity conferences not only enhances their skills but also boosts morale and engagement.

Emotionally charged situations, such as responding to a ransomware attack or mitigating a breach, can lead to impulsive decision-making (Virtanen, 2024). These hasty actions, driven by fear or urgency, may worsen the situation or lead to incomplete resolutions. Encouraging team-based decision-making during critical incidents ensures a more measured approach (Virtanen, 2024). For example, establishing incident response playbooks with predefined escalation procedures provides clear guidance and reduces reliance on emotional reactions.

Regular mental health check-ins and fostering an environment of psychological safety ensure that cybersecurity professionals feel supported in their roles (Virtanen, 2024). Organizations can also provide tools and resources to improve emotional resilience, such as mindfulness apps or on-site wellness programs. When professionals feel emotionally balanced, they are better equipped to make thoughtful decisions, collaborate effectively, and adapt to the demands of their work (Virtanen, 2024). Addressing emotional and psychological states holistically enhances both individual performance and organizational security.

## CHAPTER SUMMARY

This chapter explores the psychological, social, and behavioral elements influencing cybersecurity professionals and the security systems they manage. It emphasizes that human behavior is one of the most significant vulnerabilities in cybersecurity, often exploited by attackers through social engineering and cognitive manipulation (Hakimi et al., 2024). This chapter highlights key learning objectives, including recognizing human behavior as a security risk, understanding how social engineering exploits psychological tendencies, and leveraging behavioral analysis to strengthen security strategies. By addressing these human factors, organizations can develop more effective security policies that account for decision-making biases, stress, and collaboration challenges.

A core discussion in this chapter is the impact of cognitive biases on cybersecurity decision-making. Biases such as overconfidence, confirmation bias, and optimism bias can lead to flawed risk assessments and misjudgments (Darley, 2023). Overreliance on technology is another prevalent bias, where professionals assume that automated security systems can detect all threats, leading to complacency (Rohan et al., 2021). These cognitive distortions highlight the need for structured decision-making frameworks, continuous training, and diverse team perspectives to improve security assessments and incident response strategies. By mitigating cognitive biases, cybersecurity professionals can make more balanced, evidence-based decisions that enhance overall security posture.

This chapter also underscores the significance of teamwork dynamics in cybersecurity operations. Effective security measures require collaboration across multidisciplinary teams, yet poor communication, conflicting priorities, and lack of trust can weaken security efforts (Papatsaroucha et al., 2021). The text advocates for strong interpersonal skills, clear communication protocols, and a culture of collaboration to ensure cohesive security responses. Similarly, the interaction between professionals and technology is explored, emphasizing that poorly designed security tools can lead to errors, while intuitive, human-centric designs can enhance efficiency and reduce risks (Axon et al., 2021). Ensuring that cybersecurity technologies align with human cognitive processes can reduce misconfigurations and overlooked vulnerabilities.

A major focus of this chapter is social engineering, a tactic that manipulates human psychology to bypass security defenses. Social engineers exploit trust, fear, and urgency to deceive individuals into revealing sensitive information or taking actions that compromise security (Mitnick & Simon, 2011). Various attack methods such as phishing, pretexting, and tailgating are examined, with case studies illustrating how these techniques have been used to infiltrate organizations (Pollini et al., 2022). This chapter stresses the importance of security awareness training, behavioral reinforcement techniques, and zero trust verification practices to counteract these threats. Organizations must adopt proactive strategies such as role-playing exercises, phishing simulations, and MFA to reduce susceptibility to social engineering attacks.

Additionally, insider threats are identified as a significant cybersecurity risk. This chapter categorizes insider threats into malicious, negligent, and accidental actions, each requiring distinct mitigation strategies (Mimecast, 2024). Behavioral indicators such as financial stress, sudden work pattern changes, or dissatisfaction with management are explored as early warning signs (Greitzer et al., 2008). This chapter advocates for trust-based organizational cultures, role-based security training, and AI-driven monitoring tools to detect and prevent insider threats while balancing security and privacy concerns. Addressing insider risks requires a combination of technical controls, employee engagement strategies, and continuous behavioral monitoring to prevent data breaches and unauthorized access.

Lastly, this chapter examines the role of human emotions and psychological states in cybersecurity decision-making. Stress, fatigue, and cognitive overload can impair professionals' ability to assess threats accurately and respond effectively (Nobles, 2022). Cybersecurity professionals working under extreme pressure may overlook crucial security measures or fall victim to cognitive shortcuts that increase vulnerabilities. This chapter concludes by recommending strategies such as structured workflows, AI-driven automation, and mental health support to mitigate the effects of emotional strain on cybersecurity professionals. Ethical considerations, including responsible

AI use, surveillance concerns, and professional integrity, are also discussed, reinforcing the need for cybersecurity teams to uphold ethical standards in their decision-making processes (Flechais & Chalhoub, 2023).

Overall, this chapter presents a comprehensive analysis of how human behavior influences cybersecurity, emphasizing that even highly trained professionals are susceptible to cognitive biases, stress, and social engineering tactics. It underscores the need for organizations to integrate behavioral science into cybersecurity strategies, ensuring that security measures account for human limitations rather than relying solely on technical controls. By investing in continuous education, fostering a culture of collaboration, and implementing structured decision-making frameworks, organizations can mitigate the risks associated with human factors. Additionally, balancing security with ethical considerations such as privacy, transparency, and fairness is essential to maintaining trust and effectiveness in cybersecurity operations. This chapter ultimately reinforces that addressing human vulnerabilities is just as crucial as deploying advanced security technologies, as sustainable cybersecurity resilience depends on the intersection of human behavior, organizational culture, and technological innovation.

## REFERENCES


Abdelrahman, Y., Alt, F., Dingler, T., Hadnagy, C., Maroño, A., & Distler, V. (2023). Defining and fortifying against cognitive vulnerabilities in social engineering (Dagstuhl Seminar 23462). *Dagstuhl Reports*, *13*(11), 103–129. https://doi.org/10.4230/DagRep.13.11.103

Agbangla, N., Audiffren, M., Pylouster, J., & Albinet, C. (2022). Load-dependent prefrontal cortex activation assessed by continuous-wave near-infrared spectroscopy during two executive tasks with three cognitive loads in young adults. *Brain Sciences*, *12*(11), Article 1462. https://doi.org/10.3390/brainsci12111462

Ajani, S., Vaghasiya, D., Kapadia, D., Chauhan, D., Thakkar, M., & Sanmugam, R. (2024). Behind closed doors: Insider threats in the world of cybersecurity. In *2024 IEEE International Conference on Computing, Power and Communication Technologies (IC2PCT)*, 5, 216–222. https://doi.org/10.1109/IC2PCT60090.2024.10486311

Allahrakha, N. (2023). *Balancing cyber-security and privacy: Legal and ethical considerations in the digital age*. Legal Issues in the Digital Age. https://doi.org/10.17323/10.17323/2713-2749.2023.2.78.121

Alsharif, M., Mishra, S., & AlShehri, M. (2022). Impact of human vulnerabilities on cybersecurity. *Computer Systems Science and Engineering*, *40*(3), 1153–1166. https://doi.org/10.32604/csse.2022.019938

Anderson, C. L., & Agarwal, R. (2010). Practicing safe computing: A multimedia empirical examination of home computer user security behavioral intentions. *MIS Quarterly*, *34*(3), 613–643. https://doi.org/10.2307/25750694

Andrade, R. O., Fuertes, W., Cazares, M., Ortiz-Garcés, I., & Navas, G. (2022). An Exploratory Study of Cognitive Sciences Applied to Cybersecurity. *Electronics*, *11*(11), 1692. https://doi.org/10.3390/electronics11111692

AP News. (2023, September 29). IronNet, cybersecurity firm founded by former NSA director, shuts down amid financial struggles. Associated Press. https://apnews.com/article/keith-alexander-ironnet-cybersecurity-nsa-bankruptcy-eddd67f3a1b312face21c29c59400e05

Asasfeh, A., Alnawayseh, S., AbdElkareem, R., & Salahat, M. (2024). Human factors in security management: Understanding and mitigating insider threats. In *2024 2nd International Conference on Cyber Resilience (ICCR)*, 1–10. https://doi.org/10.1109/ICCR61006.2024.10532956

Axon, L., Erola, A., Janse van Rensburg, A., Nurse, J. R. C., Goldsmith, M., & Creese, S. (2021). Practitioners' views on cybersecurity control adoption and effectiveness. In *Proceedings of the 16th International Conference on Availability, Reliability and Security* (Article 91). Association for Computing Machinery. https://doi.org/10.1145/3465481.3470038

Ayoola, V. B., Ugoaghalam, U. J., Idoko, P. I., Ijiga, O. M., & Olola, T. M. (2024). Effectiveness of social engineering awareness training in mitigating spear phishing risks in financial institutions from a cybersecurity perspective. *Global Journal of Engineering and Technology Advances*, *20*(03), 094–117. https://doi.org/10.30574/gjeta.2024.20.3.0164

Beautement, A., Becker, I., Parkin, S., Krol, K., & Sasse, M. A. (2016). Productive security: A scalable methodology for analysing employee security behaviours. In *SOUPS '16: twelfth symposium on usable privacy and security*. USENIX Association.

Ben-Asher, N., & Meyer, J. (2018). The triad of risk-related behaviors (TriRB): A three-dimensional model of cyber risk taking. *Human Factors: The Journal of Human Factors and Ergonomics Society*, *60*(8), 1163–1178. https://doi.org/10.1177/0018720818783953

Bollarino, S., Ceschi, A., Monti, M., & Sartori, R. (2023). Development and validation of a noise in decision inventory for organizational settings. *Informing Science: The International Journal of an Emerging Transdiscipline*, *26*, 173–189. https://doi.org/10.28945/5138

Budniok, S., Callaerts-Végh, Z., Bakermans-Kranenburg, M. J., Bosmans, G., & D'Hooge, R. (2024). Oxytocin enhances acquisition in a social trust task in mice, whereas both oxytocin and its antagonist block trust violation learning. bioRxiv. https://doi.org/10.1101/2024.12.13.628349

Bundala, N. (2024). Understanding cybercrime modus operandi: Techniques, psychological tricks, and countermeasures. *Asian Journal of Research in Computer Science*, *17*(1), 1–15. https://doi.org/10.9734/ajrcos/2024/v17i12541

Burda, P., Allodi, L., & Zannone, N. (2024). Cognition in social engineering empirical research: A systematic literature review. *ACM Transactions on Computer-Human Interaction*, *31*(2), Article 19. https://doi.org/10.1145/3635149

Chamberlain, L., Davis, L., Stanley, M., & Gattoni, B. (2020). Automated decision systems for cybersecurity and infrastructure security. In *2020 IEEE Security and Privacy Workshops (SPW)* (pp. 196–201). IEEE. https://doi.org/10.1109/SPW50608.2020.00048

Chinta, M., Alaparthi, J., & Kodali, E. (2016). A study on social engineering attacks and defence mechanisms. *International Journal of Computer Science and Information Security. IJCSIS*, *14*, 225–231.

Choi, Y. B., & Rubin, J. (2023). Social engineering cyber threats. *Journal of Global Awareness*, *4*(2), Article 8. https://doi.org/10.24073/jga/4/02/08

Chowdhury, N. H., Adam, M. T., & Teubner, T. (2020). Time pressure in human cybersecurity behavior: Theoretical framework and countermeasures. *Computers & Security*, *97*, 101963. https://doi.org/10.1016/j.cose.2020.101963

D'Arcy, J., Herath, T., & Shoss, M. K. (2014). Understanding employee responses to stressful information security requirements: A coping perspective. *Journal of Management Information Systems*, *31*(2), 285–318. https://doi.org/10.2753/MIS0742-1222310210

Darley, H.-M. (2023, March 1). Dangers of succumbing to bias in cyber security: An evaluation of the impact of cognitive biases on threat assessments and cyber security strategies. *Cyber Security: A Peer-Reviewed Journal*, *6*(3). https://doi.org/10.69554/JQHH7665

Donovan, C. (2022). Examining employee engagement amid a crisis: Reactions to mandatory stay-at-home orders during the COVID-19 pandemic. *Psychology of Leaders and Leadership*, *25*(2), 114–143. https://doi.org/10.1037/mgr0000127

Eskander, E., Sanders, N., & Nam, C. S. (2020). Neural correlates and mechanisms of trust. In C. S. Nam (Ed.), *Neuroergonomics. Cognitive Science and Technology* (pp. 451–461). Springer. https://doi.org/10.1007/978-3-030-34784-0_22

FedScoop. (2015, July 9). OPM Hack: The Complete Timeline. FedScoop. https://fedscoop.com/opm-hack-the-complete-timeline/

Fenech, J., Richards, D., & Formosa, P. (2024). Ethical principles shaping values-based cybersecurity decision-making. *Computers & Security*, *140*, 103795. https://doi.org/10.1016/j.cose.2023.103795

Flechais, I., & Chalhoub, G. (2023). Practical cybersecurity ethics: Mapping CyBOK to ethical concerns. In *Proceedings of the 2023 New Security Paradigms Workshop*. https://doi.org/10.1145/3633500.3633505

Furnell, S., & Clarke, N. (2012). Power to the people? The evolving recognition of human aspects in security. *Computers & Security*, *31*(8), 983–988.

Garr, A. K. (2023). The role of the ventromedial prefrontal cortex in moral cognition: A value-centric hypothesis. *Philosophical Psychology*, *37*(6), 970–987. https://doi.org/10.1080/09515089.2023.2166820

Georgiadou, A., Mouzakitis, S., Bounas, K., & Askounis, D. (2020). A cyber-security culture framework for assessing organization readiness. *Journal of Computer Information Systems*, *62*(3), 452–462. https://doi.org/10.1080/08874417.2020.1845583

Greitzer, F., Moore, A., Cappelli, D., Andrews, D., Carroll, L., & Hull, T. (2008). Combating the insider cyber threat. *IEEE Security & Privacy*, *6*(1), 61–64. https://doi.org/10.1109/MSP.2008.8

Gupta, A. (2024). Can leading questions result in reconstructions of memory? *International Journal of Science and Research (IJSR)*, *13*(7), 1362–1363. https://doi.org/10.21275/sr24724161732

Hadlington, L. (2017). Human factors in cybersecurity: Examining the link between Internet addiction, impulsivity, attitudes towards cybersecurity, and risky cybersecurity behaviours. *Heliyon*, *3*(7), Article e00346. https://doi.org/10.1016/j.heliyon.2017.e00346

Hakimi, M., Quchi, M. M., & Fazil, A. W. (2024). Human factors in cybersecurity: An in-depth analysis of user-centric studies. *Jurnal Ilmiah Multidisiplin Indonesia (JIM-ID)*, *3*(1), 20–33. https://doi.org/10.58471/esaprom.v3i01.3832

Herley, C. (2009). So long, and no thanks for the externalities: The rational rejection of security advice by users. In *Proceedings of the 2009 Workshop on New Security Paradigms* (pp. 133–144). Association for Computing Machinery. https://doi.org/10.1145/1719030.1719050

Ilangakoon, S. D., & Abeywardena, K. (2018). The use of subliminal and supraliminal messages in phishing and spear phishing based social engineering attacks: Feasibility study. In *2018 13th International Conference on Computer Science & Education (ICCSE)* (pp. 1–5). IEEE. https://doi.org/10.1109/ICCSE.2018.8468681

Kahneman, D. (2011). *Thinking, fast and slow*. Farrar, Straus and Giroux.

Kahneman, D., Sibony, O., & Sunstein, C. R. (2021). *Noise: A flaw in human judgment*. Little, Brown Spark.

Karlsson, N., Loewenstein, G., & Seppi, D. (2009). The ostrich effect: Selective attention to information. *Journal of Risk and Uncertainty*, *38*(2), 95–115.

Kumar, I. (2023). Emerging threats in cybersecurity: A review article. *International Journal of Applied and Natural Sciences*, *1*(1), 1–8. https://bluemarkpublishers.com/index.php/IJANS/article/view/2

La Fleur, C., Hoffman, B., Gibson, C., & Buchler, N. (2021). Team performance in a series of regional and national US cybersecurity defense competitions: Generalizable effects of training and functional role specialization. *Computers & Security*, *104*, 102229. https://doi.org/10.1016/j.cose.2021.102229

Lau, J., Rashid, A., Jacob, A. D., Frankland, P., Schacter, D., & Josselyn, S. (2020). The role of neuronal excitability, allocation to an engram and memory linking in the behavioral generation of a fSalse memory in mice. *Neurobiology of Learning and Memory*, *174*, 107284. https://doi.org/10.1016/j.nlm.2020.107284

Maalem Lahcen, R. A., Caulkins, B., Mohapatra, R., & Kumar, M. (2020). Review and insight on the behavioral aspects of cybersecurity. *Cybersecurity*, *3*(1), Article 10. https://doi.org/10.1186/s42400-020-00050-w

Marvin, C. B., Tedeschi, E., & Shohamy, D. (2020). Curiosity as the impulse to know: Common behavioral and neural mechanisms underlying curiosity and impulsivity. *Current Opinion in Behavioral Sciences*, *35*, 92–98. https://doi.org/10.1016/j.cobeha.2020.08.003

Mihailescu, M., Nita, S. L., Rogobete, M., & Marascu, V. (2023). Unveiling threats: Leveraging user behavior analysis for enhanced cybersecurity. In *2023 15th International Conference on Electronics, Computers and Artificial Intelligence (ECAI)* (pp. 1–6). https://doi.org/10.1109/ECAI58194.2023.10194039

Mimecast. (2024). *The state of email security 2024*. Mimecast Ltd.

Mitchell, J. P., Sullivan, A. L., Schacter, D. L., & Budson, A. E. (2006). Mis-attribution errors in Alzheimer's disease: The illusory truth effect. *Neuropsychology*, *20*(2), 185–192. https://doi.org/10.1037/0894-4105.20.2.185

Mitnick, K. D., & Simon, W. L. (2011). *The art of deception: Controlling the human element of security*. Wiley.

Montañez R, Golob E and Xu S (2020) Human Cognition Through the Lens of Social Engineering Cyberattacks. Front. Psychol. 11:1755. https://doi.org/10.3389/fpsyg.2020.01755

Murphy, G., Loftus, E., Grady, R., Levine, L., & Greene, C. (2020). Fool me twice: How effective is debriefing in false memory studies? *Memory*, *28*(9), 938–949. https://doi.org/10.1080/09658211.2020.1803917

Nobles, C. (2022). Stress, burnout, and security fatigue in cybersecurity: A human factors problem. *HOLISTICA – Journal of Business and Public Administration*, *13*(2), 49–72. https://doi.org/10.2478/hjbpa-2022-0003

Ofoegbu, K. D. O., Osundare, O. S., Ike, C. S., Fakeyede, O. G., & Ige, A. B. (2023). Data-driven cyber threat intelligence: Leveraging behavioral analytics for proactive defense mechanisms. *Computer Science & IT Research Journal*, *4*(3), 502–524. https://doi.org/10.51594/csitrj.v4i3.1501

Pacella, J. M. (2016). The cybersecurity threat: Compliance and the role of whistleblowers. *Brook. J. Corp. Fin. & Com. L.*, 11, 39–68. https://doi.org/10.2139/ssrn.2803995

Papatsaroucha, D., Nikoloudakis, Y., Kefaloukos, I., Pallis, E., & Markakis, E. K. (2021). A survey on human and personality vulnerability assessment in cyber-security: Challenges, approaches, and open issues. *arXiv preprint arXiv: 2106.09986*.

Parsons, K., McCormac, A., Butavicius, M., & Ferguson, L. (2014). *Human factors and information security: Individual, culture and security environment*. Australian Defence Science and Technology Organisation.

Peltzman, S. (1975). The effects of automobile safety regulation. *Journal of Political Economy*, *83*(4), 677–725.

Petropoulou, F., & Varouchas, E. (2024). Cracking the code: How social media and human behavior shape cybersecurity challenges. In A. Moallem (Ed.), *Human factors in cybersecurity* (AHFE (2024) International Conference, AHFE Open Access, Vol. 127). AHFE International, USA. http://doi.org/10.54941/ahfe1004783

Pfleeger, S. L., & Caputo, D. D. (2012). Leveraging behavioral science to mitigate cyber security risk. *Computers & Security*, *31*(4), 597–611. https://doi.org/10.1016/j.cose.2011.12.010

Pollini, A., Callari, T. C., Tedeschi, A., et al. (2022). Leveraging human factors in cybersecurity: An integrated methodological approach. *Cognition Technology Work, 24*, 371–390. https://doi.org/10.1007/s10111-021-00683-y

Putnam, P. T., & Chang, S. W. C. (2021). Toward a holistic view of value and social processing in the amygdala: Insights from primate behavioral neurophysiology. *Behavioural Brain Research*, *411*, 113356. https://doi.org/10.1016/j.bbr.2021.113356

Reeves, A., Delfabbro, P., & Calic, D. (2021). Encouraging employee engagement with cybersecurity: How to tackle cyber fatigue. *SAGE Open*, *11*(1). https://doi.org/10.1177/21582440211000049

Renaud, K., Musarurwa, A., & Zimmermann, V. (2021). Contemplating blame in cyber security. In J. Lopez, A. Siraj, & K. Perumalla (Eds.), *Proceedings of the 16th International Conference on Cyber Warfare and Security: ICCWS 2021* (pp. 309–317).

Rohan, R., Funilkul, S., Pal, D., & Chutimaskul, W. (2021). Understanding of human factors in cybersecurity: A systematic literature review. In *2021 International Conference on Computational Performance Evaluation (ComPE)* (pp. 133–140). IEEE. https://doi.org/10.1109/ComPE53109.2021.9752358

Ross, L., Greene, D., & House, P. (1977). The false consensus effect: An egocentric bias in social perception and attribution processes. *Journal of Experimental Social Psychology*, *13*(3), 279–301. https://doi.org/10.1016/0022-1031(77)90049-X

Rys, M., Ślusarek, A., & Zieliński, K. (2025). Caught off guard: When experts fall for quishing, is awareness enough? *Security and Privacy*, *8*(1), Article e486. https://doi.org/10.1002/spy2.486

Sachs, D. S. (2024). Deciphering the supply chain chessboard: The science of decision-making in risk management. *The Pinnacle: A Journal by Scholar-Practitioners*, 2(2). https://doi.org/10.61643/c30815

Singh, B., & Cheema, S. S. (2024). Psychology in cybersecurity: Unveiling the human dimensions of digital resilience. *International Journal of Advanced Networking and Applications*, *16*(1), 6281–6290.

Siponen, M., Mahmood, M. A., & Pahnila, S. (2014). Employees' adherence to information security policies: An exploratory field study. *Information & Management*, *51*(2), 217–224. https://doi.org/10.1016/j.im.2013.08.006

Thite, M., & Iyer, R. (2025). Addressing the gap in information security: An HR-centric and AI-driven framework for mitigating insider threats. *Personnel Review*, *54*(3), 935–951. https://doi.org/10.1108/PR-04-2023-0358

Tsanov, I. (2024). Social engineering threats in cybersecurity: Risk mitigation through behavioral insights. In *2024 International Conference Automatics and Informatics (ICAI)* (pp. 136–141). IEEE. https://doi.org/10.1109/ICAI63388.2024.10851536

Tversky, A., & Kahneman, D. (1974). Judgment under uncertainty: Heuristics and biases. *Science*, *185*(4157), 1124–1131. https://doi.org/10.1126/science.185.4157.1124

Virtanen, T. (2024). Psychological effects of continuity-threatening cyber incidents. *European Conference on Cyber Warfare and Security*. https://doi.org/10.34190/eccws.23.1.2268

Volz, K. G., & Hertwig, R. (2016). Emotions and decisions: Beyond conceptual vagueness and the rationality muddle. *Perspectives on Psychological Science*, *11*(1), 101–116. https://doi.org/10.1177/1745691615619608

Wang, J., Li, Y., & Rao, H. R. (2016). Overconfidence in phishing email detection. *Journal of the Association for Information Systems*, *17*(1), Article 1. https://doi.org/10.17705/1jais.00442

Wantenaar, L. (2022, December 15). Social engineering and the use of persuasion to commit cyber fraud. In Cyber Security: A Peer-Reviewed Journal, Volume 6, Issue 2. https://doi.org/10.69554/KCCT5734

West, R. (2008). The psychology of security. *Communications of the ACM, 51*(4), 34–40.

Wibowo, B. (2024). Social engineering as a major cybersecurity threat: Analysis of challenges and solutions for organizations. *International Journal of Science Education and Cultural Studies*, *3*(2), 57–65. https://doi.org/10.58291/ijsecs.v3i2.306

Workman, M., Bommer, W. H., & Straub, D. (2008). Security lapses and the omission of information security measures: A threat control model and empirical test. *Computers in Human Behavior*, *24*(6), 2799–2816. https://doi.org/10.1016/j.chb.2008.04.005

Zheltyakova, M., Kireev, M., Korotkov, A., & Medvedev, S. (2020). Neural mechanisms of deception in a social context: An fMRI replication study. *Scientific Reports*, *10*, 10713. https://doi.org/10.1038/s41598-020-67721-z

Chapter 4

# Impacts on Organizational Culture

## LEARNING OBJECTIVES

- Examine how the shared values, beliefs, and behaviors within an organization influence its approach to managing and mitigating cyber risks.
- Learn how effective leadership can shape a proactive security mindset, integrate cybersecurity into strategic initiatives, and set the tone for a secure organizational environment.
- Explore actionable methods to shift organizational culture, empowering security teams and practitioners to embed security as a core organizational value.

## THE CRITICAL IMPORTANCE OF ORGANIZATIONAL CULTURE IN CYBERSECURITY

Organizational culture can be defined as the shared assumptions, values, and beliefs that govern how people behave in organizations. When it comes to cybersecurity, culture manifests in how teams prioritize security, how information is shared, and how decision-making occurs around risk management (Corradini, 2020; Dahmer, 2020). A robust security culture ensures that security is not an afterthought but is integrated into the fabric of the organization. This is particularly important for security teams and practitioners, who are responsible not only for implementing technical defenses but also for shaping the mindset that guides everyday decision-making in the face of cyber threats (Huang & Pearlson, 2019; Marotta & Pearlson, 2019).

In an era of sophisticated cyberattacks and an ever-evolving threat landscape, organizations that embrace a proactive, security-conscious culture tend to be more resilient (Aksoy, 2024; Neri et al., 2024). The interplay between technology and people is especially critical in the security domain; even the most advanced technical solutions can be undermined by human error, miscommunication, or a lack of awareness (De Silva, 2023; Lie et al., 2021). Hence, a strong cultural foundation becomes essential in

DOI: 10.1201/9781003606345-4

aligning the organization's overall mission with robust cybersecurity practices (Aldulaimi et al., 2023; Pankajakshan & Bangur, 2024).

## FOCUSING ON SECURITY TEAMS AND PRACTITIONERS

Unlike approaches that primarily target end-user awareness or training, the focus here is on the inner workings of security teams and the professionals who defend organizations from cyber threats. These teams are on the front lines, handling critical tasks such as threat detection, incident response, and vulnerability management (Ioannou et al., 2019; Yulianto & Soewito, 2023). Their expertise and rapid decision-making are essential in mitigating risks and ensuring the organization remains secure. Additionally, the culture within these teams fosters collaboration, continuous improvement, and innovation in the face of evolving threats (Corradini, 2020; Dahmer, 2020). Overall organizational culture also plays a significant role by providing support, resources, and a framework that encourages proactive security measures. Together, these factors determine the effectiveness of a security team in protecting the organization from cyber-attacks (Neri et al., 2023; Onumo et al., 2021).

For security practitioners, the organizational environment determines not only the resources available to them but also the degree of support they receive from leadership (Aksoy, 2024; Aldulaimi et al., 2023). A culture that values continuous learning, open communication, and proactive risk management enables these professionals to stay ahead of emerging threats and adapt to new challenges (Bowen & Sethi, 2022; Lie et al., 2021). In contrast, a culture that is resistant to change or that prioritizes short-term gains over long-term security can stifle innovation and undermine the effectiveness of even the most skilled security professionals (De Silva, 2023; Pankajakshan & Bangur, 2024).

## UNDERSTANDING ORGANIZATIONAL CULTURE

Unlike approaches that primarily target end-user awareness or training, the focus here is on the inner workings of security teams and the professionals who defend organizations from cyber threats. These teams are on the front lines, handling critical tasks such as threat detection, incident response, and vulnerability management (Ioannou et al., 2019; Yulianto & Soewito, 2023). Their expertise and rapid decision-making are essential in mitigating risks and ensuring the organization remains secure. Additionally, the culture within these teams fosters collaboration, continuous improvement, and innovation in the face of evolving threats (Corradini, 2020; Dahmer, 2020). Overall organizational culture also plays a significant role by providing support, resources, and a framework that encourages proactive security measures. Together, these factors determine the effectiveness of a security team in protecting the organization from cyberattacks (Neri et al., 2023; Onumo et al., 2021).

For security practitioners, the organizational environment determines not only the resources available to them but also the degree of support they receive from leadership (Aksoy, 2024; Aldulaimi et al., 2023). A culture that values continuous learning, open communication, and proactive risk management enables these professionals to stay ahead of emerging threats and adapt to new challenges (Bowen & Sethi, 2022; Lie et al., 2021). In contrast, a culture that is resistant to change or that prioritizes short-term gains over long-term security can stifle innovation and undermine the effectiveness of even the most skilled security professionals (De Silva, 2023; Pankajakshan & Bangur, 2024).

The way an organization's culture is structured can either serve as a powerful enabler of robust cybersecurity practices or become a significant impediment. A positive culture fosters an environment where security is woven into every decision and process, enabling teams to respond quickly and effectively to threats. When the values and norms prioritize risk management and collaboration, security practices become more proactive and resilient (Corradini, 2020; Dahmer, 2020). In contrast, a fragmented or apathetic culture can lead to overlooked vulnerabilities and delayed responses, severely compromising an organization's defenses (Dorairajan, 2024).

Historically, organizational cultures have evolved alongside technological advancements and emerging cybersecurity challenges. In the early days of computing, security was often an afterthought, with organizations focusing primarily on operational efficiency rather than risk management. As cyber threats have grown in sophistication, the need for a culture that values security has become increasingly apparent (Pankajakshan & Bangur, 2024). This evolution has underscored the importance of integrating security practices into the organizational DNA rather than treating them as isolated technical concerns.

Today, the multifaceted nature of organizational culture is recognized as a key driver in the effectiveness of cybersecurity measures. Culture encompasses not only the formal policies and procedures but also the underlying beliefs, attitudes, and behaviors of employees. These cultural elements shape how security protocols are implemented and adhered to on a daily basis. An organization that nurtures a culture of continuous learning, open communication, and shared responsibility tends to be better prepared to handle the dynamic landscape of cyber threats (Aldulaimi et al., 2023; Neri et al., 2023).

This analysis examines the various dimensions of organizational culture and its direct impact on cybersecurity practices. By understanding how values, communication styles, and leadership behaviors influence security outcomes, organizations can better align their strategies to support robust defenses (De Silva, 2023). The interplay between these cultural factors and technical measures is critical, as even the most advanced security technologies can be undermined by poor cultural practices. Addressing these cultural elements can lead to a more cohesive and effective security posture (De Silva, 2023).

Finally, the way organizational culture influences the behavior and effectiveness of security teams cannot be overstated. Security professionals operate within the framework of the broader organizational mindset, and their ability to innovate and respond to threats is deeply affected by the cultural environment (Yulianto & Soewito, 2023). A supportive culture not only provides the necessary resources but also fosters an atmosphere where security concerns are openly discussed and addressed. Ultimately, by analyzing and reshaping their cultural foundations, organizations can empower their security teams to perform at their highest potential in the face of evolving cyber challenges.

## DEFINING ORGANIZATIONAL CULTURE IN THE CONTEXT OF CYBERSECURITY

Organizational culture encompasses the underlying values, beliefs, and behaviors that define how work is approached within an entity. In cybersecurity, this culture determines how rigorously policies are followed, how incidents are reported and addressed, and the overall attitude toward risk (Dahmer, 2020; Huang & Pearlson, 2019). Culture is not something that can be altered overnight; it is built over time through shared experiences, leadership examples, and the continuous reinforcement of norms (Corradini, 2020).

- **Risk Awareness:** It is the degree to which an organization understands and prioritizes the management of risk. A culture that emphasizes risk awareness ensures that potential threats are identified, communicated, and mitigated in a timely fashion (Mizrak, 2023; Parsola, 2023).
- **Accountability and Ownership:** In a healthy security culture, every team member, from security practitioners to support staff, takes responsibility for their role in safeguarding the organization's digital assets. This shared ownership is critical for a coordinated response to threats (De Silva, 2023; Lie et al., 2021).
- **Communication and Transparency:** Effective communication channels within an organization allow for quick dissemination of information, particularly in crisis situations. When teams communicate openly about vulnerabilities and incidents, it fosters an environment where continuous improvement is possible (Parkin et al., 2023).

- **Adaptability and Learning:** Cyber threats evolve rapidly. An organization that values continuous learning, adaptation, and innovation is better positioned to respond to new challenges as they emerge (Aksoy, 2024; Domańska-Szaruga, 2020).

These dimensions underscore that a company's culture is not simply an abstract concept but a dynamic force that directly shapes cybersecurity practices at every level. For security teams and practitioners, the cultural environment can either empower them to take decisive action or hamper their efforts by creating bureaucratic or adversarial conditions (Dahmer, 2020).

## HISTORICAL PERSPECTIVES AND EVOLVING CYBER THREATS

Over the past few decades, the landscape of cybersecurity has undergone dramatic shifts. In the early days of computing, security was largely an IT issue, something that could be addressed by installing antivirus software or a firewall. However, as organizations have grown more interconnected and cyber threats have become more sophisticated, the need for a holistic, culture-driven approach has become evident (Corradini, 2020; Dahmer, 2020).

Historically, many organizations operated under a "security through obscurity" model, assuming that keeping their systems hidden would protect them. As cyberattacks became more publicized and their impacts more severe, this model proved insufficient. The need for a proactive and comprehensive security culture emerged as companies began to realize that effective cybersecurity depends as much on people and processes as it does on technology (Falco & Rosenbach, 2022).

For security teams, this shift has meant a transition from purely reactive measures to a more strategic, proactive stance. The evolution of cyber threats, from simple viruses to complex state-sponsored attacks, has forced organizations to rethink their approaches. The interplay between evolving threats and organizational culture now requires that security practitioners be not only technically proficient but also adept at influencing and working within a culture that values vigilance, continuous improvement, and proactive risk management (Bowen & Sethi, 2022; Nasrullayev & Holubkin, 2024).

## HOW CULTURE SHAPES SECURITY PRACTICES

At its core, the relationship between organizational culture and cybersecurity practices is one of cause and effect. A security-conscious culture naturally leads to more rigorous security practices, while a lax or adversarial culture may leave vulnerabilities unaddressed. Several key factors illustrate this connection:

- **Policy Adoption and Enforcement:** Organizations with a strong security culture are more likely to adopt comprehensive security policies and enforce them consistently. When leadership prioritizes security, policies are taken seriously, and compliance becomes part of the everyday workflow of security teams (Dahmer, 2020; Huang & Pearlson, 2019).
- **Incident Response and Reporting:** In organizations where a blame-free culture exists, one that emphasizes learning from mistakes rather than punishing error-security practitioners are more likely to report incidents promptly. This open communication is vital for early detection and rapid response (Corradini, 2020; Parkin et al., 2023).
- **Investment in Training and Resources:** A culture that values security is reflected in the allocation of resources toward continuous training and professional development. For security teams, this means regular opportunities to update their skills and stay abreast of emerging threats (De Silva, 2023; Mizrak, 2023).
- **Cross-Functional Collaboration:** Cybersecurity is a team sport. Organizations that foster a culture of collaboration see improved coordination between different departments, enabling security teams to work more effectively with IT, risk management, and even legal and compliance units (Nasrullayev & Holubkin, 2024; Parsola, 202;).

For security practitioners, the benefits of a supportive culture are profound. They not only gain access to better training and tools but also operate within an environment that encourages innovation and proactive risk management. In contrast, when the organizational culture is misaligned with security goals, practitioners may find themselves hamstrung by outdated practices, insufficient resources, or internal resistance to change (Bowen & Sethi, 2022; Falco & Rosenbach, 2022).

## THE ROLE OF VALUES, NORMS, AND BELIEFS

The everyday actions of security teams are deeply influenced by the underlying values and norms of their organizations. For instance, if an organization places a high value on rapid innovation without corresponding attention to risk, security teams might struggle to implement robust controls (Corradini, 2020). Conversely, if the organizational belief system recognizes cybersecurity as a core component of business success, then security teams are empowered to take a leadership role in shaping strategy (Dahmer, 2020).

Some of the core values that can enhance a security-conscious culture include:

- **Integrity and Trust:** When security practitioners are trusted to make decisions and act in the organization's best interest, they are more likely to adopt innovative and effective security measures (De Silva, 2023).
- **Collaboration and Transparency:** Open lines of communication allow for the free flow of information, ensuring that potential vulnerabilities are identified and addressed before they can be exploited (Aksoy, 2024).
- **Continuous Improvement:** A commitment to learning and development fosters an environment where security teams regularly update their skills and adapt their practices to meet new challenges (Triplett, 2022).

By embedding these values into the very DNA of an organization, leaders can create an environment where security practices are not just a set of rules to follow but a shared mission that unites all members of the security team.

## IMPACT ON SECURITY TEAMS AND PRACTITIONERS

For those charged with protecting their organizations, the impact of a well-defined and supportive culture cannot be overstated. Security teams and practitioners who work in environments that prioritize cybersecurity tend to exhibit higher morale, improved performance, and greater innovation in problem-solving (Pankajakshan & Bangur, 2024). They are more likely to experiment with new technologies, share intelligence on emerging threats, and collaborate across departmental boundaries to implement holistic security strategies (Yulianto & Soewito, 2023).

In contrast, a culture that is indifferent or hostile to security can lead to burnout, disengagement, and, ultimately, an increased risk of security breaches. Security practitioners in such environments might feel undervalued or even blamed when incidents occur, leading to a vicious cycle of reduced reporting and less effective incident response (Jones, 2024). Clearly, aligning organizational culture with robust cybersecurity practices is not only a strategic imperative but also a moral one, ensuring that the professionals who shoulder the enormous responsibility of defending digital assets are supported at every level.

## DEVELOPING STRATEGIES FOR LEADERSHIP-DRIVEN CULTURE

A transformative security culture begins at the top. Without engaged and proactive leadership, even the most well-designed security policies can fall short (Falco & Rosenbach, 2022). Leadership is the catalyst for cultural change. Leaders, ranging from board members to C-suite executives and middle management, must not only endorse but actively embody the principles of cybersecurity. Their actions, communications, and decisions send

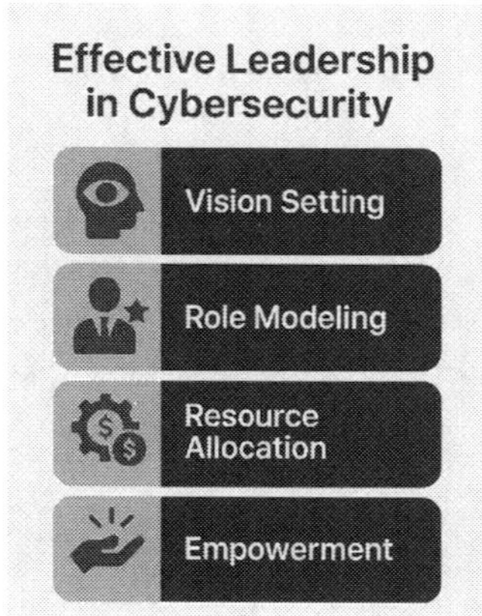


*Figure 4.1* Effective Cybersecurity Leadership Essentials

powerful signals to the entire organization about what is valued (Dahmer, 2020). For security teams, having leaders who understand and prioritize cybersecurity translates into tangible benefits, such as more resources, greater autonomy, and a clearer strategic mandate (Huang & Pearlson, 2019) (Figure 4.1).

Effective leadership in cybersecurity involves:

- **Vision Setting**: Leaders must articulate a clear vision for cybersecurity that aligns with the broader goals of the organization. This vision should emphasize the long-term value of investing in robust security practices (De Silva, 2023).
- **Role Modeling**: When leaders visibly follow best practices, such as routinely participating in security briefings or advocating for rigorous security standards, they set an example for others (Alghazo et al., 2023).
- **Resource Allocation**: By prioritizing cybersecurity in budgeting and strategic planning, leaders can ensure that security teams have the tools and training they need to stay ahead of threats (Marotta & Pearlson, 2019).
- **Empowerment**: Leaders who empower their security teams to make decisions and take calculated risks help foster an environment where innovation and proactive threat management are the norm (Triplett, 2022).

## Strategies for Engaging Executive Leadership

To build a culture of security that resonates throughout an organization, it is essential to secure buy-in from executive leadership. This involves not only demonstrating the technical aspects of cybersecurity but also framing security as a business imperative (Parkin et al., 2023). Key strategies include:

- **Linking Security to Business Outcomes**: Executives are more likely to support security initiatives when they understand how these measures protect the organization's reputation, revenue streams, and long-term viability. Presenting clear, quantifiable risks, and the potential cost of breaches, helps create a compelling business case (Falco & Rosenbach, 2022).
- **Regular Communication**: Establishing a cadence of regular briefings and updates ensures that executives remain informed about the latest threats, vulnerabilities, and security initiatives. This communication should be clear, jargon-free, and focused on strategic implications rather than technical minutiae (Burrell, 2019).
- **Establishing Metrics and Key Performance Indicators (KPIs)**: Defining KPIs for cybersecurity can help leaders track progress and identify areas for improvement. Metrics might include incident response times, vulnerability remediation rates, or the number of reported near-miss events (De Silva, 2023).
- **Involving Leadership in Training and Simulations**: Engaging executives in cybersecurity drills and tabletop exercises not only enhances their understanding of potential threats but also reinforces the message that security is everyone's responsibility (Dahmer, 2020).

## Communication, Visibility, and Accountability

A transparent and communicative environment is essential for fostering leadership-driven security awareness. Leaders should create platforms for open dialogue where security concerns can be raised and addressed promptly. For security teams and practitioners, this means having clear channels for reporting, receiving feedback, and collaborating across functions (Triplett, 2022).

Key aspects include:

- **Visible Leadership Support**: When executives are seen actively participating in security initiatives, it reinforces the importance of these measures and sets the tone for the rest of the organization (Parkin et al., 2023).
- **Accountability Mechanisms**: Establishing clear accountability structures ensures that every team and individual understands their role in the broader cybersecurity strategy. This may involve regular audits, performance reviews focused on security outcomes, and clear reporting lines (Falco & Rosenbach, 2022).
- **Cross-Departmental Collaboration**: Security is inherently interdisciplinary. Leaders must foster an environment where different departments, such as IT, risk management, and compliance, work together

seamlessly. For security practitioners, this cross-functional collaboration can lead to a more integrated and effective response to emerging threats (Triplett, 2022).
- **Feedback Loops**: Constructive feedback from both leadership and peer groups helps refine security practices over time. A culture that values continuous improvement is one in which security teams feel empowered to suggest innovations and improvements without fear of retribution (Dahmer, 2020).
- Integrating Security Goals into Organizational Objectives

One of the most effective ways to ensure that security is taken seriously is by integrating cybersecurity objectives into the overall strategic plan of the organization. When security goals are embedded in the organization's key performance metrics, they become part of the daily operational fabric (Aksoy, 2024).

- **Strategic Alignment**: Leaders should ensure that cybersecurity goals are seen not as separate or secondary but as integral to the organization's mission. This can be achieved by aligning security metrics with business performance indicators and risk management frameworks (Parkin et al., 2023).
- **Incentive Structures**: Reward systems that recognize proactive security behavior, from both leaders and security teams, can significantly enhance motivation and performance. Incentives might include recognition programs, bonuses for exceeding security benchmarks, or professional development opportunities (Burrell, 2019).
- **Regular Review and Adaptation**: As the threat landscape evolves, so too must the organization's security goals. Regular reviews of cybersecurity policies and practices ensure that the organization remains agile and responsive to new challenges (De Silva, 2023). For security practitioners, this iterative process fosters a culture of learning and resilience.

## EMPOWERING SECURITY PRACTITIONERS THROUGH LEADERSHIP

Finally, leadership-driven security awareness must translate into tangible empowerment for security teams on the front lines. Leaders should ensure that practitioners have the autonomy, resources, and strategic backing needed to make critical decisions. Empowerment involves not only providing technical tools and training but also fostering an environment where practitioners feel their expertise is trusted and valued (Aksoy, 2024).

This empowerment can take many forms:

- **Decentralized Decision-Making**: Allowing security practitioners to make decisions in real time, especially during incidents, can be the difference between a contained threat and a full-scale breach (De Silva, 2023).

- **Continuous Professional Development:** Leaders must prioritize ongoing training and certifications for security teams, ensuring they remain current on the latest technologies, threats, and best practices (De Silva, 2023).
- **Mentorship and Coaching:** Establishing mentorship programs where experienced security professionals guide and support newer team members helps build a strong internal community and facilitates knowledge transfer (Bowen & Sethi, 2022).
- **Access to Cutting-Edge Tools:** Investment in state-of-the-art security tools not only improves threat detection and response but also signals to practitioners that their work is valued and supported at the highest levels (Ofoegbu et al., 2023).

## Building Through Cultural Transformation

A truly resilient organization is one where security is woven into every facet of its operations. Cultural transformation is the process of reshaping an organization's attitudes, behaviors, and practices to create an environment in which security is a core value (Dahmer, 2020). This section lays out a comprehensive framework for achieving such a transformation, with a focus on strategies and roadmaps that empower security teams and practitioners. Cultural transformation involves a deliberate, sustained effort to shift the underlying beliefs and practices within an organization.

Transformation means moving from a reactive, compliance-driven approach to one that is proactive, integrated, and adaptive. The goal is to create a "security-first" mindset where every decision, process, and project is evaluated through the lens of risk management and threat mitigation (Marotta & Pearlson, 2019). For security teams, this transformation can mean transitioning from a siloed, tool-centric mindset to a more holistic, collaborative approach that emphasizes strategic thinking, continuous improvement, and proactive risk management (Przekota, 2024). It involves not only updating policies and procedures but also changing the way people think about and engage with security on a daily basis.

# FRAMEWORKS FOR ORGANIZATIONAL CHANGE

Several established frameworks can serve as models for cultural transformation in cybersecurity. These frameworks offer structured approaches that guide organizations through the complex process of change.

Some of the most prominent include:

- **The ADKAR Model:** Focused on individual change, the ADKAR framework emphasizes Awareness, Desire, Knowledge, Ability, and Reinforcement. By applying these principles, organizations can drive lasting change at the individual and team levels (Burton, 2024) (Figure 4.2).

- **Kotter's 8-Step Process for Leading Change**: This model outlines steps, from establishing a sense of urgency to consolidating gains, that help organizations systematically address cultural barriers and build momentum for transformation (Burton, 2024) (Figure 4.3).
- **The National Institute of Standards and Technology (NIST) Cybersecurity Framework (CSF)**: Although primarily a technical framework, the NIST CSF's emphasis on governance, risk assessment, and continuous improvement can be adapted to support cultural change initiatives (National Institute of Standards and Technology, 2024) (Figure 4.4).

Security frameworks provide practitioners with a structured approach to managing change by outlining the stages of transformation and necessary actions at each step. These frameworks emphasize that security is not a one-time initiative but an ongoing process of adaptation and improvement. By fostering a security-first mindset, organizations can better respond to emerging threats, regulatory changes, and technological advancements. They also help security leaders anticipate resistance, address behavioral challenges, and embed cybersecurity practices into daily operations. Integrating behavioral science with security strategies ensures that changes are not only implemented but also sustained over time. Ultimately, this proactive approach strengthens resilience, enhances risk management, and aligns cybersecurity efforts with long-term business objectives (Dahmer, 2020).

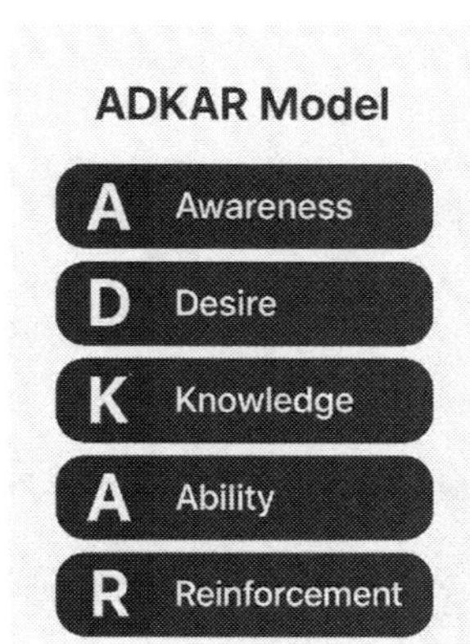


*Figure 4.2* ADKAR Change Management Model

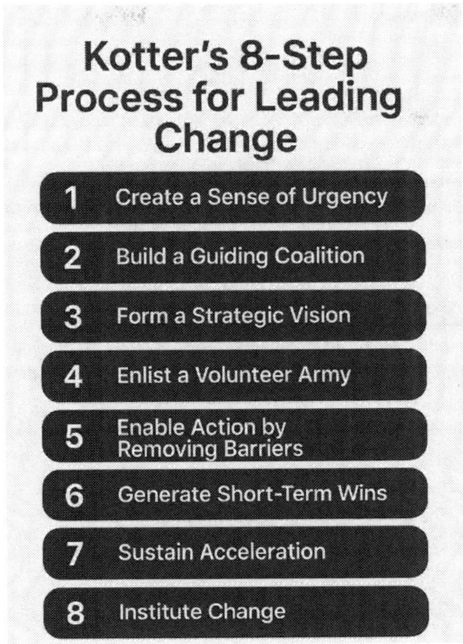


*Figure 4.3* Kotter's 8-Step Change Process

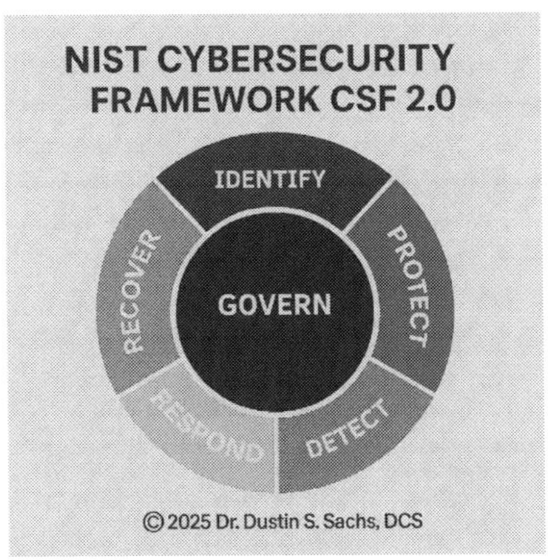


*Figure 4.4* NIST Cybersecurity Framework CSF 2.0

## ROADMAPS FOR BUILDING SECURITY-CENTRIC TEAMS

A successful cultural transformation in cybersecurity requires a clear and actionable roadmap that integrates security into the organization's core values and daily operations. This roadmap should focus on building agile, well-trained teams that align with strategic business objectives. Leadership commitment is essential, ensuring that cybersecurity is prioritized and embedded in decision-making processes. Continuous education and cross-departmental collaboration help foster a shared responsibility for security, preventing silos and improving overall awareness. Regular assessments and feedback loops ensure ongoing progress and adaptation to evolving threats. Ultimately, a strong security culture enhances resilience, drives innovation, and supports long-term business success.

- **Assessment and Benchmarking**: Conducting a thorough evaluation of the current cultural state is the first step. This includes gathering data on employee attitudes, existing practices, and the level of leadership support for cybersecurity initiatives. Benchmarking against industry standards or peer organizations can help identify gaps and opportunities for improvement (Dahmer, 2020).
- **Defining the Vision and Strategy**: With a clear understanding of the current state, leaders and security practitioners must work together to define a vision for a security-conscious culture. This vision should be translated into a detailed strategy with measurable objectives and timelines (Handri et al., 2024).
- **Engagement and Communication**: Transparent communication is critical during the transformation process. Leaders must articulate the benefits of change and involve security teams in the planning process. Regular updates, town hall meetings, and cross-functional workshops help maintain momentum and ensure that everyone is aligned with the vision (Silva, 2024).
- **Training and Skill Development**: A central pillar of the roadmap is continuous professional development. Tailored training programs, certifications, and mentorship initiatives ensure that security practitioners are equipped with the skills and knowledge necessary to drive change (Sabillon, 2022).
- **Implementation and Iteration**: Cultural transformation is not a one-off event; it requires ongoing monitoring, feedback, and adaptation. Organizations should establish mechanisms for regular review and update their strategies based on lessons learned and emerging trends in the cybersecurity landscape (Aksoy, 2025).

## TRAINING, DEVELOPMENT, AND CONTINUOUS IMPROVEMENT

For security practitioners, ongoing training is not just a benefit; it's a necessity in an ever-changing digital landscape. The rapid pace of technological advancement, coupled with the constantly evolving threat landscape, means that security professionals must stay ahead of emerging risks, vulnerabilities, and attack techniques to protect their organizations effectively. Continuous learning should be a core tenet of any security-conscious organization, ensuring that teams are well equipped to adapt to new tools, methodologies, and regulatory requirements. Training programs must go beyond just technical skills like penetration testing, threat intelligence, and incident response; they should also focus on developing soft skills such as leadership, communication, and crisis management, which are essential for effective decision-making under pressure (Sabillon, 2022). By fostering a culture of lifelong learning, organizations can strengthen their cybersecurity posture, enhance collaboration across departments, and ensure that security teams remain proactive rather than reactive in the face of evolving cyber threats.

- **Technical Certifications and Workshops**: Providing opportunities for certifications in areas such as penetration testing, threat intelligence, and incident response ensures that practitioners remain at the forefront of industry best practices (Pankajakshan & Bangur, 2024).
- **Scenario-Based Exercises and Simulations**: Tabletop exercises and simulated incident response drills help security teams practice their skills in realistic environments. These exercises build confidence, improve coordination, and reveal areas for further improvement (Angafor et al., 2023).
- **Leadership and Soft Skills Development**: For many security practitioners, technical expertise is only part of the picture. Training in leadership, communication, and strategic planning empowers them to advocate for security initiatives and drive organizational change from within (Dalal et al., 2021).
- **Feedback Mechanisms and Continuous Improvement**: Establishing regular feedback loops, through peer reviews, performance evaluations, and after-action reports, ensures that lessons learned from both successes and failures are systematically integrated into future strategies (Parsola, 2023).

### Metrics and Continuous Monitoring

No cultural transformation is complete without effective mechanisms for measuring progress, as tracking improvements ensures that initiatives are driving meaningful change. For security teams and practitioners, KPIs serve as essential tools to gauge the effectiveness of cybersecurity initiatives and overall security posture. Metrics such as cybersecurity awareness levels, incident response times, and training effectiveness provide tangible evidence of progress, helping organizations identify areas that require further attention. Regularly analyzing these KPIs allows teams to refine their strategies, allocate resources efficiently, and reinforce behaviors that contribute to a strong security culture. Without these measurement mechanisms, organizations risk investing in security initiatives without fully understanding their impact or whether they are achieving long-term behavioral and operational improvements.

- Incident Detection and Response Rates: Tracking how quickly security teams detect and mitigate threats provides a direct measure of operational efficiency and preparedness. Studies highlight the importance of developing situational awareness scoring systems to evaluate cybersecurity response times effectively (Damianou et al., 2024).
- Training Completion and Certification Levels: Monitoring the uptake of training programs and the achievement of certifications can help gauge the overall skill level of the security team. Research has shown that AI-based security awareness training significantly improves employees' risk scores and cybersecurity knowledge (Ansari, 2022). Additionally, integrating machine learning for training effectiveness evaluation provides more accurate assessments (Sheng, 2020).
- Employee Engagement and Satisfaction: Surveys and feedback mechanisms can assess how security practitioners perceive the organizational culture and leadership support, highlighting areas where further improvements are needed. The development of cybersecurity awareness training programs, particularly those utilizing gamification, has been found to increase engagement and knowledge retention (Taherdoost, 2024).
- Audit and Compliance Scores: Regular internal and external audits help ensure that security practices are aligned with organizational policies and industry best practices. Studies propose structured cybersecurity awareness program evaluations using defined performance metrics to assess their impact on organizational security posture (Chaudhary et al., 2022).

By setting clear benchmarks, organizations establish measurable goals that provide a structured framework for tracking progress throughout the transformation process. Regularly reviewing these benchmarks allows leaders to assess the effectiveness of implemented strategies, identify areas requiring adjustment, and ensure alignment with overarching business objectives. This continuous evaluation fosters a culture of accountability, encouraging employees to remain engaged and committed to the organization's evolving vision. Additionally, it enables organizations to proactively address emerging challenges, adapt to industry trends, and refine their approach based on real-time insights. Through this iterative process, organizations can sustain momentum, reinforce desired cultural behaviors, and drive long-term success in an ever-changing environment.

## CASE STUDIES, BEST PRACTICES, AND IMPLEMENTATION GUIDELINES

Building on the foundational understanding of how organizational culture and leadership drive cybersecurity practices, this segment delves into practical examples, actionable guidelines, and strategic frameworks. Research highlights that organizational cybersecurity culture must integrate leadership engagement, cross-functional collaboration, and continuous education to build resilience against cyber threats (Dahmer, 2020). Through case studies, lessons learned, and best practices, this analysis offers a roadmap for security-centric teams and highlights emerging trends shaping the cybersecurity landscape (Corradini, 2020).

## REAL-WORLD EXAMPLES OF CULTURAL TRANSFORMATION

Organizational transformation is best understood when illustrated by real-world examples, as practical scenarios provide valuable insights into the complexities of change. In this section, we examine several hypothetical yet highly realistic case studies that reflect common challenges faced by enterprises striving to embed a strong security culture. These cases highlight the strategic interventions implemented to address issues such as employee resistance, leadership buy-in, and the integration of security into daily operations. By analyzing the outcomes, we gain a deeper understanding of the key factors that drive successful cultural change and the potential roadblocks that organizations must navigate. Through these examples, leaders can extract actionable lessons to apply within their own enterprises, fostering a more resilient and security-conscious workforce.

## CASE STUDY: FINSECURE CORP

### Background

FinSecure Corp, a mid-sized financial institution, was traditionally known for its rapid innovation in digital banking solutions. However, with increased exposure to cyber risks and the rising sophistication of attacks targeting the financial sector, the company found its traditional "security through obscurity" methods increasingly inadequate. Initially, cybersecurity was seen as an IT concern, a siloed function with little influence over broader strategic decisions.

## Challenges Identified

- **Fragmented Security Practices:** Security teams operated in isolation, leading to inconsistencies in incident reporting and response.
- **Leadership Disconnect:** The executive leadership did not fully grasp the long-term implications of cybersecurity risks, leading to underinvestment in necessary tools and training.
- **Reactive Culture:** A lack of proactive risk management meant that most security measures were implemented in response to incidents rather than as part of a preventive strategy.
- **Inadequate Cross-Functional Communication:** There was minimal coordination between the IT, legal, and risk management departments, which hampered a unified response to emerging threats.

## Interventions and Strategies

FinSecure's transformation journey began with a comprehensive cultural assessment. Senior leadership, spurred by a near-miss cybersecurity incident, commissioned an external audit and a series of internal focus groups to diagnose the gaps in their approach. The following key interventions were introduced:

1. **Executive Sponsorship and Vision Setting:**
    - The Chief Executive Officer (CEO) and Chief Financial Officer (CFO) publicly committed to making cybersecurity a core strategic pillar.
    - Regular "cybersecurity briefings" were instituted at board meetings, and KPIs related to security were integrated into the executive dashboard.
2. **Restructuring and Empowering the Security Team:**
    - A Chief Information Security Officer (CISO) with a clear mandate was appointed.
    - The security team was reorganized to include representatives from IT, risk management, legal, and compliance, breaking down silos and fostering cross-functional collaboration.
3. **Comprehensive Training and Professional Development:**
    - The organization launched an internal certification program for security practitioners, coupled with regular scenario-based exercises and simulated incident responses.
    - Investments were made in state-of-the-art monitoring tools and threat intelligence platforms.

4. **Cultural Initiatives and Communication:**
    - A "security champion" program was rolled out to identify and empower advocates within every department who could help bridge the gap between technical teams and operational units.
    - Transparent reporting channels were established to ensure that lessons learned from incidents were shared across the organization without fear of punitive repercussions.

### Outcomes

Within 18 months, FinSecure reported a marked improvement in its incident response times, a significant increase in internal reporting of near-miss events, and an overall boost in employee morale among security practitioners. The transformation not only mitigated risks but also fostered an environment where security was seen as a business enabler rather than an operational burden.

## CASE STUDY: TECHFORWARD SOLUTIONS

### Background

TechForward Solutions, a leading technology firm with a global presence, was renowned for its cutting-edge product development and rapid market expansion. However, its security posture lagged behind its pace of innovation. Despite the presence of a dedicated cybersecurity team, the organizational culture was predominantly "development-first," where speed and agility often overshadowed risk management.

### Challenges Identified

- **Prioritization Conflicts:** The drive for innovation led to security measures being sidelined, especially during product launch phases.
- **Limited Leadership Engagement:** Although technical teams recognized the importance of security, executive leadership was more focused on market performance, resulting in insufficient strategic backing for cybersecurity initiatives.
- **Siloed Operations:** Communication between the development, operations, and security teams was infrequent, leading to inconsistent application of security protocols in product development cycles.

### Interventions and Strategies

Recognizing that the security team's recommendations were not resonating at the executive level, TechForward's leadership embarked on a cultural transformation journey. Key measures included:

- **Reframing Security as a Competitive Advantage:**
  - The leadership worked closely with the security team to articulate how robust cybersecurity measures could serve as a market differentiator, building trust with customers and stakeholders.
  - Detailed risk assessments were conducted to translate potential financial and reputational losses into tangible business impacts.

1. **Leadership Integration in Security Initiatives:**
   - Executive members participated in cybersecurity training sessions and crisis simulation exercises, ensuring that they experienced firsthand the complexities of managing cyber threats.
   - A regular "security roundtable" was introduced, inviting cross-departmental representatives to discuss current threats, challenges, and strategic responses.
2. **Embedding Security in Product Development:**
   - A "security by design" philosophy was institutionalized within the product development lifecycle.
   - Security teams were assigned early in the product development process, ensuring that risk assessments and secure coding practices became integral components of innovation efforts.
3. **Cross-Functional Collaboration and Transparency:**
   - An internal portal was launched to share security updates, threat intelligence, and best practices across departments.
   - Regular postmortem analyses of security incidents and near-misses were conducted and shared, fostering a learning culture.

### Outcomes

TechForward Solutions experienced a significant cultural shift over two years. Security became a shared responsibility, embedded in the product development ethos rather than viewed as an afterthought. Enhanced collaboration led to quicker remediation of vulnerabilities, and the company's reputation as a secure, forward-thinking organization grew, ultimately contributing to an increase in customer trust and market share.

## ADDITIONAL CASE EXAMPLES: SMALL AND MEDIUM ENTERPRISES

Not every organization undergoing cultural transformation is a large enterprise with vast resources and dedicated security teams. Many small and medium enterprises (SMEs) have also recognized the critical need for a security-first mindset, understanding that cyber threats do not discriminate based on company size. These organizations are increasingly prioritizing cybersecurity awareness, training, and best practices to protect their assets, customer data, and overall business continuity. Despite often having limited budgets and fewer dedicated security personnel, SMEs are finding innovative ways to embed security into their operations, leveraging automation, employee education, and third-party security providers. By fostering a culture where cybersecurity is viewed as a shared responsibility rather than a technical afterthought, SMEs can build resilience against evolving threats and ensure long-term sustainability in an increasingly digital world.

Consider the following aggregated examples:

- SME in Healthcare:
  A regional healthcare provider revamped its cybersecurity culture after a ransomware attack nearly paralyzed its operations. By establishing a dedicated security task force and promoting a culture of transparency, the provider not only improved its incident response but also ensured compliance with stringent healthcare data protection regulations. Leadership-led initiatives included regular briefings on evolving threats and mandatory training sessions for security practitioners, leading to a 70% improvement in reported security incidents.
- **SME in Manufacturing:**
  A mid-sized manufacturing company with a growing digital footprint undertook a cultural transformation after experiencing repeated industrial control system (ICS) vulnerabilities. By integrating cybersecurity goals into its overall business strategy and emphasizing cross-departmental collaboration, the company managed to secure its operational technology (OT) environment. Security practitioners were empowered through hands-on workshops and scenario-based drills that simulated cyber-physical attacks, significantly reducing downtime and operational risk.

These examples underscore that, regardless of an organization's size, fostering a security-centric culture is not just an option but a necessity for sustainable business operations. Security should be embedded into the very fabric of an organization's strategy, ensuring that it is treated not as separate or reactive function but as an integral component of business success. While the scale and complexity of implementing a security-first approach may differ across organizations, the foundational principles remain unchanged: strong leadership commitment, seamless cross-functional collaboration, a proactive and adaptive approach to risk management, and an unwavering dedication to continuous learning and improvement. Leadership plays a critical role in setting the tone for security priorities, driving accountability, and ensuring alignment with business objectives. By embracing these principles, organizations can build resilient security postures that not only mitigate risks but also create a competitive advantage in an increasingly threat-laden digital landscape.

## LESSONS LEARNED AND PITFALLS TO AVOID

Cultural transformation in cybersecurity is a challenging journey, requiring sustained commitment from leadership, employee engagement, and structural changes. Despite technological advancements, cybersecurity remains heavily dependent on human factors, with employees' behaviors and attitudes significantly impacting security outcomes (Aksoy, 2024). Organizations that fail to address cultural barriers often struggle with security implementation, leading to increased vulnerability. Lessons from past implementations indicate that a combination of leadership advocacy, continuous training, and an inclusive approach to cybersecurity policy adoption is critical for success. Additionally, companies must remain agile, adapting security practices based on emerging threats and lessons learned from past incidents.

### Importance of Early and Ongoing Executive Buy-In

One of the most critical lessons is that without strong, sustained executive support, transformation initiatives falter. Executives set the tone for cybersecurity culture by prioritizing security initiatives, allocating necessary resources, and ensuring consistent messaging (Huang & Pearlson, 2019). However, short-term thinking often undermines cybersecurity efforts, with many organizations treating security measures as temporary solutions rather than long-term strategic investments (Dorairajan, 2024). In addition, communication gaps between technical teams and business leadership can create disconnects in security priorities. To ensure ongoing executive buy-in, organizations should foster a culture where cybersecurity is integrated into broader business objectives and is regularly reviewed by top management (Falco & Rosenbach, 2022).

### Overcoming Silo Mentality

The entrenchment of siloed operations leads to fragmented security strategies, making organizations more susceptible to cyber threats. Many organizations still operate with cybersecurity teams working in isolation, limiting collaboration and reducing the effectiveness of security measures (Marotta & Pearlson, 2019). To counteract this, organizations should implement integrative processes such as cross-functional teams, shared communication platforms, and cybersecurity training for non-IT departments. Research suggests that establishing clear accountability structures fosters cooperation and shared responsibility, ensuring that security is embedded in all business functions (Neri et al., 2023). Additionally, regular interdepartmental meetings can improve information sharing, helping organizations anticipate and respond to security threats more effectively.

### The Challenge of Cultural Inertia

Resistance to change is a common barrier in cybersecurity cultural transformation. Employees accustomed to established norms often resist new cybersecurity measures, viewing them as unnecessary or disruptive (Bowen & Sethi, 2022). To address this, organizations should adopt a gradual, iterative approach that allows employees to adjust to new security practices over time. Research emphasizes the importance of feedback loops where employees can voice concerns, suggest improvements, and take an active role in shaping security initiatives (Olaniyi et al., 2023). Celebrating small wins, such as recognizing employees who adhere to security protocols, helps build momentum and fosters a security-positive culture. By reinforcing cybersecurity as an ongoing process rather than a one-time initiative, organizations can sustain long-term cultural change.

### Avoiding Overreliance on Technology

While cybersecurity tools and systems play a vital role in securing an organization, relying solely on technology without addressing human factors can undermine transformation efforts. Organizations that focus exclusively on implementing advanced security solutions often neglect the importance of fostering a security-conscious workforce (De Silva, 2023). A holistic approach that includes employee education, leadership commitment, and well-defined security policies is necessary to mitigate risks effectively (Triplett, 2022). Human-centric training programs that incorporate scenario-based exercises and role-playing simulations have been found to enhance employees' ability to respond to cyber threats (Jones, 2024). Organizations should prioritize developing security leaders who can bridge the gap between technological defenses and behavioral strategies to ensure a comprehensive security posture.

## BEST PRACTICES FOR DEVELOPING SECURITY TEAMS

Based on recent case studies and lessons learned, organizations seeking to develop and nurture security teams within a transformed cultural framework should adopt several key best practices. First, fostering a strong security culture requires leadership buy-in and a commitment to integrating cybersecurity into the organization's core values, ensuring that security is prioritized at all levels. Additionally, continuous training and development programs tailored to different roles within the security team can enhance both technical expertise and behavioral competencies, reinforcing a proactive security mindset. Encouraging cross-departmental collaboration and communication is also essential, as it helps bridge the gap between security teams and other business units, fostering a shared responsibility for cybersecurity. Lastly, implementing metrics and feedback loops to assess security awareness, team effectiveness, and incident response capabilities allows organizations to refine their strategies and maintain a resilient security culture over time (Figure 4.5).

## REMOTE WORK FROM A BEHAVIORAL SCIENCE PERSPECTIVE

The rapid expansion of remote work has not only transformed organizational structures but also fundamentally shifted human behaviors in cybersecurity. Employees working remotely exhibit varied risk perceptions, cognitive biases, and decision-making tendencies that impact security practices. Behavioral science suggests that remote workers often underestimate cyber threats due to optimism bias, assuming they are less likely to

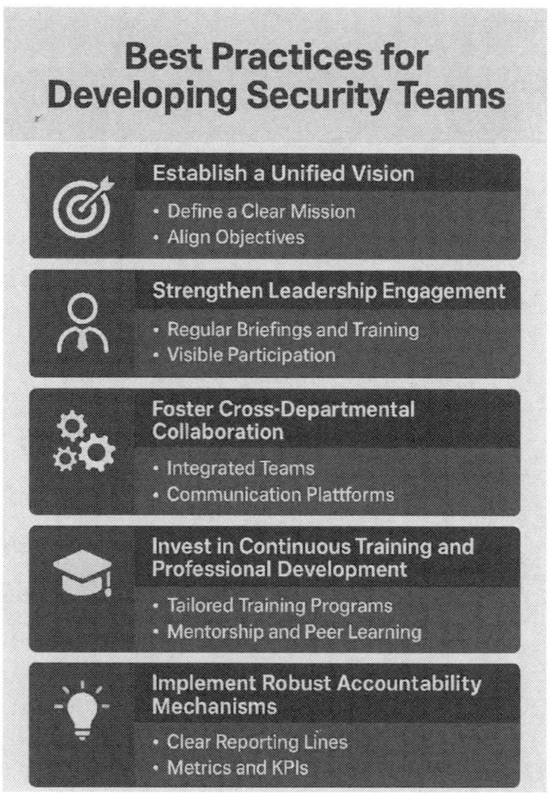


*Figure 4.5* Security Team Development Practices

be targeted than traditional office-based employees (Nwankpa & Datta, 2023). Additionally, decision fatigue and digital overload in remote work environments can lead to riskier behaviors, such as reusing passwords or ignoring security warnings (Reeves et al., 2025).

## Cognitive Load and Security Fatigue

Remote employees often juggle various tools, platforms, and communication channels, which can lead to significant cognitive overload. This mental strain makes it harder to consistently follow complex security protocols, especially when under pressure or facing tight deadlines. As a result, individuals may prioritize convenience over safety, opting to bypass security measures such as disabling multifactor authentication (MFA) or using unsecured personal devices for work-related tasks (Nobles, 2022). Over time, this behavior can increase an organization's vulnerability to cyber threats and data breaches.

## Social Norms and Compliance

Without the physical presence of a traditional workplace, employees rely heavily on social norms and the behaviors of their virtual colleagues to navigate expectations, including cybersecurity practices. In the absence of direct supervision and visible workplace cues, individuals look to their peers for guidance on acceptable behavior, often adopting the prevailing attitudes within their teams. If security policies are perceived as optional, burdensome, or inconsistently enforced, employees may deprioritize compliance, assuming that strict adherence is not essential. Furthermore, when colleagues openly dismiss or circumvent security protocols without consequence, it reinforces a culture of lax security, making it more likely that others will follow suit (Madnick et al., 2023). This erosion of compliance can introduce significant vulnerabilities, ultimately undermining the organization's cybersecurity posture and increasing the risk of security breaches.

## Perceived Anonymity and Moral Licensing

Remote work can lead to a sense of detachment from direct organizational oversight, which can, in turn, increase the likelihood of employees engaging in risky cybersecurity behaviors. Without the physical presence of managers or colleagues reinforcing security expectations, employees may feel a reduced sense of accountability, making them more prone to cutting corners on security protocols. This phenomenon is particularly concerning because individuals who typically comply with cybersecurity policies in an office setting may unknowingly or deliberately engage in unsafe practices while working remotely. They might rationalize minor violations, such as using personal devices for work, disabling MFA for convenience, or sharing passwords informally, as insignificant or justified due to productivity pressures. Over time, these small infractions can accumulate, creating vulnerabilities that cybercriminals can exploit, ultimately increasing an organization's overall security risk (Mingo, 2024).

## BEHAVIORAL SCIENCE-BASED STRATEGIC RESPONSES

Creating a culture of cybersecurity resilience requires more than just policies and technical controls; it demands behavioral reinforcement that encourages secure habits. By leveraging behavioral nudges, gamification, social influence, and mindful security practices, organizations can drive long-term engagement and compliance. Subtle, well-timed prompts and framing security in terms of loss aversion can nudge employees toward better security decisions without resistance. Similarly, positive reinforcement through rewards and recognition sustains motivation. Empowering security champions within teams fosters a sense of collective responsibility, while simplifying security choices and integrating mindfulness into training help mitigate decision fatigue. By aligning these strategies with human behavior, organizations can transform security from an obligation into an ingrained, everyday practice.

### Reinforcing Secure Behaviors Through Habit Formation

- **Leverage Behavioral Nudges:**
  Subtle, well-timed prompts can encourage employees to adopt secure behaviors without feeling coerced. For instance, framing security messages in a loss-aversion context (e.g., "90% of data breaches occur due to weak passwords") increases compliance (Ariely, 2020).
- **Gamification and Positive Reinforcement:**
  Rewarding security-conscious behavior with incentives, recognition, or friendly competitions helps sustain engagement. Leaderboards, badges, or peer acknowledgment has been shown to improve adherence to cybersecurity practices (Jun & Lucas, 2024).

### Social Influence and Security Culture Transformation

- **Empowering Security Champions:**
  Employees are more likely to adopt security behaviors if they see respected colleagues practicing them. Establishing internal "security ambassadors" within teams can shift norms and reinforce positive peer influence (Zairon et al., 2023).

- **Framing Security as a Collective Responsibility:**
  Messages emphasizing "we" rather than "you" foster a shared sense of duty. Group accountability models, where teams are collectively responsible for security metrics, drive higher engagement than top-down mandates (Black, 2023).

### Mitigating Decision Fatigue and Encouraging Mindful Security

- **Simplify Security Choices:**
  Reducing the number of decisions employees must make about security lowers fatigue and increases compliance. Default settings, such as auto-enabling MFA, reduce friction and enhance security adherence (Sachs, 2025).
- **Mindfulness-Based Security Training:**
  Integrating mindfulness techniques into cybersecurity training helps employees recognize impulsive, risk-prone behaviors and respond thoughtfully to security threats rather than reactively dismissing warnings (Roghanizad et al., 2021).

## IMPLEMENTATION GUIDELINES AND ROADMAP

Effective cybersecurity strategies extend beyond technical solutions; they must address the human element by shaping behaviors, attitudes, and decision-making patterns. This roadmap outlines a structured, behaviorally informed approach to integrating security into workplace culture. By leveraging insights from behavioral science, organizations can proactively identify risk tendencies, refine security communications, and embed secure behaviors into daily workflows. The phased approach begins with understanding the behavioral landscape, followed by optimizing communication strategies, embedding security behaviors into processes, and ensuring continuous learning and reinforcement. Through these targeted interventions, organizations can cultivate a security-first mindset that enhances resilience and reduces human-related cyber risks (Figure 4.6).

### Phase I: Understanding the Behavioral Landscape

- **Conduct Behavioral Audits:**
  Analyze employee decision-making patterns, attitudes, and biases related to cybersecurity. Behavioral assessments provide insights into subconscious risk-taking tendencies.
- **Identify Behavioral Stakeholders:**
  Engage behavioral scientists, psychologists, and HR teams in security strategy planning.

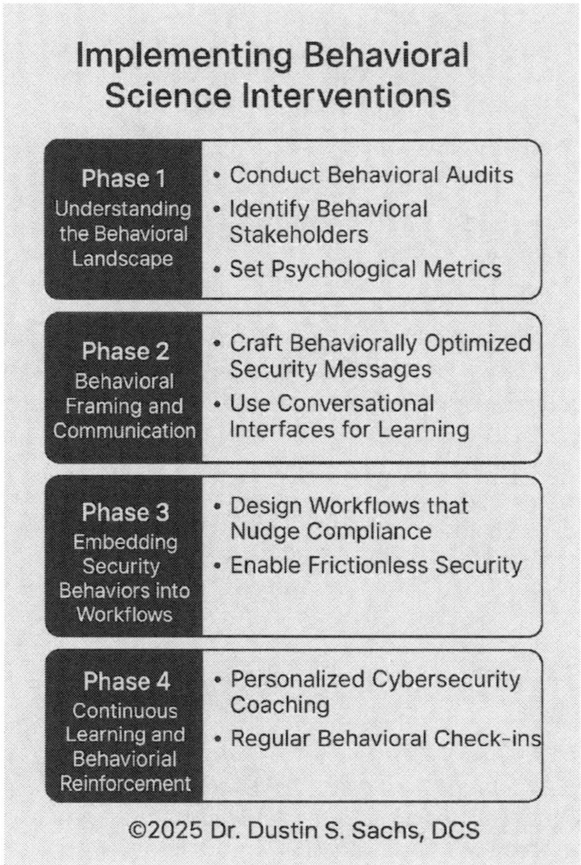


*Figure 4.6* Behavioral Science Interventions Phases

- **Set Psychological Metrics:**
  Instead of only tracking security incidents, measure behavioral indicators like security training retention rates and policy adherence changes over time.

## Phase 2: Behavioral Framing and Communication

- **Craft Behaviorally Optimized Security Messages:**
  Adjust security communication to align with principles of behavioral economics. Messages framed around social proof, scarcity, or urgency can be more effective than generic security reminders (Tversky & Kahneman, 2022).

- **Use Conversational Interfaces for Learning:**
  Chatbots and interactive modules that simulate security decision-making in real time help employees internalize secure behaviors (Thawbaan et al., 2024).

### Phase 3: Embedding Security Behaviors into Workflows

- **Design Workflows That Nudge Compliance:**
  Place security confirmations at natural workflow interruptions (e.g., requiring password updates at the start of the workday rather than mid-task).
- **Enable Frictionless Security:**
  Minimize unnecessary authentication prompts to prevent habituation and disengagement.

### Phase 4: Continuous Learning and Behavioral Reinforcement

- **Personalized Cybersecurity Coaching:**
  Instead of one-size-fits-all training, adaptive learning systems that provide tailored advice based on past behaviors can improve long-term security habits (Delso-Vicente et al., 2025).
- **Regular Behavioral Check-Ins:**
  Short, reflective surveys about security attitudes can help organizations track shifts in perception and engagement.

## INTEGRATING BEHAVIORAL SCIENCE INTO BUSINESS STRATEGY

Integrating behavioral science into business strategy shifts cybersecurity from a purely technical focus to a human-centered approach that enhances both security and employee well-being. By leveraging predictive models, organizations can identify and mitigate high-risk behaviors before they lead to security incidents. Framing cybersecurity as a way to reduce stress and uncertainty makes it more personally meaningful, while fostering habitual security practices ensures compliance becomes second nature. This behavior-centric model recognizes that long-term cybersecurity success depends not just on technology but on the psychological and social factors influencing human decision-making.

- **Quantify Behavioral Risks:**
  Develop predictive models that assess which employees are most likely to engage in high-risk behaviors and provide targeted interventions.

- **Tie Security to Employee Well-Being:**
  Position cybersecurity not just as protecting data but as reducing stress and uncertainty, making it personally relevant.
- **Make Cybersecurity a Habitual, Unconscious Action:**
  The goal is to make security as automatic as checking a seatbelt, an ingrained, reflexive behavior rather than an additional cognitive task.

This shift from a tool-centric to a behavior-centric security model acknowledges that technology alone cannot ensure long-term cybersecurity success. Instead, it emphasizes the importance of understanding the psychological and social mechanisms that influence human decision-making in digital environments. By integrating behavioral science, organizations can identify patterns of risky behavior, implement targeted interventions, and create environments where secure actions become second nature. This approach not only strengthens security but also enhances employee engagement by reducing stress and uncertainty around cybersecurity practices. Ultimately, fostering a security-first mindset at the human level leads to more resilient organizations, where individuals play an active role in maintaining a strong cybersecurity posture.

## CHAPTER SUMMARY

Organizational culture plays a critical role in shaping cybersecurity practices by influencing how security teams operate, how information is shared, and how leadership prioritizes risk management. A security-conscious culture ensures that cybersecurity is integrated into daily operations rather than treated as an isolated function. Research suggests that organizations with a proactive security culture are more resilient to cyber threats, as they align their security practices with their overall mission and values (Corradini, 2020; Dahmer, 2020). However, without cultural alignment, even the most advanced technical defenses can be undermined by human error, miscommunication, or a lack of awareness (Huang & Pearlson, 2019; Marotta & Pearlson, 2019).

Security teams and practitioners are at the forefront of defending organizations against cyber threats, and their effectiveness is directly influenced by the culture in which they operate. A supportive culture fosters collaboration, continuous improvement, and innovation, allowing security professionals to respond swiftly to evolving threats (Ioannou et al., 2019; Yulianto & Soewito, 2023). When leadership prioritizes cybersecurity and provides necessary resources, security teams are better equipped to handle challenges. Conversely, a culture resistant to change or one that values short-term gains over long-term security can hinder the effectiveness of security teams and create vulnerabilities within the organization (Bowen & Sethi, 2022; Lie et al., 2021).

Leadership plays a pivotal role in driving a security-aware culture by setting expectations, allocating resources, and demonstrating a commitment to cybersecurity. Leaders who integrate cybersecurity into strategic initiatives and decision-making processes help establish a security-first mindset across the organization (Parkin et al., 2023). Strategies such as executive sponsorship, structured training programs, and cross-functional collaboration are essential for embedding security into the organization's DNA (Falco & Rosenbach, 2022). Organizations that invest in leadership-driven security awareness not only enhance their cybersecurity posture but also build a culture where security is viewed as a collective responsibility.

Cultural transformation in cybersecurity requires a structured approach that aligns security initiatives with business objectives. Frameworks such as the NIST CSF and Kotter's 8-Step Process for Leading Change provide structured methodologies for organizations to embed security into their culture (Burton, 2024). Key steps include assessing the current cultural landscape, defining a vision for security integration, fostering continuous education, and establishing accountability mechanisms (Marotta & Pearlson, 2019). Effective cultural change is not a one-time initiative but an ongoing process that requires adaptation to emerging threats, evolving regulatory requirements, and shifting business priorities.

Organizations that successfully cultivate a security-conscious culture benefit from improved resilience and increased employee engagement. Case studies of organizations undergoing cultural transformation highlight the importance of leadership commitment, proactive risk management, and cross-departmental collaboration in achieving cybersecurity maturity (Neri et al., 2023). By embedding security into every aspect of the organization, businesses can ensure long-term sustainability in an increasingly threat-laden digital landscape. Ultimately, security culture is about shaping behaviors, fostering accountability, and creating an environment where cybersecurity is an integral part of the organizational ethos.

## REFERENCES

Aksoy, C. (2024). Building a cyber security culture for resilient organizations against cyber attacks. *İşletme Ekonomi ve Yönetim Araştırmaları Dergisi*, 7(1), 96–110. https://doi.org/10.33416/baybem.1374001

Aksoy, C. (2025). Building effective cybersecurity leadership: The crucial role of leaders in protecting businesses against cyber threats. *Kalite ve Strateji Yönetimi Dergisi*, 5(1), 33–49. https://doi.org/10.56682/ksydergi.1539408

Aldulaimi, S. H., Abdeldayem, M. M., & Abo Keir, M. Y. (2023). Formulating the cyber security culture in organizations: Proposing and arguing insights. *International Journal of Professional Business Review*, 8(5), e01660. https://doi.org/10.26668/businessreview/2023.v8i5.1660

Alghazo, S. H. A., Humaidi, N., & Noranee, S. (2023). Assessing information security competencies of firm leaders towards improving procedural information security countermeasure: Awareness and cybersecurity protective behavior. *Information Management and Business Review*, *15*(1(I)SI), 1–13. https://doi.org/10.22610/imbr.v15i1(I)SI.3408

Angafor, G. N., Yevseyeva, I., & Maglaras, L. (2023). Scenario-based incident response training: Lessons learnt from conducting an experiential learning virtual incident response tabletop exercise. *Information and Computer Security, 31*(4), 404–426. https://doi.org/10.1108/ICS-05-2022-0085

Ansari, M. F. (2022). A quantitative study of risk scores and the effectiveness of AI-based cybersecurity awareness training programs. *International Journal of Smart Sensor and Adhoc Network*, *3*(3), Article 1. https://doi.org/10.47893/IJSSAN.2022.1212

Ariely, D. (2020). *Predictably irrational: The hidden forces that shape our decisions* (Revised ed.). HarperCollins.

Black, P. W. (2023). The effect of peer-to-peer recognition systems on helping behavior: The influence of rewards and group affiliation. *Accounting, Organizations and Society, 109*, 101454. https://doi.org/10.1016/j.aos.2023.101454

Bowen, G., & Sethi, A. (2020). Internal marketing cybersecurity-conscious culture. In S. Dadwal (Ed.), *Handbook of research on innovations in technology and marketing for the connected consumer* (pp. 135–154). IGI Global. https://doi.org/10.4018/978-1-7998-0131-3.ch007

Burrell, D. N. (2019). Assessing the value of executive leadership coaches for cybersecurity project managers. *International Journal of Human Capital and Information Technology Professionals (IJHCITP)*, *10*(2), 20–32. https://doi.org/10.4018/IJHCITP.2019040102

Burton, S. L. (2024). Securing tomorrow: Synergizing change management and cybersecurity in the digital era. *Holistica*, *15*(1), 1. https://doi.org/10.2478/hjbpa-2024-0001

Chaudhary, S., Gkioulos, V., & Katsikas, S. (2022). Developing metrics to assess the effectiveness of cybersecurity awareness program. Journal of Cybersecurity, 8(1), 1–19. https://doi.org/10.1093/cybsec/tyac006

Corradini, I. (2020). Building a cybersecurity culture. In *Building a cybersecurity culture in organizations: How to bridge the gap between people and digital technology* (pp. 63–86). Springer International Publishing. https://doi.org/10.1007/978-3-030-43999-6_4

Dahmer, L. J. N. (2020). The role of organizational culture in cybersecurity: A path to resilience. *REVISTA FIT*, *24*(82), 14–15. https://doi.org/10.69849/revistaft/ar10202001010814

Dalal, R. S., Howard, D. J., Bennett, R. J., Posey, C., Zaccaro, S. J., & Brummel, B. J. (2022). Organizational science and cybersecurity: Abundant opportunities for research at the interface. *Journal of Business and Psychology*, *37*(1), 1–29. https://doi.org/10.1007/s10869-021-09732-9

Damianou, A., Mazi, M. S., Rizos, G., Voulgaridis, A., & Votis, K. (2024, September). Situational awareness scoring system in cyber range platforms. In *2024 IEEE International Conference on Cyber Security and Resilience (CSR)* (pp. 520–525). IEEE. https://doi.org/10.1109/CSR61664.2024.10679451

Delso-Vicente, A. T., Diaz-Marcos, L., Aguado-Tevar, O., & de Blanes-Sebastián, M. G. (2025). Factors influencing employee compliance with information security policies: A systematic literature review of behavioral and technological aspects in cybersecurity. *Future Business Journal*, *11*(1), 28. https://doi.org/10.1186/s43093-025-00452-7

De Silva, B. (2023). Exploring the relationship between cybersecurity culture and cyber-crime prevention: A systematic review. *International Journal of Information Security and Cybercrime (IJISC)*, *12*(1), 23–29. https://doi.org/10.19107/IJISC.2023.01.03

Domańska-Szaruga, B. (2020). Maturity of risk management culture. *Entrepreneurship and Sustainability Issues*, *7*(3), 2060–2078. https://doi.org/10.9770/jesi.2020.7.3(41)

Dorairajan, V. (2024). Cybersecurity and organisational performance – the interplay. *ARPHA Conference Abstracts*, *7*, e129255. https://doi.org/10.3897/aca.7.e129255

Falco, G., & Rosenbach, E. (2022). Who is responsible for cybersecurity? In G. J. Falco & E. Rosenbach (Eds.), *Confronting cyber risk: An embedded endurance strategy for cybersecurity* (pp. 79–103). Oxford University Press.

Handri, E. Y., Sensuse, D. I., & Tarigan, A. (2024). Developing an agile cybersecurity framework with organizational culture approach using Q methodology. *IEEE Access*, *12*, 108835–108850. https://doi.org/10.1109/ACCESS.2024.3432160

Huang, K., & Pearlson, K. (2019, January 8). For what technology can't fix: Building a model of organizational cybersecurity culture. In *Proceedings of the 52nd Hawaii International Conference on System Sciences* (pp. 6398–6407). https://doi.org/10.24251/HICSS.2019.769

Ioannou, M., Stavrou, E., & Bada, M. (2019). Cybersecurity culture in computer security incident response teams: Investigating difficulties in communication and coordination. *2019 International Conference on Cyber Security and Protection of Digital Services (Cyber Security)* (pp. 1–4). https://doi.org/10.1109/CyberSecPODS.2019.8885240

Jones, L. A. (2024). Unveiling human factors: Aligning facets of cybersecurity leadership, insider threats, and arsonist attributes to reduce cyber risk. *SocioEconomic Challenges*, *8*(2), 44–63. https://doi.org/10.61093/sec.8(2).44-63.2024

Jun, M., & Lucas, T. (2024). Gamification elements and their impacts on education: A review. *Multidisciplinary Reviews*, *8*(5), 2025155. https://doi.org/10.31893/multirev.2025155

Lie, L. B., Utomo, P., & Winarno, P. M. (2021, December). Investigating the impact of cybersecurity culture on employees' cybersecurity protection behaviours: A conceptual paper. In *Conference Series* (Vol. 3, No. 2, pp. 295–305). https://doi.org/10.34306/conferenceseries.v3i2.598

Madnick, B., Huang, K., & Madnick, S. (2023). The evolution of global cybersecurity norms in the digital age: A longitudinal study of the cybersecurity norm development process. *Information Security Journal: A Global Perspective*, *33*(3), 204–225. https://doi.org/10.1080/19393555.2023.2201482

Malmquist, K. (2020). *Information security ambassadors' perceptions of peer-led motivation in phishing detection*. (Doctoral dissertation, Walden University).

Marotta, A., & Pearlson, K. (2019). A culture of cybersecurity at banca popolare di sondrio. In *AMCIS 2019 Proceedings* (p. 24). https://aisel.aisnet.org/amcis2019/info_security_privacy/info_security_privacy/24

Mingo, H. C. (2024). *Emerging vulnerabilities in cyberspace: A qualitative content analysis of organizational behaviors and complexities that drive cybersecurity risks*. (Doctoral dissertation, Marymount University).

Mızrak, F. (2023). Integrating cybersecurity risk management into strategic management: A comprehensive literature review. *Research Journal of Business and Management*, *10*(3), 98–108. https://doi.org/10.17261/Pressacademia.2023.1807

Nasrullayev, R., & Holubkin, S. (2024). The organizational and economic mechanism of risk management in enterprises under digitalization. *Ukrainian Journal of Applied Economics and Technology*, *2024*(3), 118–121. https://doi.org/10.36887/2415-8453-2024-3-21

National Institute of Standards and Technology. (2024). The NIST Cybersecurity Framework (CSF) 2.0.

Neri, M., Niccolini, F., & Martino, L. (2024). Organizational cybersecurity readiness in the ICT sector: a quanti-qualitative assessment. *Information and Computer Security*, *32*(1), 38–52. https://doi.org/10.1108/ICS-05-2023-0084

Nobles, C. (2022). Stress, burnout and security fatigue in cybersecurity: A human factors problem. *Holistica Journal of Business and Public Administration*, *13*(1), 49–72. https://doi.org/10.2478/hjbpa-2022-0003

Nwankpa, J. K., & Datta, P. M. (2023). Remote vigilance: The roles of cyber awareness and cybersecurity policies among remote workers. *Computers & Security*, *130*, 103266. https://doi.org/10.1016/j.cose.2023.103266

Obiki-Osafiele, A. N., Agu, E. E., & Chiekezie, N. R. (2024). Protecting digital assets in Fintech: Essential cybersecurity measures and best practices. *Computer Science & IT Research Journal*, *5*(8), 1884–1896. https://doi.org/10.51594/csitrj.v5i8.1449

Ofoegbu, K., Osundare, O., Ike, C., & Fakeyede, O. (2023). Enhancing cybersecurity resilience through real-time data analytics and user empowerment strategies. *Engineering Science & Technology Journal*, *4*(6). https://doi.org/10.51594/estj.v4i6.1527

Olaniyi, O. O., Asonze, C. U., Ajayi, S. A., Olabanji, S. O., & Adigwe, C. S. (2023). A regressional study on the impact of organizational security culture and transformational leadership on social engineering awareness among bank employees: The interplay of security education and behavioral change. *Asian Journal of Economics, Business and Accounting*, *23*(23), 128–143. https://doi.org/10.9734/ajeba/2023/v23i231176

Onumo, A., Ullah-Awan, I., & Cullen, A. (2021). Assessing the moderating effect of security technologies on employees compliance with cybersecurity control procedures. *ACM Transactions on Management Information Systems (TMIS)*, *12*(2), 1–29. https://doi.org/10.1145/3424282

Pankajakshan, J., & Bangur, D. (2024). Organizational strategies and policies for implementing emerging cybersecurity technologies. *International Journal of Information Technology and Management*, *19*(1), 81–92. https://doi.org/10.29070/m75p4s25

Parkin, S., Kuhn, K., & Shaikh, S. A. (2023). Executive decision-makers: A scenario-based approach to assessing organizational cyber-risk perception. *Journal of Cybersecurity*, *9*(1), 1–13. https://doi.org/10.1093/cybsec/tyad018

Parsola, J. (2022). Cybersecurity risk assessment and management for organizational security. *NeuroQuantology*, *20*(5), 5330. https://doi.org/10.48047/nq.2022.20.5.nq22815

Pramod, D. (2025). Gamification in cybersecurity education; a state of the art review and research agenda. *Journal of Applied Research in Higher Education*, *17*(4), 1162–1180. https://doi.org/10.1108/JARHE-02-2024-0072

Przekota, G. (2024). Investment in cybersecurity companies in times of political and economic instability. *Applied Cybersecurity & Internet Governance*, *3*(1), 170–184. https://doi.org/10.60097/ACIG/190342

Reeves, A., Calic, D., & Delfabbro, P. (2025). How to De-CyFa the actor-observer bias in cybersecurity fatigue: Building the CyFa measure of attribution styles and mitigation strategies. *Computers & Security, 150*, 104179. https://doi.org/10.1016/j.cose.2024.104179

Roghanizad, M., Choi, E., Mashatan, A., & Turetken, O. (2021). Mindfulness and cybersecurity behavior: A comparative analysis of rational and intuitive cybersecurity decisions. In *Proceedings Americas Conference on Information Systems 2021 (AMCIS 2021)* (p. 1360). https://aisel.aisnet.org/amcis2021/info_security/info_security/13

Sabillon, R. (2022). Cybersecurity incident response and management. In I. Management Association (Ed.), *Research anthology on business aspects of cybersecurity* (pp. 611–620). IGI Global Scientific Publishing. https://doi.org/10.4018/978-1-6684-3698-1.ch028

Sachs, D. S. (2025). Decision overload: Cybersecurity in the age of big data. *The Pinnacle: A Journal by Scholar-Practitioners, 3*(1). https://doi.org/10.61643/c21537

Saiz-Alvarez, J. M., & Leal, G. C. (2020). Cybersecurity best practices and cultural change in global business: Some perspectives from the European Union. In I. Management Association (Ed.), *Cyber warfare and terrorism: Concepts, methodologies, tools, and applications* (pp. 1566–1584). IGI Global Scientific Publishing. https://doi.org/10.4018/978-1-7998-2466-4.ch092

Sheng, Q. W. (2020). Effectiveness evaluation of network security knowledge training based on machine learning. In Z. Cai, D. Zou, J. Li, & H. Xie (Eds.), *e-Learning, e-Education, and Online Training: 6th EAI International Conference, eLEOT 2020, Changsha, China, June 20–21, 2020, Proceedings, Part II* (pp. 25–37). Springer International Publishing. https://doi.org/10.1007/978-3-030-66444-2_3

Silva, J. F. (2024). Navigating cybersecurity challenges: Legal implications and organizational strategies. *International Seven Journal of Multidisciplinary*, *2*(1). https://doi.org/10.56238/isevmjv2n1-012

Taherdoost, H. (2024). Towards an innovative model for cybersecurity awareness training. *Information*, *15*(9), 512. https://doi.org/10.3390/info15090512

Thawbaan, A., Emmanuel, S., Dusserre, G., Ahmed, N. B., Babatunde, Z., Isa, L. M., & Job, D. A. (2024). Chatbots in cybersecurity: Enhancing security chatbot efficacy through iterative feedback loops and user-centric approaches. *American Journal of Innovation in Science and Engineering*, *3*(3), 77–87. https://doi.org/10.54536/ajise.v3i3.2919

Triplett, W. J. (2022). Addressing human factors in cybersecurity leadership. *Journal of Cybersecurity and Privacy,* 2(3), 573–586. https://doi.org/10.3390/jcp2030029

Tversky, A., & Kahneman, D. (1990). Judgment under uncertainty: Heuristics and biases. In P. K. Moser (Ed.), *Rationality in action: Contemporary approaches* (pp. 171–188). Cambridge University Press. (Reprinted from "Science" 185 (1974), 1124–31)

Yulianto, S., Soewito, B., Gaol, F. L., & Kurniawan, A. (2023, November). Metrics and red teaming in cyber resilience and effectiveness: A systematic literature review. In *2023 29th International Conference on Telecommunications (ICT)* (pp. 1–7). IEEE. https://doi.org/10.1109/ICT60153.2023.10374053

Zairon, I. Y., Wook, T. S. M. T., Salleh, S. M., & Dahlan, H. A. (2023). Gamification adaptive elements in virtual learning to improve behaviour and collaborative interaction. In *2023 International Conference on Electrical Engineering and Informatics (ICEEI)* (pp. 1–6). IEEE. https://doi.org/10.1109/ICEEI59426.2023.10346688

Chapter 5

# Technology Strategy Needs Pyramid

## LEARNING OBJECTIVES

- Examine how fundamental human motivations, such as safety, belonging, and self-actualization, influence cybersecurity behaviors, risk perception, and compliance within organizations.
- Explore how unmet psychological needs can lead to security fatigue, noncompliance, and risky behaviors, and develop strategies to align security initiatives with user motivations.
- Implement a structured approach to balancing technical controls with human-centric security measures, ensuring that cybersecurity policies are both effective and sustainable within an organization's culture.

## MASLOW'S HIERARCHY OF NEEDS

Maslow's Hierarchy of Needs, a psychological framework introduced by Abraham Maslow in 1943, categorizes human motivation into five levels: physiological needs, safety, social belonging, esteem, and self-actualization. While traditionally applied to human psychology and workplace motivation, this model is highly relevant to cybersecurity practitioners. Understanding human needs and motivations can help cybersecurity professionals design better security strategies, improve user behavior, and strengthen an organization's security culture. Given that many cyber threats exploit human psychology rather than technical vulnerabilities alone, cybersecurity practitioners must consider both the technical and behavioral aspects of security (Dar & Sakthivel, 2022).

At the most fundamental level, cybersecurity professionals must recognize that their role is directly tied to the second tier of Maslow's hierarchy: safety. Digital security is an extension of physical and financial security in the modern world. Protecting data, systems, and infrastructure ensures that individuals and organizations feel safe in their digital environments. Whether mitigating ransomware attacks, securing cloud environments, or preventing identity theft, cybersecurity practitioners are responsible for

DOI: 10.1201/9781003606345-5

upholding this essential need. Without security, businesses and individuals cannot function effectively, as fear and uncertainty erode trust in digital systems (Omodan & Abejide, 2022).

Cybersecurity practitioners must also consider the impact of security on social and esteem needs. Poorly implemented security measures, such as restrictive policies, cumbersome authentication processes, or ineffective training, can lead to frustration, noncompliance, and even resentment among users. Cybersecurity teams must balance security and usability to ensure that employees and customers do not feel alienated by security policies. Moreover, a breach or cyber incident can damage an organization's reputation, leading to a loss of customer trust and employee morale. Practitioners who understand the human side of security can design strategies that align with how people interact with technology, making security more intuitive and less burdensome (Wei & Ma, 2022).

For cybersecurity professionals themselves, esteem and self-actualization are critical motivators. The field is highly demanding, requiring constant learning, adaptability, and resilience. Burnout is a real challenge, particularly for practitioners dealing with incident response, threat intelligence, and risk management. Understanding Maslow's hierarchy can help cybersecurity leaders support their teams by ensuring they have opportunities for professional growth, recognition, and work-life balance. Encouraging certifications, mentorship, and career progression not only helps individuals reach self-actualization but also strengthens the overall cybersecurity workforce (Bahar & Özen, 2024).

Additionally, cybersecurity training and awareness programs should be designed with human psychology in mind. Many security awareness initiatives fail because they do not align with employees' needs and motivations. If security policies are viewed as a barrier rather than an enabler, employees may ignore or circumvent them. By recognizing how security affects different levels of Maslow's hierarchy, especially safety, belonging, and esteem, practitioners can create more effective engagement strategies that foster a culture of cybersecurity rather than one of fear or compliance-driven behavior (Shi et al., 2021).

Cyber practitioners who understand Maslow's hierarchy can design security strategies that align closely with intrinsic human behavior, recognizing and addressing users' fundamental needs before progressing to higher-level motivations. Research suggests that Maslow's framework remains relevant in contemporary contexts, including cybersecurity, where psychological insights enhance user compliance and trust (Dar & Sakthivel, 2022). By ensuring security measures do not conflict with essential human desires for safety, belonging, and self-esteem, organizations can create environments where security practices feel intuitive rather than restrictive (Omodan, 2022). Furthermore, studies highlight that organizations applying Maslow's principles effectively enhance user motivation and engagement by balancing security requirements with psychological well-being (Wei & Ma, 2022).

Such an approach ensures security is both effective and sustainable, enabling individuals and organizations to thrive confidently and resiliently in an increasingly complex digital landscape.

## PHYSIOLOGICAL NEEDS

Physiological needs form the foundation of Maslow's hierarchy, encompassing essential elements for human survival such as food, water, air, shelter, and sleep. Without these necessities, an individual cannot sustain life, making them the most fundamental requirements of human existence (Maslow, 1943). Proper nutrition is crucial, as deficiencies in essential nutrients can lead to malnourishment and chronic health conditions that impair physical and cognitive functions (World Health Organization [WHO],2021). Hydration is equally vital; the human body relies on water for cellular processes, digestion, and temperature regulation, and prolonged dehydration can result in severe health complications or death (Popkin et al., 2018). Without adequate food and water intake, the body begins to break down muscle mass and fat reserves, leading to weakened immunity and organ failure (Gibney et al., 2016).

Shelter provides protection from environmental elements and plays a crucial role in overall well-being. Studies show that inadequate housing conditions contribute to stress, disease, and psychological distress, making secure housing a fundamental physiological necessity (Braveman et al., 2011). Homelessness or living in unsafe environments can expose individuals to extreme weather conditions, violence, and health hazards, further exacerbating physical and mental health concerns (Mejia-Lancheros et al., 2021). Having stable housing allows individuals to focus on fulfilling other essential needs, such as employment, healthcare, and education (Carrere et al., 2022).

Furthermore, sleep is essential for cognitive function, immune system regulation, and emotional stability. Sleep deprivation has been linked to increased risks of mental health disorders, cardiovascular diseases, and impaired decision-making abilities (Kahn, 2023). A lack of quality sleep affects memory retention, reaction times, and mood regulation, which can impact an individual's daily functioning and overall quality of life (Kredlow et al., 2015). Chronic sleep deprivation may also contribute to long-term health complications such as obesity, diabetes, and neurodegenerative diseases (Grandner, 2022).

In addition to these, proper clothing and temperature regulation are crucial physiological requirements. Exposure to extreme cold or heat can lead to hypothermia or heatstroke, both of which pose significant health risks (Zhao et al., 2024). Clothing serves as a barrier against environmental hazards, preventing conditions such as frostbite or heat exhaustion (Gauer & Meyers, 2019). Access to weather-appropriate attire is particularly important for vulnerable populations, such as the elderly and young children, who may struggle to regulate body temperature efficiently (Guo et al., 2016).

The human body is unable to function optimally without maintaining homeostasis, and physiological needs ensure that individuals can sustain life before progressing to higher levels of Maslow's hierarchy. When these basic needs are not met, the body prioritizes survival, often at the expense of higher-order cognitive functions and emotional well-being (Sapolsky, 2017). Addressing physiological needs is a prerequisite for personal development, as individuals cannot focus on safety, relationships, or self-fulfillment without a stable foundation (Tushir et al., 2023). Public health policies and social support systems play a crucial role in ensuring that people have access to food, water, shelter, and medical care (WHO, 2021).

## SAFETY NEEDS

Once physiological needs are met, individuals seek safety and security in various aspects of life. Safety needs encompass personal security, financial stability, health and well-being, and a secure living environment (Maslow, 1943). In contemporary society, personal safety involves protection from physical harm, crime, and violence. A sense of security contributes to mental well-being, and individuals living in unsafe environments often experience chronic stress, anxiety, and reduced quality of life (Taylor et al., 2023). Without a stable sense of safety, individuals may become hypervigilant, experiencing difficulty concentrating and engaging in social or occupational activities (Porges, 2022).

Financial stability is a critical component of safety needs, as financial insecurity can lead to stress and an inability to afford basic necessities. Research indicates that economic instability is a major contributor to mental health disorders, family conflicts, and reduced life satisfaction (Diener et al., 2018). Without a reliable source of income, individuals may struggle to pay for housing, healthcare, and education, leading to a cycle of poverty and hardship (Wilkinson & Pickett, 2020). Access to stable employment and financial resources enables individuals to plan for the future and reduce the anxiety associated with economic uncertainty (Sharma & Chaurasia, 2023).

Health and well-being also fall under this category, as individuals require access to healthcare, disease prevention, and a safe living environment. Lack of access to healthcare can result in untreated illnesses and lower life expectancy (Marmot & Allen, 2014). Preventative care, such as vaccinations and regular medical checkups, helps mitigate the risks of serious diseases and enhances overall quality of life (McNeill et al., 2022). Additionally, mental health support is essential for ensuring that individuals can cope with stress and maintain emotional resilience (Fatima et al., 2024).

## ESTEEM NEEDS

Esteem needs, as defined in Maslow's hierarchy, encompass the human desire for respect, self-esteem, and recognition. These needs can be categorized into two distinct types: the need for self-respect and the need for respect from others. Self-respect, or internal esteem, relates to an individual's confidence, competence, independence, and sense of achievement. External esteem, on the other hand, involves recognition, status, appreciation, and validation from others. Achieving these needs contributes to a person's overall mental well-being, allowing them to feel valued and motivated to pursue higher aspirations (Uka & Prendi, 2021).

Esteem needs play a crucial role in an individual's personal and professional life. In educational settings, students who feel recognized for their achievements tend to perform better academically and are more motivated to engage in learning activities (Fabella, 2023). Similarly, in workplaces, employees who receive acknowledgment and positive feedback from supervisors exhibit increased productivity and job satisfaction. Esteem needs also extend to social relationships, where individuals seek validation and appreciation from peers, family members, and society at large.

The fulfillment of esteem needs has been linked to psychological resilience and overall mental health. Studies suggest that individuals who receive consistent validation and respect tend to exhibit lower levels of anxiety and depression. Conversely, when esteem needs are not met, individuals may struggle with feelings of inadequacy, inferiority, and a lack of motivation. Social comparison theory posits that people evaluate their self-worth by comparing themselves to others, further underscoring the importance of recognition in self-esteem development (Powdthavee, 2023).

Moreover, esteem needs are culturally influenced, reflecting varying priorities and expectations shaped by societal values and norms. In individualistic societies, self-esteem is often built through personal achievements, independence, and individual distinction, highlighting personal success as a key metric of worth. Conversely, in collectivist cultures, esteem tends to be derived from group harmony, social approval, and contributions to collective goals, emphasizing interconnectedness and social integration over personal accolades. Additionally, the role of digital media has further complicated esteem needs, as social media platforms provide new avenues for recognition and affirmation, while simultaneously fostering unrealistic comparisons, anxiety, and validation-seeking behaviors that may undermine authentic self-esteem (Carducci, 2020).

In sum, esteem needs are integral to an individual's psychological development and social interactions, influencing how one perceives oneself and engages with others. Whether through personal achievements, workplace recognition, or societal validation, fulfilling these needs enhances self-worth, fosters motivation for further growth, and promotes a sense of belonging and accomplishment. Conversely, unmet esteem needs can lead to emotional distress, decreased self-confidence, and hindered personal progress, underscoring the critical role that positive reinforcement and acknowledgment play in maintaining mental health. Therefore, cultivating a supportive environment that recognizes and values individual contributions is essential, as it not only bolsters self-esteem but also encourages continuous personal and professional development.

## SELF-ACTUALIZATION

Self-actualization, the pinnacle of Maslow's hierarchy, represents the fulfillment of one's potential, creativity, and personal growth. Maslow described self-actualization as an ongoing process of becoming rather than a final state of perfection. Individuals who reach this stage exhibit qualities such as autonomy, creativity, problem-solving skills, deep relationships, and a strong sense of purpose (D'souza et al., 2015). Self-actualized individuals often pursue activities that align with their values and contribute positively to society.

One of the primary characteristics of self-actualization is intrinsic motivation, which refers to an individual's internal drive to pursue personal fulfillment and growth. Unlike individuals who are primarily driven by external rewards such as money, recognition, or societal approval, self-actualized people derive satisfaction directly from engaging in activities aligned with their passions and personal values. They actively seek out experiences and tasks that challenge them intellectually, emotionally, and creatively, viewing these challenges as opportunities for ongoing learning and self-improvement. Consequently, self-actualized individuals consistently strive for deeper meaning, personal excellence, and continuous development throughout their lives (Dar & Sakthivel, 2022).

Self-actualization is often associated with peak experiences, a concept introduced by Maslow to describe moments of intense joy, creativity, and fulfillment. These experiences can occur in various contexts, such as artistic expression, intellectual discovery, spiritual enlightenment, or deep human connections. During peak experiences, individuals frequently experience a heightened sense of clarity, harmony, and interconnectedness with the world around them, enabling profound insights into their personal potential and life's meaning. Such moments not only reinforce an individual's sense of purpose but also serve as powerful motivators, inspiring continued personal growth and the relentless pursuit of self-discovery and authenticity (Guesmi, 2022).

However, self-actualization is not a static achievement but a continuous, evolving process that unfolds throughout an individual's life. Maslow acknowledged that external factors such as financial constraints, societal pressures, and personal crises could temporarily hinder an individual's ability to pursue self-actualization, indicating that the journey toward one's full potential is often marked by periods of struggle and regression. Additionally, cultural and religious perspectives significantly influence how self-actualization is perceived, pursued, and ultimately attained, demonstrating that this concept is interpreted differently across diverse societies. For example, some traditions emphasize personal enlightenment as the primary path to self-actualization, while others highlight community service, spiritual transcendence, and collective harmony as essential components of achieving one's fullest human potential (Compton, 2018).

Despite these variations, the pursuit of self-actualization remains a fundamental aspect of human motivation. Individuals continuously strive to realize their fullest potential by exploring personal talents, developing unique abilities, and embracing growth opportunities that align with their values and aspirations. By striving for personal excellence, engaging in meaningful activities, and cultivating a sense of purpose, people not only enhance their own well-being but also positively influence those around them. In doing so, individuals can achieve fulfillment, leave enduring legacies, and make lasting contributions to society, fostering a more connected and purposeful community.

Maslow's Hierarchy of Needs provides a structured framework for understanding human motivation. While esteem needs focus on the desire for respect and recognition, self-actualization represents the pursuit of personal growth and fulfillment. Although Maslow originally proposed a sequential progression through the hierarchy, contemporary research suggests that individuals may pursue higher-level needs even when lower ones remain unmet (Dellaert et al., 2018). The interplay between these needs highlights the dynamic and individualized nature of human development.

## BUILDING THE PYRAMID

Cybersecurity is a field that requires both technical precision and a deep understanding of human behavior. Security is not solely about firewalls, encryption, and compliance; rather, it is about how people interact with technology, make decisions, and respond to risks. Organizations that fail to consider human psychology in their cybersecurity strategies often experience gaps where user behavior conflicts with security policies (Sangwan, 2024). By leveraging behavioral science, cybersecurity practitioners can create security measures that are intuitive, sustainable, and effective in fostering secure behaviors (Triplett, 2022).

This chapter builds upon the concepts introduced in previous chapters and brings them together into a new framework and paradigm. While past discussions may have addressed security controls, risk management, or compliance requirements separately, the Technology Strategy Needs Pyramid integrates these elements into a hierarchical model that aligns security priorities with human psychology. Just as Maslow's Hierarchy of

Needs explains how individuals prioritize physiological and psychological needs, the Technology Strategy Needs Pyramid illustrates how organizations and users prioritize security needs, progressing from basic accessibility to collective impact (Kadena & Gupi, 2021)

A major challenge in cybersecurity is bridging the gap between what security teams expect and how users behave. Traditional security policies often assume that users will comply without questioning the rationale behind security controls. However, behavioral research shows that individuals are influenced by cognitive biases, immediate rewards, and perceived effort, all of which shape their cybersecurity decisions (Corradini, 2020). This framework acknowledges these influences and provides a structured approach to overcoming them (Gopireddy, 2022).

By understanding how security decisions align with human psychology, organizations can craft policies that naturally encourage secure behaviors rather than relying solely on enforcement. Instead of security being an external requirement imposed on employees, it should be embedded seamlessly into the workflow, culture, and technology people engage with every day (Qashqari et al., 2020). The Technology Strategy Needs Pyramid provides a structured model for achieving this balance, ensuring that security measures are both technically sound and behaviorally effective. Ultimately, when organizations integrate psychological insights into their cybersecurity strategies, employees become active participants in security efforts, fostering a more resilient and secure organizational environment (Jeong et al., 2019) (Figure 5.1).

This approach shifts cybersecurity from a reactive, compliance-driven model to a proactive, user-centric paradigm. By aligning security strategies with the way people think and act, organizations can foster a cybersecurity culture where security is not an afterthought but a natural part of how individuals interact with technology (Morgan et al., 2020). Instead of merely responding to threats after they occur, this methodology emphasizes understanding human behaviors, motivations, and cognitive biases to anticipate potential security risks before they materialize (Rohan et al., 2021). By embedding cybersecurity into everyday decision-making processes and routines, organizations not only strengthen their defensive posture but also empower employees to become active participants in maintaining security, ultimately driving sustainable, long-term resilience (Zimmermann & Renaud, 2019). The sections that follow will explore each level of the Technology Strategy Needs Pyramid, providing insights into how organizations can implement these principles effectively.

## RELIABLE ACCESS (DIGITAL ACCESSIBILITY AND INFRASTRUCTURE RELIABILITY)

At the foundation of the Technology Strategy Needs Pyramid lies reliable access, which ensures that individuals and organizations have stable and

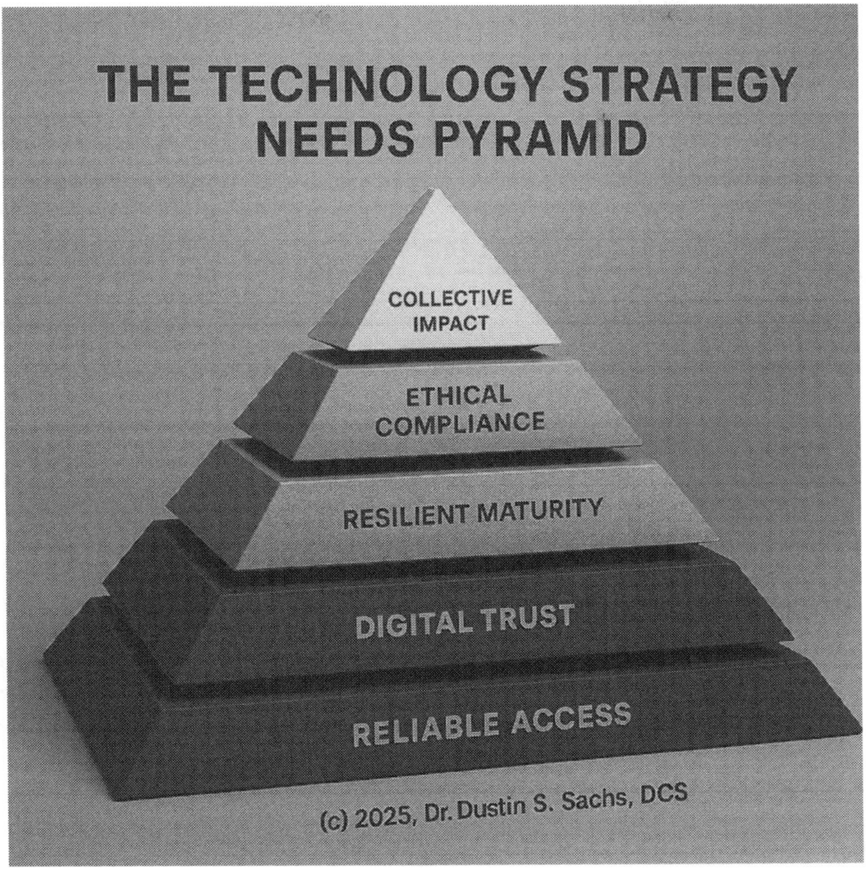


*Figure 5.1* Technology Strategy Needs Pyramid

secure digital infrastructure. Just as Maslow's Hierarchy of Needs identifies food, water, and shelter as basic necessities, cybersecurity begins with access to reliable technology, networks, and computing resources. Without this foundation, even the most well-designed security policies become irrelevant, as users will seek workarounds when systems are slow, unreliable, or inaccessible (Teh et al., 2020). Reliable access thus serves not only as a cornerstone for cybersecurity best practices but also as a critical factor influencing user behavior, driving individuals toward compliance rather than circumvention. By providing consistent and dependable infrastructure, organizations can significantly reduce security risks stemming from frustration-induced shortcuts or shadow IT solutions (Banire et al., 2021). Ultimately, reliable access creates the essential environment in which effective security behaviors and cultures can flourish.

Behavioral science reveals that when people experience cognitive overload or technology frustration, they are more likely to ignore security protocols. For instance, if an employee consistently faces slow authentication processes or unreliable Virtual Private Network (VPN) connections, they may start using unsecured networks or personal devices as an alternative (Naqvi et al., 2024). This tendency toward efficiency bias, where people prioritize convenience over security, illustrates why infrastructure must be not only secure but also user-friendly (Folorunsho et al., 2024). Organizations aiming to improve cybersecurity must therefore design systems that reduce cognitive strain, streamline user experiences, and provide accessible support, ultimately aligning secure practices with natural human behaviors.

To minimize these risks, organizations must invest in high-availability infrastructure, redundant networks, and failover systems that reduce downtime (Mohsin et al., 2023). Ensuring that security does not interfere with daily workflows encourages compliance rather than resistance. For example, single sign-on (SSO) solutions reduce authentication friction, allowing users to access multiple systems with minimal effort while maintaining security. Additionally, automated security updates can enhance system stability without requiring users to take additional steps (Vitla, 2023).

Another key element of reliable access is ensuring equitable access to cybersecurity tools and training. In many organizations, security resources are not distributed evenly, leading to security gaps between departments, locations, or remote workers (Bhagat, 2023). A lack of access to secure infrastructure can create vulnerabilities that adversaries exploit. By ensuring that all users, regardless of their location or technical proficiency, have the tools, knowledge, and connectivity they need, organizations can significantly reduce the likelihood of shadow IT and other insecure behaviors.

Ultimately, reliable access is about removing barriers to secure technology use. If security is too complex or unreliable, users will find ways to bypass it, creating vulnerabilities that attackers can exploit (Carlson et al., 2023). Security should not feel like an obstacle to productivity; rather, it should be embedded seamlessly into an organization's digital environment. By prioritizing access, availability, and ease of use, security teams can strengthen user engagement while reducing overall risk.

## SECURE SYSTEMS (CYBERSECURITY AND PSYCHOLOGICAL SAFETY)

Once infrastructure reliability is established, the next priority is Secure Systems, ensuring that security measures protect users without causing excessive friction or fear of punitive consequences. Traditional security policies often frame security as a restrictive force, creating resistance rather than compliance. However, behavioral research shows that people engage in security behaviors more consistently when they feel psychologically safe and supported (Santana et al., 2024).

A major challenge in security implementation is hyperbolic discounting, where users prioritize immediate convenience over long-term security. For instance, employees may ignore reminders to change their passwords because they see the inconvenience of updating credentials as more immediate than the long-term security risk. Organizations that rely on punitive security policies, such as account lockouts or strict compliance-based enforcement, often face higher levels of noncompliance, as users find ways to bypass security restrictions to complete their tasks (Virtanen, 2024).

To mitigate this, security should be designed to work with user behavior rather than against it. Secure defaults, such as enabling multifactor authentication (MFA) by default, help ensure security without requiring users to make complex decisions. Similarly, security nudges, such as gentle reminders or automated security updates, can reinforce good security habits without feeling intrusive. Behavioral research has shown that framing security as a benefit rather than an obligation increases user compliance and engagement (Singh & Cheema, 2024).

Another critical aspect of Secure Systems is psychological safety in incident reporting. If employees fear punishment for making security mistakes, they are less likely to report phishing attempts, malware infections, or accidental data breaches. This delay in reporting can significantly increase an organization's exposure to cyber threats. A supportive security culture, where employees are encouraged to report incidents without fear of blame, leads to faster threat detection and remediation (Katcher et al., 2024).

Security must feel like an integrated part of daily operations, rather than a set of external rules that users must obey. When security is seamless, intuitive, and free from excessive complexity, users are more likely to comply with security policies without resentment or avoidance. By focusing on security through support rather than restriction, organizations can cultivate an environment where users feel both protected and empowered to maintain cybersecurity best practices. This user-centric approach transforms security from an obligation into a natural component of the workflow, thereby fostering greater awareness, reducing friction, and encouraging proactive engagement from all stakeholders (Al-Hashem & Saidi, 2023).

## TRUSTED IDENTITY (TRUST, DIGITAL IDENTITY, AND SOCIAL ENGINEERING AWARENESS)

The third level of the Technology Strategy Needs Pyramid focuses on Trusted Identity, emphasizing the critical role of trust, authentication, and social engineering awareness in digital security. In a world where cybercriminals exploit human psychology more than technical vulnerabilities, ensuring that users understand and protect their digital identities is essential. Attackers frequently take advantage of cognitive biases such as authority bias, social proof, and urgency bias to manipulate individuals into revealing sensitive information. Therefore, organizations must not only implement robust authentication systems but also educate users to recognize and counteract psychological manipulation tactics, fostering a culture of vigilance and informed skepticism in interactions involving their digital identities (Singh & Cheema, 2024).

One of the most common attack methods in this category is phishing, where adversaries impersonate trusted entities to deceive users into providing credentials or downloading malware. Business Email Compromise (BEC) scams further exploit trust in workplace communication, tricking employees into transferring funds or sharing confidential data. These attacks succeed because people naturally trust authority figures and familiar communication styles, often failing to verify authenticity before taking action. Additionally, attackers frequently create a sense of urgency or pressure, encouraging users to act quickly without careful consideration, which further increases the likelihood of successful exploitation. Strengthening employee awareness through targeted training and consistent reinforcement of verification practices can significantly reduce susceptibility to these attacks (Taylor & Whitty, 2024).

To counter these threats, organizations must implement Identity and Access Management (IAM) systems that enforce strict authentication protocols while maintaining usability. MFA, passwordless authentication, and biometric verification enhance security without adding excessive user friction. Additionally, Zero Trust security models, which require continuous verification rather than implicit trust, have become essential in mitigating identity-based cyber threats. By combining these strategies, organizations can significantly reduce their attack surface, protect sensitive information, and maintain operational efficiency, thus strengthening their overall cybersecurity posture (Singh & Cheema, 2024).

Beyond technical controls, security awareness training must emphasize psychological manipulation tactics rather than just procedural compliance. Employees should be trained to question urgency critically, as attackers often exploit time pressure to bypass rational decision-making processes. Additionally, verifying unexpected or unusual requests through alternative communication channels can prevent falling victim to social engineering schemes. Recognizing deception techniques, such as emotional appeals, authoritative demands, or fabricated emergencies, empowers employees to resist manipulation effectively (Alshammari et al., 2024).

## ETHICAL COMPLIANCE (REGULATORY COMPLIANCE AND ETHICAL CYBER GOVERNANCE)

Compliance with cybersecurity regulations is a fundamental requirement, but true security extends beyond simply meeting legal standards. Regulations serve as the baseline that defines minimal acceptable security practices, yet these standards cannot anticipate every potential cyber threat or organizational vulnerability (Stevens, 2022). Organizations that view compliance solely through the lens of regulatory adherence may overlook critical risks that exist outside the bounds of mandated requirements. Achieving robust cybersecurity demands proactive measures that anticipate threats rather than reactive strategies focused exclusively on avoiding legal repercussions.

The fourth level of the Technology Strategy Needs Pyramid, Ethical Compliance, addresses the need for organizations to build a culture of ethical cybersecurity governance rather than treating compliance as a checkbox exercise. Ethical Compliance emphasizes the integration of security awareness into the core values and daily activities of all organizational members, from leadership to frontline employees. When cybersecurity is embedded ethically into organizational culture, individuals are motivated by a sense of responsibility rather than by fear of penalties or enforcement actions (Deciu, 2022). This approach transforms compliance from an administrative burden into a strategic advantage, fostering a proactive environment that actively seeks continuous improvement.

A compliance-driven approach often leads to moral licensing, where organizations believe that fulfilling regulatory requirements is enough, even when security gaps remain. Moral licensing occurs when an organization justifies reduced vigilance in cybersecurity practices because it perceives itself as compliant with established regulations. This false sense of security can result in complacency, reducing motivation to identify and address non-mandatory security weaknesses. Ultimately, reliance on minimal regulatory standards without broader ethical considerations can leave an organization exposed to cyber threats that compliance alone is insufficient to prevent (Boeken, 2024).

Regulations such as General Data Protection Regulation (GDPR), Health Insurance Portability and Accountability Act(HIPAA), Payment Card Industry-Data Security Standard (PCI-DSS), and the (National Institute of Standards and Technology) NIST Cybersecurity Framework (CSF) establish critical security baselines that organizations are mandated or strongly advised to follow. These frameworks provide structured guidelines designed to reduce risk by promoting consistent and measurable security practices across industries. However, despite adherence to these regulatory standards, many organizations continue to experience cybersecurity incidents, indicating that compliance alone is insufficient for comprehensive protection (Itani et al., 2024). Such breaches underscore the reality that compliance is just the starting point, not the complete solution, highlighting significant gaps in security effectiveness that extend beyond regulatory checklists.

Compliance frameworks predominantly emphasize formal risk management processes, documentation, and structured assessments, often overlooking the nuanced aspects of organizational culture and human behavior. Although these frameworks provide essential safeguards against known threats and encourage standardization of security practices, they rarely address the deeper challenge of ingraining security values into employee attitudes and behaviors. Employees may understand security policies intellectually, but without fully internalizing these principles or valuing their importance, they may fail to act responsibly or ethically when confronted with real-world cybersecurity decisions (Mamaysky, 2021). Thus, the effectiveness of compliance frameworks remains limited if the organization's workforce lacks intrinsic motivation and a personal commitment to upholding ethical cybersecurity standards.

In the absence of a strong ethical security culture, organizations might technically fulfill compliance requirements yet still demonstrate gaps in critical security practices that are not explicitly regulated. Ethical cultures encourage employees at all levels to proactively identify vulnerabilities, make responsible security decisions, and uphold best practices even in scenarios where compliance regulations do not explicitly dictate behavior. Conversely, when organizations rely solely on regulatory compliance as the metric for security success, employees may adopt a mindset that minimal compliance is sufficient, resulting in overlooked vulnerabilities and reactive rather than proactive cybersecurity measures (Folorunsho et al., 2024). This limited approach creates significant blind spots, making companies vulnerable to emerging threats and social engineering attacks that thrive in environments with weak ethical commitments.

Ultimately, a robust cybersecurity posture requires organizations to transcend mere regulatory compliance and intentionally cultivate an ethical security culture embedded within their operational DNA. This shift involves fostering genuine awareness, accountability, and moral responsibility among employees, enabling them to prioritize security best practices even beyond formal compliance mandates. By embedding ethical decision-making into daily activities and rewarding proactive security behaviors, organizations create a self-sustaining cybersecurity culture that actively anticipates and mitigates risks (Sadeghi et al., 2023). Organizations that successfully integrate compliance frameworks with a strong ethical culture will ultimately achieve greater resilience, safeguarding not only their systems but also their reputations and stakeholder trust.

A strong ethical compliance framework requires transparency, accountability, and proactive risk management. Organizations should clearly communicate their security practices and decisions internally and externally, fostering an environment of openness that builds trust among stakeholders. Regularly scheduled audits and evaluations can help ensure accountability by verifying adherence to ethical and security standards. Additionally, proactive risk management should involve continuous threat monitoring and the adaptation of security practices to address emerging vulnerabilities before they become significant issues (Aljarrah et al., 2024).

Organizations should go beyond minimum legal requirements by adopting internal security policies that foster security-first mindsets at all levels. This involves not only creating robust policy documents but also actively embedding security considerations into daily operational decisions. Leadership should champion security-first practices through visible actions, such as publicly recognizing teams or individuals who contribute to security improvements. For example, public security reporting, responsible vulnerability disclosure programs, and ethical hacking initiatives such as bug bounty programs can encourage security improvements beyond regulatory mandates.

Security awareness training should not only cover regulatory requirements but also highlight ethical dilemmas in cybersecurity. Training programs must delve into real-world scenarios where employees confront choices between convenience, productivity, and security, prompting critical thinking about potential ethical consequences. Employees should be encouraged to speak up about potential security risks, question decisions that prioritize convenience over security, and challenge unethical behavior (Hess, 2021). To foster this openness, organizations need to establish clear reporting channels and assurances that ethical concerns will be treated seriously and without retaliation.

Security leaders must lead by example, demonstrating that cybersecurity is a shared ethical responsibility rather than a compliance burden. Leaders should actively participate in training sessions and clearly communicate the importance of cybersecurity ethics through their behavior and decision-making processes. By regularly engaging with staff on cybersecurity issues and emphasizing the organization's commitment to ethical practices, leaders can embed a culture of collective accountability. This approach helps shift perspectives, positioning cybersecurity as a vital ethical commitment rather than merely an administrative requirement.

## RESILIENT MATURITY (CYBER RESILIENCE, ADAPTATION, AND CONTINUOUS SECURITY GROWTH)

Cybersecurity is an ever-evolving field, requiring organizations to develop resilience, adapt to new threats, and continuously improve their security posture. As cyber threats become increasingly sophisticated and pervasive, organizations must remain vigilant and proactive to defend against potential breaches. Effective cybersecurity requires not just technological advancements but also a strong emphasis on organizational culture and employee behavior (Ofoegbu et al., 2023). To maintain robust defenses, organizations should regularly update their security strategies, invest in employee training, and foster a culture of continuous improvement.

The fifth level of the Technology Strategy Needs Pyramid, Resilient Maturity, shifts the focus from compliance-based security to dynamic, proactive security strategies. Unlike traditional compliance-driven approaches that focus on meeting minimum requirements, Resilient Maturity emphasizes anticipating and preparing for future threats. Organizations that achieve this level actively seek out vulnerabilities, anticipate attacker behavior, and consistently adapt their strategies to counter evolving threats (Woods & Alderson, 2021). This shift from a reactive stance to a proactive, forward-thinking mindset ensures organizations are better equipped to handle sophisticated cyberattacks.

A key concept in resilient security is the growth mindset, where security teams actively seek opportunities to refine defenses, anticipate threats, and learn from security incidents. Teams with a growth mindset do not view incidents as merely negative outcomes but rather as opportunities for valuable learning and improvement. These teams continually assess and reassess their security posture, recognizing that cybersecurity is not a static process but a dynamic, evolving challenge (Xu, 2020). By embracing continuous improvement and actively seeking feedback, organizations can enhance their defenses and stay ahead of emerging threats.

Organizations that fail to evolve remain vulnerable to emerging attack vectors, as adversaries constantly develop new tactics, techniques, and procedures (TTPs). Cyber adversaries are highly adaptive, frequently innovating their approaches to bypass traditional security measures. Organizations that rely solely on outdated or static defenses expose themselves to significant risks and potential breaches. Therefore, it is crucial for organizations to proactively adapt and update their security strategies to match the evolving threat landscape (Itani et al., 2024).

Security programs should incorporate threat modeling, adversary simulation, and Red Team/Blue Team exercises to identify weaknesses before attackers exploit them. These proactive measures allow organizations to test their security posture under realistic conditions, revealing vulnerabilities and gaps that traditional assessments may miss. Red Team exercises simulate real-world attacks, challenging the organization's defenses and identifying areas for improvement. Meanwhile, Blue Team exercises focus on defensive strategies, ensuring the team can effectively detect, respond to, and mitigate simulated attacks, thus preparing for real-world scenarios (Yulianto et al., 2024).

Another critical component of Resilient Maturity is incident response readiness. While many organizations have response plans in place, few conduct regular drills, tabletop exercises, or real-world simulations to test their effectiveness. Regular practice helps ensure that incident response teams can quickly and effectively manage real cyber incidents when they occur. Conducting realistic simulations also provides valuable insights into potential flaws in existing response strategies, enabling continuous refinement and improvement (Al-Hawamleh, 2024).

Security teams must train in real-time crisis scenarios, ensuring that employees know how to detect, contain, and recover from cyber incidents. Training should include clearly defined roles and responsibilities, effective communication protocols, and procedures for incident containment and recovery. Regular scenario-based exercises allow teams to practice decision-making under pressure, enhancing their ability to respond swiftly and effectively during actual crises (Skopik & Leitner, 2021). Organizations that embrace scenario-driven training are better equipped to minimize damage and rapidly recover from cyber incidents.

The ability to fail fast and learn faster is essential in refining an organization's security defenses. Organizations should create an environment where mistakes and incidents are viewed as critical learning opportunities rather than merely failures. This mindset encourages security teams to openly discuss incidents, analyze root causes, and implement improvements without fear of blame or repercussions. By fostering a culture of transparency and learning, organizations can rapidly strengthen their security posture and better defend against future threats (Pfaller et al., 2024).

Artificial intelligence (AI) and machine learning (ML) have become valuable tools in enhancing resilience by identifying patterns, automating threat detection, and reducing response time. These technologies allow security teams to analyze large datasets rapidly, identify anomalies, and predict potential threats with greater accuracy (Dhanushkodi & Thejas, 2024). Automated systems powered by AI and ML can significantly reduce response times, enhancing an organization's ability to contain and mitigate cyber incidents quickly. However, organizations must also recognize the limitations of technology and ensure AI and ML are integrated thoughtfully into broader security strategies.

However, technology alone is not enough; human adaptability and strategic foresight remain critical. Cybersecurity fundamentally involves human behavior, and effective security strategies must account for the human factor in both defensive and offensive operations. Organizations must empower employees with the knowledge, skills, and tools to make informed decisions and recognize potential threats. A security culture that encourages critical thinking, innovation, and continuous learning complements technological advancements, ensuring a more holistic and effective security posture (Luo et al., 2024).

Resilient Maturity ensures that cybersecurity remains a continuous journey rather than a static destination. Mature organizations recognize that security requires ongoing vigilance, adaptation, and continuous improvement to stay effective. Security threats evolve continuously, demanding an equally adaptive and proactive response from organizations. By committing to perpetual improvement and resilience, organizations can safeguard themselves against emerging threats and maintain robust defenses over the long term (Babatunde et al., 2022).

## COLLECTIVE IMPACT (CYBERSECURITY COLLABORATION AND INDUSTRY-WIDE DEFENSE)

At the highest level of the Technology Strategy Needs Pyramid is Collective Impact, recognizing that cybersecurity is not an isolated effort but a shared responsibility across organizations, industries, and nations. This level underscores the necessity of widespread cooperation, as cybersecurity threats are complex, evolving, and too significant for any single entity to address independently. Cyber adversaries frequently leverage inconsistencies and vulnerabilities resulting from disconnected and uncoordinated defensive measures. By emphasizing collaboration and unified action, organizations and nations can create a comprehensive defense framework capable of addressing the increasingly sophisticated and interconnected nature of cyber threats (Roobini et al., 2024).

One of the most effective ways to enhance security at an industry level is through threat intelligence sharing. Organizations participating in Information Sharing and Analysis Centers (ISACs) or public-private cybersecurity partnerships significantly improve their defensive capabilities by accessing real-time threat data, detailed attack patterns, and proven best practices. This collaborative exchange of critical information enables faster detection and response to threats, greatly reducing the overall risk to all participants (Gillard et al., 2022). Consequently, shared intelligence fosters a unified security front, enhancing the resilience of the entire cybersecurity ecosystem.

Governments and private organizations must also work together to develop global cybersecurity policies that align with ethical, legal, and technological standards. Policies advocating responsible vulnerability disclosure, coordinated incident response strategies, and international cooperation are essential to effectively combat cyber threats at a global scale. Such collaboration ensures consistent standards and frameworks that transcend geographic and organizational boundaries, thereby reducing exploitation by malicious actors (Brilingaitė et al., 2022). By pursuing collective policy alignment, organizations can better address systemic cybersecurity issues, creating a more secure and robust global digital infrastructure.

By fostering a culture of cybersecurity collaboration, organizations contribute significantly to creating a resilient digital environment, ensuring that no single entity remains excessively vulnerable to cyber threats. A collaborative approach promotes shared knowledge, consistent best practices, and mutual support, leading to quicker identification, response, and recovery from cyber incidents. Collective Impact epitomizes the highest level of cybersecurity maturity, signifying a shift from reactive, isolated defenses to proactive, cooperative strategies. Ultimately, achieving Collective Impact ensures that cybersecurity transcends internal priorities and becomes a shared, industry-wide commitment integral to the stability of global digital ecosystems (Eltayeb, 2024).

## CHAPTER SUMMARY

This chapter introduces the Technology Strategy Needs Pyramid, linking cybersecurity directly with human psychology through Maslow's Hierarchy of Needs. Maslow's model, ranging from physiological needs to self-actualization, offers valuable insights for understanding cybersecurity behaviors. At the fundamental level, cybersecurity relates directly to safety needs, emphasizing the importance of digital security as a prerequisite for individuals and organizations to function effectively. Without assured security, users face anxiety and distrust, undermining overall operational effectiveness.

This chapter further explores how social and esteem needs influence cybersecurity behaviors. Poorly designed security controls can frustrate users, negatively impacting their sense of belonging and esteem, which may lead to noncompliance or security fatigue. Cybersecurity strategies should therefore balance usability and security, ensuring users feel valued rather than alienated by security processes. Effective cybersecurity considers psychological impacts, aiming to create intuitive, empowering security measures rather than restrictive burdens.

Esteem and self-actualization also significantly impact cybersecurity practitioners themselves. High-pressure cybersecurity roles demand continuous learning, adaptability, and emotional resilience, often leading to burnout. Organizations must support these professionals by fostering career development, recognition, and work-life balance, which are vital for maintaining motivation and effectiveness within cybersecurity teams. Supporting practitioners' psychological needs directly contributes to the resilience and sustainability of cybersecurity initiatives.

Addressing psychological motivations, this chapter emphasizes the importance of aligning cybersecurity training and awareness programs with user needs. Security policies often fail when perceived solely as barriers rather than enablers, causing employees to bypass controls or ignore guidance. By connecting cybersecurity directly with Maslow's hierarchy, especially safety, belonging, and esteem, organizations can develop more effective and engaging security awareness programs, promoting intrinsic motivation rather than compliance-based behavior.

Reliable Access forms the base of the Technology Strategy Needs Pyramid, paralleling Maslow's physiological needs. This foundational level underscores the necessity of stable, user-friendly digital infrastructure. When users face unreliable systems or overly complex security protocols, they naturally seek workarounds, creating vulnerabilities. Ensuring reliable, accessible technology helps minimize security risks by aligning secure practices with natural human tendencies, reducing frustration-induced security circumvention.

The next level, Secure Systems, advocates for cybersecurity measures that provide psychological safety and minimize friction. Rather than employing restrictive, punitive policies, security should support user behavior with secure defaults and intuitive security nudges. Psychological safety, especially regarding incident reporting, encourages timely threat identification and reduces risk exposure. A supportive security culture promotes proactive compliance, embedding cybersecurity seamlessly into everyday workflow.

Trusted Identity focuses on authentication, digital identity security, and social engineering awareness. Recognizing that attackers frequently exploit cognitive biases; organizations must combine robust technical controls with comprehensive training. Simulated phishing exercises and continuous education enhance employees' abilities to recognize and resist manipulation tactics. Strong identity management solutions, such as MFA and zero trust models, further mitigate vulnerabilities associated with identity-based attacks.

Ethical Compliance emphasizes moving beyond mere regulatory adherence to embedding cybersecurity ethics into organizational culture. Regulatory compliance alone often results in security gaps, complacency, and moral licensing. Ethical cybersecurity governance integrates proactive risk management, transparency, accountability, and continuous ethical reflection into operational DNA. Encouraging employees to proactively address cybersecurity dilemmas fosters a resilient security culture that surpasses compliance-based security.

Resilient Maturity highlights the importance of ongoing adaptation and continuous security improvement. Organizations must proactively anticipate threats, regularly test their defenses through adversary simulations and incident response exercises, and encourage a growth mindset within security teams. Leveraging technologies like AI and ML enhances threat detection, though human adaptability remains essential. Continuous improvement ensures organizations remain prepared for emerging threats.

At the peak of the pyramid, Collective Impact calls for industry-wide cybersecurity collaboration. Cyber threats transcend individual organizations, requiring collective defense strategies. Sharing threat intelligence, aligning global cybersecurity policies, and fostering industry collaboration significantly enhance resilience. Collective Impact ensures cybersecurity becomes an integral, collaborative priority, essential for sustaining robust global digital infrastructure.

## REFERENCES

Al-Hashem, N., & Saidi, A. (2023). The psychological aspect of cybersecurity: Understanding cyber threat perception and decision-making. *International Journal of Applied Machine Learning and Computational Intelligence*, *13*(8), 11–22. https://neuralslate.com/index.php/Machine-Learning-Computational-I/article/view/41

Al-Hawamleh, A. M. (2024). Cyber Resilience Framework: Strengthening Defenses and Enhancing Continuity in Business Security. *International Journal of Computing and Digital Systems*, *15*(1), 1315–1331. https://doi.org/10.12785/ijcds/150193

Aljarrah, S. J., Cherbal, S., Mashaleh, A. S., Al Karaki, J., & Gawanmeh, A. (2024). On the comparative analysis of trends in cybersecurity risk assessment, governance, and compliance frameworks. In *2024 International Jordanian Cybersecurity Conference (IJCC)*, (pp. 136–142). https://doi.org/10.1109/IJCC64742.2024.10847280

Alshammari, A., Benson, V., & Batista, L. (2024). The influences of employees' emotions on their cybersecurity protection motivation behaviour: A theoretical framework. In *Proceedings of the 26th International Conference on Enterprise Information Systems - Volume 2: ICEIS* (pp. 524–531). SciTePress. https://doi.org/10.5220/0012681600003690

Babatunde, G. O., Amoo, O. O., Mustapha, S. D., & Ige, A. B. (2022). Improving cybersecurity readiness with a maturity framework for organizations in U.S. and Canada. *International Journal of Science and Technology Research Archive*, *3*(1), 232–250. https://doi.org/10.53771/ijstra.2022.3.1.0068

Bahar, B., & Özen, Ü. (2024). Research on the motivational factors of information technologies department employees in the context of Abraham Harold Maslow's Hierarchy of Needs. *Trends in Business and Economics*, *38*(4), 245–253. https://doi.org/10.16951/trendbusecon.1536281

Banire, B., Al Thani, D., & Yang, Y. (2021, July). Addressing cybersecurity accessibility: A qualitative study. In *34th British HCI Workshop and Doctoral Consortium (HCI2021-WDC): Post-pandemic HCI – Living Digitally*. https://doi.org/10.14236/ewic/HCI2021-W5.2

Bhagat, N. (2023). Cybersecurity in a remote work era: Strategies for securing distributed workforces. *Journal of Mathematical & Computer Applications*, *2023*(2), 1–5. https://doi.org/10.47363/JMCA/2023(2)E137

Boeken, J. (2024). From compliance to security, responsibility beyond law. *Computer Law & Security Review*, *52*, 105926. https://doi.org/10.1016/j.clsr.2023.105926

Braveman, P., Egerter, S., & Williams, D. R. (2011). The social determinants of health: Coming of age. *Annual Review of Public Health*, *32*, 381–398. https://doi.org/10.1146/annurev-publhealth-031210-101218

Brilingaitė, A., Bukauskas, L., Juozapavičius, A., & Kutka, E. (2022). Overcoming information-sharing challenges in cyber defence exercises. *Journal of Cybersecurity*, *8*(1), tyac001. https://doi.org/10.1093/cybsec/tyac001

Carducci, B. J. (2020). Maslow's hierarchy of needs. In B. J. Carducci, C. S. Nave & C. S. Nave (Eds.), *The Wiley Encyclopedia of Personality and Individual Differences: Models and Theories*, 269–273. https://doi.org/10.1002/9781118970843.ch45

Carlson, B., Rohde, K., Crepeau, M., Salinas, S. et al., "Consequence-Driven Cybersecurity for High-Power Electric Vehicle Charging Infrastructure," SAE Technical Paper 2023-01-0047, 2023, https://doi.org/10.4271/2023-01-0047.

Carrere, J., Vásquez-Vera, H., Pérez-Luna, A., Novoa, A. M., & Borrell, C. (2022). Housing insecurity and mental health: The effect of housing tenure and the coexistence of life insecurities. *Journal of Urban Health*, *99*(2), 268–276. https://doi.org/10.1007/s11524-022-00619-5

Compton, W. C. (2018). Self-actualization myths: What did Maslow really say? *Journal of Humanistic Psychology*, *64*(5), 743–760. https://doi.org/10.1177/0022167818761929

Corradini, I. (2020). Security: Human nature and behaviour. In *Building a cybersecurity culture in organizations* (Vol. 284, Studies in Systems, Decision and Control, pp. 23–47). Springer, Cham. https://doi.org/10.1007/978-3-030-43999-6_2

Dar, S. A., & Sakthivel, P. (2022). Maslow's hierarchy of needs is still relevant in the 21st century. *Journal of Learning and Educational Policy, 2*(5), 1–9. https://doi.org/10.55529/jlep25.1.9

Deciu, V. (2022). Psychological factors to consider when adopting an ethics and compliance program. *Psychology, 13*(1), 89–100. https://doi.org/10.4236/psych.2022.131007

Dellaert, B. G. C., Swait, J., Adamowicz, W. L. V., et al. (2018). Individuals' decisions in the presence of multiple goals. *Customer Needs and Solutions, 5*(1), 51–64. https://doi.org/10.1007/s40547-017-0071-1

Dhanushkodi, K., & Thejas, S. (2024). AI enabled threat detection: Leveraging artificial intelligence for advanced security and cyber threat mitigation. *IEEE Access, 12*, 173127–173136. https://doi.org/10.1109/ACCESS.2024.3493957

Diener, E., Oishi, S., & Tay, L. (2018). Advances in subjective well-being research. *Nat Hum Behav, 2*, 253–260. https://doi.org/10.1038/s41562-018-0307-6

Dong, K., Zhen, J., Xie, Z., & Chen, L. (2025). Building cybersecurity resilience: Integrating defense and recovery investment strategies in an expected resilience framework. *Journal of Enterprise Information Management, 38*(2), 502–531. https://doi.org/10.1108/JEIM-04-2023-0189

D'Souza, J. F., Adams, C. K., & Fuss, B. (2015). A pilot study of self-actualization activity measurement. *Journal of the Indian Academy of Applied Psychology, 41*(3), 28–33.

Eltayeb, O. E. O. (2024). The crucial significance of cyber threat intelligence in mitigating cyber attacks. *Journal of Ecohumanism, 3*(4), 2422–2434. https://doi.org/10.62754/joe.v3i4.3767

Fabella, F. E. T. (2023). Investigating the applicability of Maslow's theory of hierarchy of needs on selected Filipino teachers. *International Journal of Research and Innovation in Social Science*, *7*(9), 1892–1916. https://dx. doi.org/10.47772/IJRISS.2023.71053

Fatima, F., Hyatt, J. C., Rehman, S. U., De La Cruz, E., Nadella, G. S., & Meduri, K. (2024). Resilience and risk management in cybersecurity: A grounded theory study of emotional, psychological, and organizational dynamics. *Journal of Economy and Technology, 2*, 247–257. https://doi.org/10.1016/j.ject.2024.08.004

Folorunsho, S. O., Adenekan, O. A., Ezeigweneme, C., Somadina, I. C., & Okeleke, P. A. (2024). Ensuring cybersecurity in telecommunications: Strategies to protect digital infrastructure and sensitive data. *Computer Science & IT Research Journal, 5*(8), 1855–1883. https://doi.org/10.51594/csitrj.v5i8.1448

Gauer, R., & Meyers, B. K. (2019). Heat-related illnesses. *American Family Physician*, *99*(8), 482–489.

Gibney, M. J., Lanham-New, S. A., Cassidy, A., & Vorster, H. H. (2016). *Introduction to human nutrition* (2nd ed.). Wiley-Blackwell.

Gillard, S., David, D. P., Mermoud, A., & Maillart, T. (2022). Efficient collective action for tackling time-critical cybersecurity threats. *arXiv preprint arXiv:2206.15055*. https://doi.org/10.48550/arXiv.2206.15055

Gopireddy, R. R., & Bodipudi, A. (2022). Human-centric cybersecurity: Addressing the human element in cyber defense and ethical considerations in cybersecurity. *Journal of Artificial Intelligence & Cloud Computing, 1*(4), 2–5. https://doi.org/10.47363/JAICC/2022(1)E118

Grandner, M. A. (2022). Sleep, health, and society. *Sleep Medicine Clinics, 17*(2), 117–139. https://doi.org/10.1016/j.jsmc.2022.03.001

Guesmi, M., Chatti, M. A., Tayyar, A., Ain, Q. U., & Joarder, S. (2022). Interactive Visualizations of transparent user models for self-actualization: A human-centered design approach. *Multimodal Technologies and Interaction*, *6*(6), 42. https://doi.org/10.3390/mti6060042

Guo, Y., Gasparrini, A., Armstrong, B. G., Tawatsupa, B., Tobias, A., Lavigne, E., ... & Tong, S. (2016). Temperature variability and mortality: A multi-country study. *Environmental Health Perspectives, 124*(10), 1554–1559. https://doi.org/10.1289/EHP149

Hess, D. (2021). Ethics and compliance training. In B. van Rooij & D. D. Sokol (Eds.), *The Cambridge handbook of compliance* (pp. 616–625). Cambridge University Press.

Itani, D., Itani, R., Eltweri, A. A., Faccia, A., & Wanganoo, L. (2024). Enhancing cybersecurity through compliance and auditing: A strategic approach to resilience. In *2024 2nd International Conference on Cyber Resilience (ICCR)*, (pp. 1–10). https://doi.org/10.1109/ICCR61006.2024.10532959

Jeong, J., Mihelcic, J., Oliver, G., & Rudolph, C. (2019). Towards an improved understanding of human factors in cybersecurity. In *2019 IEEE 5th International Conference on Collaboration and Internet Computing (CIC)* (pp. 338–345). Los Angeles, CA, USA. IEEE. https://doi.org/10.1109/CIC48465.2019.00047

Kadena, E., & Gupi, M. (2021). Human factors in cybersecurity: Risks and impacts. *Security Science Journal*, *2*(2), 51–64. https://doi.org/10.37458/ssj.2.2.3

Katcher, S., Wang, L., Yang, C., Messdaghi, C., Mazurek, M. L., Chetty, M., Fulton, K. R., & Votipka, D. (2024). A survey of cybersecurity professionals' perceptions and experiences of safety and belonging in the community. In *Twentieth Symposium on Usable Privacy and Security (SOUPS 2024)* (pp. 1–20). USENIX Association. https://www.usenix.org/conference/soups2024/presentation/katcher

Khan, M. A., & Al-Jahdali, H. (2023). The consequences of sleep deprivation on cognitive performance. *Neurosciences Journal, 28*(2), 91–99. https://doi.org/10.17712/nsj.2023.2.20220108

Kredlow, M. A., Capozzoli, M. C., Hearon, B. A., Calkins, A. W., & Otto, M. W. (2015). The effects of physical activity on sleep: A meta-analytic review. *Journal of Behavioral Medicine*, *38*, 427–449. https://doi.org/10.1007/s10865-015-9617-6

Luo, M., Cai, Y., & Zhang, M. (2024). *A Review of Research on the Influence of Organizational Culture on Employee Innovation Behavior*. SHS Web of Conferences. https://doi.org/10.1051/shsconf/202418101034

Mamaysky, I. (2021). Understanding Ethics and Compliance: A Practitioner's Guide to Effective Corporate Compliance Programs. *Loy. U. Chi. J. Reg. Compl.*, *6*, 58.

Marmot, M., & Allen, J. J. (2014). Social determinants of health equity. *American Journal of Public Health, 104*(S4), S517–S519. https://doi.org/10.2105/AJPH.2014.302200

Maslow, A. H. (1943). A theory of human motivation. *Psychological Review, 50*(4), 370–396. https://doi.org/10.1037/h0054346

McNeill, S. G., O'Donovan, D., & Hart, N. (2022). Access to healthcare for people experiencing homelessness in the post-conflict society of Northern Ireland. *Medicine, Conflict and Survival*, *38*(4), 274–279. https://doi.org/10.1080/13623699.2022.2116553

Mejia-Lancheros, C., Woodhall-Melnik, J., Wang, R., Hwang, S. W., Stergiopoulos, V., & Durbin, A. (2021). Associations of resilience with quality of life levels in adults experiencing homelessness and mental illness: A longitudinal study. *Health and Quality of Life Outcomes*, *19*, 1–9. https://doi.org/10.1186/s12955-021-01713-z

Mohsin, A., Janicke, H., Nepal, S., & Holmes, D. (2023). Digital twins and the future of their use enabling shift left and shift right cybersecurity operations. In *2023 5th IEEE International Conference on Trust, Privacy and Security in Intelligent Systems and Applications (TPS-ISA)*, (pp. 277–286). https://doi.org/10.1109/TPS-ISA58951.2023.00042

Morgan, P.L., Asquith, P.M., Bishop, L.M., Raywood-Burke, G., Wedgbury, A., Jones, K. (2020). A New Hope: Human-Centric Cybersecurity Research Embedded Within Organizations. In: Moallem, A. (eds) *HCI for Cybersecurity, Privacy and Trust*. HCII 2020. Lecture Notes in Computer Science(), vol 12210. Springer, Cham. https://doi.org/10.1007/978-3-030-50309-3_14

Naqvi, B., Kävrestad, J., & Islam, A. K. M. N. (2024). Inclusive and accessible cybersecurity: Challenges and future directions. *Computer, 57*(6), 73–81. https://doi.org/10.1109/MC.2024.3376827

Ofoegbu, K., Osundare, O., Ike, C., & Fakeyede, O. (2023). Enhancing cybersecurity resilience through real-time data analytics and user empowerment strategies. *Engineering Science & Technology Journal*, *4*, 1527. https://doi.org/10.51594/estj.v4i6.1527

Omodan, B. I., & Abejide, S. O. (2022). Reconstructing Abraham Maslow's hierarchy of needs towards inclusive infrastructure development needs assessment. *Journal of Infrastructure, Policy and Development*, *6*(2), 1483. https://doi.org/10.24294/jipd.v6i2.1483

Pfaller, T., Skopik, F., Smith, P., & Leitner, M. (2024). Towards customized cyber exercises using a process-based lifecycle model. In *Proceedings of the 2024 European Interdisciplinary Cybersecurity Conference* (pp. 37–45). Association for Computing Machinery. https://doi.org/10.1145/3655693.3655713

Popkin, B. M., D'Anci, K. E., & Rosenberg, I. H. (2018). Water, hydration, and health. *Nutrition Reviews, 68*(8), 439–458. https://doi.org/10.1111/j.1753-4887.2010.00304.x

Porges, S. W. (2022). Polyvagal theory: A science of safety. *Frontiers in Integrative Neuroscience, 16*, 871227. https://doi.org/10.3389/fnint.2022.871227

Powdthavee, N. (2023). Social comparison theory. In F. Maggino (Ed.), *Encyclopedia of quality of life and well-being research* (pp. 6518–6519). Springer, Cham. https://doi.org/10.1007/978-3-031-17299-1_2740

Qashqari, A. A., Munshi, A. M., Alturkstani, H. A., Ghwati, H. T., & Alhebshi, D. H. (2020). The human factors and cybersecurity policy. *International Journal of Computer Science and Network Security, 20*(4), 1–5. http://paper.ijcsns.org/07_book/202004/20200401.pdf

Rohan, R., Funilkul, S., Pal, D., & Chutimaskul, W. (2021). Understanding of human factors in cybersecurity: A systematic literature review. In *2021 International Conference on Computational Performance Evaluation (ComPE)* (pp. 133–140). Shillong, India. IEEE. https://doi.org/10.1109/ComPE53109.2021.9752358

Roobini, M. S., Chowdary, M. B., Srinivas, Y., Jayanthi, S., & Srividhya, E. (2024). Cloud-based threat intelligence sharing for collective defence. In *2024 Ninth International Conference on Science Technology Engineering and Mathematics (ICONSTEM)*, (pp. 1–6). https://doi.org/10.1109/ICONSTEM60960.2024.10568663

Sadeghi, B., Richards, D., Formosa, P., McEwan, M., Bajwa, M. H. A., Hitchens, M., & Ryan, M. (2023). Modelling the ethical priorities influencing decision-making in cybersecurity contexts. *Organizational Cybersecurity Journal: Practice, Process and People*, *3*(2), 127–149. https://doi.org/10.1108/OCJ-09-2022-0015

Sapolsky, R. M. (2017). *Behave: The biology of humans at our best and worst.* Penguin.

Sangwan, A. (2024). Human factors in cybersecurity awareness. In *2024 International Conference on Intelligent Systems for Cybersecurity (ISCS)* (pp. 1–7). Gurugram, India. IEEE. https://doi.org/10.1109/ISCS61804.2024.10581139

Santana, B., Freire, S., Santos, J. A. M., & Mendonça, M. (2024). Psychological safety in the software work environment. *IEEE Software, 41*(4), 86–94. https://doi.org/10.1109/MS.2024.3386532

Sharma, B., & Chaurasia, A. (2023). Does access to finance alleviates poverty: A systematic review. *Indonesian Journal of Business Analytics*, *3*(5), 1957–1964. https://doi.org/10.55927/ijba.v3i5.6560

Shi, F., Ning, H., & Dhelim, S. (2021). A tutorial of cyber-syndrome viewed from cyber-physical-social-thinking space and Maslow's hierarchy of needs. *arXiv*. https://arxiv.org/abs/2111.02775

Singh, B., & Cheema, S. S. (2024). Psychology in cybersecurity: Unveiling the human dimensions of digital resilience. *International Journal of Advanced Networking and Applications*, *16*(1), 6281–6290. https://doi.org/10.35444/IJANA.2024.16107

Skopik, F., & Leitner, M. (2021). Preparing for national cyber crises using non-linear cyber exercises. In *2021 18th International Conference on Privacy, Security and Trust (PST)* (pp. 1–5). IEEE. https://doi.org/10.1109/PST52912.2021.9647795

Stevens, R., Kokulu, F. B., Doupé, A., & Mazurek, M. L. (2022). Above and beyond: Organizational efforts to complement U.S. digital security compliance mandates. In *Proceedings 2022 Network and Distributed System Security Symposium*. https://doi.org/10.14722/ndss.2022.23107

Taylor, J., & Whitty, M. (2023). An exploration of the awareness and attitudes of psychology students regarding their psychological literacy for working in the cybersecurity industry. *Psychology Learning & Teaching, 23*(2), 298–314. https://doi.org/10.1177/14757257231214612

Teh, K., Suhendra, V., Lim, S. C., & Roychoudhury, A. (2020). Singapore's cybersecurity ecosystem. *Communications of the ACM, 63*(4), 55–57. https://doi.org/10.1145/3378552

Triplett, W. J. (2022). Addressing human factors in cybersecurity leadership. *Journal of Cybersecurity and Privacy, 2*(3), 573–586. https://doi.org/10.3390/jcp2030029

Tushir, B., Joshi, G., & Pandey, V. P. (2023). Cultural influences on motivation theories and their application. In C. Maheshkar & J. Sonwalkar (Eds.), *Handbook of research on cultural and cross-cultural psychology* (pp. 253–271). Venon Press.

Uka, A., & Prendi, A. (2021). Motivation as an indicator of performance and productivity from the perspective of employees. *Management & Marketing. Challenges for the Knowledge Society, 16*(3), 268–285. https://doi.org/10.2478/mmcks-2021-0016

Virtanen, T. (2024). Psychological effects of continuity threatening cyber incidents. In *European Conference on Cyber Warfare and Security*. https://doi.org/10.34190/eccws.23.1.2268

Vitla, S. (2023). Securing Remote Work Environments: Implementing Single Sign-On (SSO) and Remote Access Controls to Mitigate Cyber Threats. *Turkish Journal of Computer and Mathematics Education (TURCOMAT), 14*(2), 1097–1114. https://doi.org/10.61841/turcomat.v14i2.14968

Wei, Z., & Ma, Y. (2022). The limitation and optimization of Maslow's hierarchy of needs theory in enterprises' application: Perspectives based on case studies. *BCP Business & Management, 17*, 161–168. https://doi.org/10.54691/bcpbm.v17i.388

Wilkinson, R., & Pickett, K. (2020). *The inner level: How more equal societies reduce stress, restore sanity, and improve everyone's well-being*. Penguin Publishing Group.

Woods, D.D. & Alderson, D. L. (2021). Progress toward resilient infrastructures: Are we falling behind the pace of events and changing threats? *Journal of Critical Infrastructure Policy, 2*, 5–18. https://doi.org/10.18278/jcip.2.2.2

World Health Organization. (2021). *Malnutrition*. https://www.who.int/news-room/fact-sheets/detail/malnutrition

Xu, S. (2020). The Cybersecurity Dynamics Way of Thinking and Landscape. In *Proceedings of the 7th ACM Workshop on Moving Target Defense* (pp. 69–80). Association for Computing Machinery. https://doi.org/10.1145/3411496.3421225

Yulianto, S., Soewito, B., Gaol, F. L., & Kurniawan, A. (2025). Enhancing cybersecurity resilience through advanced red-teaming exercises and MITRE ATT&CK framework integration: A paradigm shift in cybersecurity assessment. *Cyber Security and Applications, 3*, 100077.

Zhao, J., Wang, Y., Ou, D., Wang, H., Li, Y., & Deng, Q. (2024). Predicting survival time for cold exposure by thermoregulation modeling. *Building and Environment, 249*, 111127. https://doi.org/10.1016/j.buildenv.2023.111127

Zimmermann, V., & Renaud, K. (2019). Moving from a "human-as-problem" to a "human-as-solution" cybersecurity mindset. *International Journal of Human-Computer Studies, 131*, 169–187. https://doi.org/10.1016/j.ijhcs.2019.05.005

Chapter 6

# Decision Hygiene in Cybersecurity

## LEARNING OBJECTIVES

- Enhance operational effectiveness by applying behavioral science principles to reduce cognitive errors and optimize risk-based decisions.
- Identify how biases like optimism, availability, and anchoring affect cybersecurity choices, and apply strategies to mitigate their impact.
- Leverage behavioral frameworks to influence secure behaviors, promote compliance, and support a proactive security culture.

## INTRODUCTION TO DECISION HYGIENE

Cybersecurity decision-making has grown increasingly complex, requiring constant vigilance, swift reactions, and accurate judgment in the face of uncertainty. As organizations digitize assets and processes, the risks of cyberattacks, data breaches, and security lapses rise sharply. While significant attention has been devoted to strengthening technical controls and system defenses, a growing body of research highlights that many breaches stem from flawed human decision-making, rather than technological shortcomings (Howell et al., 2024). In this context, "decision hygiene" has emerged as a crucial framework for improving decision quality by reducing the noise, bias, and inconsistency that often plague human judgment (Bone, 2021).

Decision hygiene refers to the disciplined practices and tools used to improve the quality of decision-making by addressing cognitive distortions, heuristic errors, and environmental factors that lead to suboptimal outcomes (Kahneman et al., 2021). In cybersecurity, these distortions can result in underestimated risks, overconfident assessments, flawed threat prioritization, and inconsistent responses to security events. Cybersecurity professionals, system administrators, and end users alike are vulnerable to these errors, particularly when operating under time pressure, information overload, or ambiguous threats (Sachs, 2024). As cybersecurity moves increasingly toward risk-informed decision processes, embedding decision hygiene

DOI: 10.1201/9781003606345-6

principles into organizational workflows becomes not only beneficial but essential.

The rise of behavioral science in cybersecurity has provided new insight into how people make decisions about threats and protections, often contradicting the assumptions made by traditional, rational-choice models. Studies show that users frequently disregard security warnings, neglect updates, reuse passwords, or fall for phishing scams, not because they lack information but because of how that information is framed, processed, or prioritized cognitively (Howell et al., 2024; Koshiya, 2025). These behaviors are not necessarily irrational; rather, they reflect the bounded rationality and mental shortcuts that humans rely on to cope with complexity and uncertainty (Bone, 2021; Berthet, 2022).

Recent cybersecurity incidents illustrate the impact of poor decision hygiene. In the SolarWinds breach, for instance, attackers exploited supply chain vulnerabilities that had previously been flagged as low priority, likely due to availability bias and miscalibrated threat perception. Similarly, in organizations responding to ransomware attacks, overconfidence in backup procedures or delayed reporting often stems from flawed assumptions and groupthink, not malicious intent (Vajpayee & Hossain, 2024). In each case, better decision structures, clearer cognitive models, and debiasing tools might have prevented or reduced the damage.

Understanding and mitigating decision-making flaws in cybersecurity is thus both a scientific and practical challenge. Several emerging models, including thoughtfully reflective decision-making (TRDM), behavioral security games, and cognitive bias-aware decision support systems (DSS), aim to tackle these flaws systematically. These approaches shift the focus from punishing individual errors to designing better environments for secure choices, highlighting the importance of decision hygiene at both the individual and the institutional level (Abdallah et al., 2020; Howell et al., 2024).

Moreover, the move toward remote work has only heightened the need for decision hygiene. With employees now operating in isolated, digitally mediated environments, susceptibility to phishing, social engineering, and weak policy compliance have risen. Factors such as fatigue, digital overload, and environmental distractions amplify cognitive biases, increasing the likelihood of risky decisions (Koshiya, 2025). Organizations must recognize these contextual effects and proactively address them through behavioral design, decision scaffolding, and targeted interventions.

This chapter explores how decision hygiene can be applied to cybersecurity contexts to improve judgment, reduce risk, and support secure behavior. It draws upon recent interdisciplinary research from cognitive science, behavioral economics, cybersecurity, and systems design to explain why decisions go wrong, how biases manifest in digital settings, and what tools and frameworks can be used to improve them. We begin by reviewing the theoretical foundations of cognitive biases and decision-making under uncertainty, then move into practical tools such as decision matrices, reflective models, and training interventions. This chapter concludes with recommendations for integrating decision hygiene into cybersecurity operations, policy, and culture.By understanding the roots of poor decision-making and addressing them with structured, evidence-based techniques, cybersecurity leaders can build more resilient systems, both technically and psychologically.

## THEORETICAL FOUNDATIONS OF DECISION HYGIENE

Decision hygiene is grounded in cognitive psychology, behavioral economics, and risk science. These disciplines converge on the insight that human decision-making is systematically fallible, not due to irrationality per se, but because of how the brain simplifies complexity using heuristics. These shortcuts, while efficient, can result in biased judgments and suboptimal outcomes. In cybersecurity, where decisions often involve high stakes and limited information, the cost of cognitive bias can be particularly severe (Sachs, 2024). Understanding the theoretical roots of these decision errors is the first step in building effective mitigation strategies.

At the heart of decision hygiene lies the concept of bounded rationality, introduced by Herbert Simon. Bounded rationality asserts that human decision-makers are constrained by cognitive limitations, time pressures, and incomplete information. Rather than optimizing, individuals satisfice, settling for a solution that is "good enough" under the circumstances (Bone, 2021). This theory is highly relevant in cybersecurity contexts, where threat landscapes evolve quickly, data can be overwhelming or unavailable, and perfect information is a luxury.

Building on Simon's work, Daniel Kahneman and Amos Tversky introduced Prospect Theory, which describes how people evaluate potential gains and losses under uncertainty. A key insight from this theory is loss aversion: people tend to weigh losses more heavily than equivalent gains. In cybersecurity, this bias can result in over-prioritizing avoidance of penalties (e.g., regulatory fines) rather than investing in proactive measures like threat detection or staff training. Additionally, framing effects, how a problem is worded, can drastically alter perceived risk and choice preference, even if the objective facts remain unchanged (Zhu, 2023).

Another central idea in decision hygiene is the dual-system theory of cognition, also known as "System 1 and System 2" thinking. System 1 is fast, intuitive, and automatic, while System 2 is slower, deliberate, and logical (Berthet, 2022) ). Most day-to-day decisions, including many in cybersecurity, are made using System 1 processes, which are prone to errors like confirmation bias, anchoring, and the availability heuristic. For instance, a system administrator under time pressure might patch only those systems they recall being vulnerable in the past (availability heuristic), ignoring recent but less salient threats (Figure 6.1).

*Figure 6.1* Cybersecurity Biases and Heuristics

Cognitive biases are predictable deviations from rational judgment. In cybersecurity, these include:

Each of these can distort threat assessments, weaken incident response, or impair prioritization of risk mitigation efforts (Vajpayee & Hossain, 2024). For example, overconfidence among technical staff might lead to complacency in reviewing code for vulnerabilities or skipping mandatory security audits.

To illustrate, Howell et al. (2024) tested the concept of TRDM in a cybersecurity context. TRDM refers to a style of decision-making that involves identifying options, weighing evidence, and reflecting on outcomes. Their study found that individuals with high TRDM scores were significantly more likely to engage in protective behaviors, such as enabling two-factor authentication (2FA) or scrutinizing suspicious emails. This reinforces the value of deliberate, reflective thinking in cybersecurity environments, especially when dealing with ambiguous or deceptive threats.

Recent theoretical advancements have explored behavioral security games, in which security decisions are modeled not as purely rational calculations but as interactions between players (e.g., defenders and attackers) who exhibit human cognitive limitations. These models acknowledge that both attackers and defenders are susceptible to biases and incomplete reasoning. For example, defenders may underinvest in protections for interdependent systems if their cognitive models of risk are fragmented or siloed

(Abdallah et al., 2020). These behavioral models are particularly useful for designing policies that account for imperfect human agents rather than idealized rational actors.

In parallel, cognitive neuroscience and human factors research have begun to map the neural correlations of cybersecurity decision-making. Findings suggest that uncertainty, time pressure, and emotional arousal activate brain regions associated with automatic responses, reducing analytical processing (Chen et al., 2024). This aligns with real-world observations: under the stress of an active incident, security professionals may revert to heuristics and groupthink, rather than calmly evaluating the full set of options. This has led to increasing interest in DSS that scaffold deliberation and "nudge" users toward more robust choices.

The domain of cognitive risk management has also evolved in recent years. This framework treats biases not as isolated errors but as systemic risks that must be identified, measured, and mitigated, much like malware or network vulnerabilities (Bone, 2021). For example, organizations can assess decision hygiene in risk reviews by identifying where intuitive judgments dominate over evidence-based assessments. By incorporating bias audits, postmortems, and scenario planning into cybersecurity governance, leaders can operationalize decision hygiene as a measurable competency.

Finally, the shift toward remote and hybrid work has amplified the relevance of these theories. Koshiya (2025) notes that remote environments increase user isolation and decrease visibility into peer behaviors, raising the likelihood of biases like optimism, neglect of threats, and inconsistency in applying security practices. In such contexts, decision hygiene practices, like digital nudges, reflective prompts, and structured choices, can help reintroduce discipline into otherwise informal or fragmented decision contexts.

In sum, decision hygiene draws from a rich theoretical base encompassing bounded rationality, behavioral economics, dual-process cognition, and cognitive risk management. It emphasizes not only the identification of biases but also the design of systems and environments that anticipate, detect, and reduce the impact of those biases. Understanding these foundations is essential to creating actionable frameworks for cybersecurity practice, which we explore in the next sections.

## COMMON BIASES IN CYBERSECURITY DECISION-MAKING

Human cognition is not naturally wired for the type of abstract, probabilistic, and long-term risk reasoning that cybersecurity demands. As a result, decision-making in this domain is highly susceptible to cognitive biases, systematic patterns of deviation from rational judgment that persist even in trained professionals. These biases distort how individuals perceive threats, prioritize risks, and respond to incidents. This section explores several of the most relevant biases in cybersecurity contexts, supported by empirical studies and real-world implications.

## Confirmation Bias

Confirmation bias refers to the tendency to favor information that confirms existing beliefs and to dismiss evidence that contradicts them. In cybersecurity, this can lead analysts to interpret ambiguous data as supporting their initial threat hypothesis, potentially overlooking alternative explanations or missing new forms of attack. For example, an incident response team might prematurely conclude that a security alert stems from known malware, failing to detect a novel exploit because they ignored anomalous data that didn't fit the expected pattern (Sachs, 2024).

The bias is especially dangerous in high-stress environments where decisions must be made quickly. A study by Berthet (2022) found that confirmation bias intensifies when decision-makers operate under time constraints, which are common in security operations centers (SOCs). This leads to premature closure, where decision-makers settle on a threat classification too early in the investigation. Training programs and playbooks that enforce consideration of alternative hypotheses can help mitigate this bias.

## Overconfidence Bias

Overconfidence bias involves the overestimation of one's knowledge, abilities, or judgment accuracy. In cybersecurity, this bias can manifest in multiple ways, overestimating the effectiveness of defenses, underestimating the likelihood of attack, or assuming that one's technical skills are sufficient to detect all threats. This has been observed particularly in IT professionals who, due to prior successes or role authority, believe they are immune to common social engineering or phishing attempts (Vajpayee & Hossain, 2024).

Howell et al. (2024) found that individuals with lower scores on TRDM were more prone to overconfidence and less likely to engage in protective behaviors such as enabling 2FA. This highlights the interplay between cognitive style and susceptibility to bias. Overconfidence is especially perilous in environments where a false sense of security may result in ignoring updates, misconfiguring firewalls, or delaying vulnerability scans.

## Anchoring Bias

Anchoring bias occurs when individuals rely too heavily on an initial piece of information (the "anchor") when making decisions. For instance, if a threat intelligence report states that a certain attack vector has a 10% likelihood, security teams might anchor on that figure, even if new evidence suggests a higher risk. Anchoring affects everything from risk assessments to patch prioritization (Zhu, 2023).

Pharmer et al. (2024) experimentally demonstrated anchoring bias in a gamelike cybersecurity simulation where participants, acting as attackers, made skewed choices based on arbitrary numerical anchors provided in pre-task instructions. Even when new data became available, participants stuck to their initial assumptions. The implication is clear: unless individuals are trained to deliberately reevaluate prior information, anchoring can undermine adaptive response in dynamic threat environments.

## Availability Heuristic

The availability heuristic is the tendency to assess the probability of events based on how easily examples come to mind. This is especially problematic in cybersecurity, where certain threats (like ransomware) receive more media coverage and thus loom larger in decision-makers' minds than others (like insider threats or configuration errors), which may be statistically more common but less memorable (Bone, 2021).

This bias can skew risk prioritization and resource allocation. For instance, after a highly publicized breach in another organization, security teams might overinvest in similar defenses while neglecting other areas of equal or greater risk. Koshiya (2025) points out that in remote work environments, the lack of peer feedback and social comparison further amplifies availability effects, as workers may rely solely on recent alerts or headlines to guide decisions.

## Optimism Bias

Optimism bias reflects the belief that negative events are less likely to happen to oneself than to others. In cybersecurity, this leads to behaviors like neglecting personal backups, reusing passwords, or delaying software updates. Despite knowing the risks, users believe they are unlikely to be targeted or affected, especially in large organizations where responsibility is perceived to be diffused (Howell et al., 2024).

This bias is also seen in leadership and organizational decision-making. Executives may underinvest in security controls or incident response planning under the assumption that their organization is less likely to be attacked than their peers, often due to wishful thinking or lack of recent incidents. Decision hygiene techniques, such as structured premortems and adversarial risk assessments, can help correct for this misplaced optimism.

## Complexity Aversion

Complexity aversion describes the tendency to avoid complex or effortful decisions, even when such decisions are necessary. In cybersecurity, this can manifest as choosing simpler but less secure configurations, avoiding multistep authentication processes, or failing to conduct deep vulnerability scans that require specialized tools or training (Aggarwal et al., 2024).

This was evident in a study where attackers in a simulated scenario preferred using a simple but unreliable shell script over a more complex and effective attack tool, suggesting that even adversaries fall prey to complexity aversion (Aggarwal et al., 2024). On the defense side, this bias can lead to reliance on outdated tools or standard settings, undermining proactive security posture. Automating decision workflows and reducing friction in secure behaviors are potential mitigation strategies.

### Default Effect

The default effect refers to the tendency to go along with preselected options. In cybersecurity, default configurations, many of which are insecure, are often left unchanged by users or even professionals due to this bias. For instance, if multifactor authentication (MFA) is not enabled by default, many users will not activate it even if prompted (Purnamawati, 2024).

This bias is particularly relevant for software developers and product designers, who shape user behavior through interface design and system defaults. Secure defaults are a powerful application of decision hygiene because they nudge users toward better outcomes without requiring conscious effort. Organizations can harness this bias by designing systems where secure choice is the path of least resistance.

Understanding the most common cognitive biases in cybersecurity decision-making is essential for developing effective interventions and tools. Each bias, whether it be confirmation, overconfidence, anchoring, or availability, distorts the perception of threats and responses to them. These distortions can occur at all organizational levels, from frontline users to executives and system architects. By recognizing the specific ways these biases manifest in digital contexts, cybersecurity professionals can begin to implement tailored mitigation strategies relaying the groundwork for a culture of better, bias-aware decisions.

## MITIGATING BIAS—TOOLS AND FRAMEWORKS FOR DECISION HYGIENE

Biases in cybersecurity decision-making cannot be eliminated, but they can be identified, managed, and reduced through structured interventions. The goal of decision hygiene is not to achieve perfect rationality, but rather to design processes and environments that promote consistent, defensible, and higher-quality judgments. This section explores practical tools and frameworks that organizations can adopt to reduce the influence of cognitive bias and improve decision outcomes in cybersecurity operations (Figure 6.2).

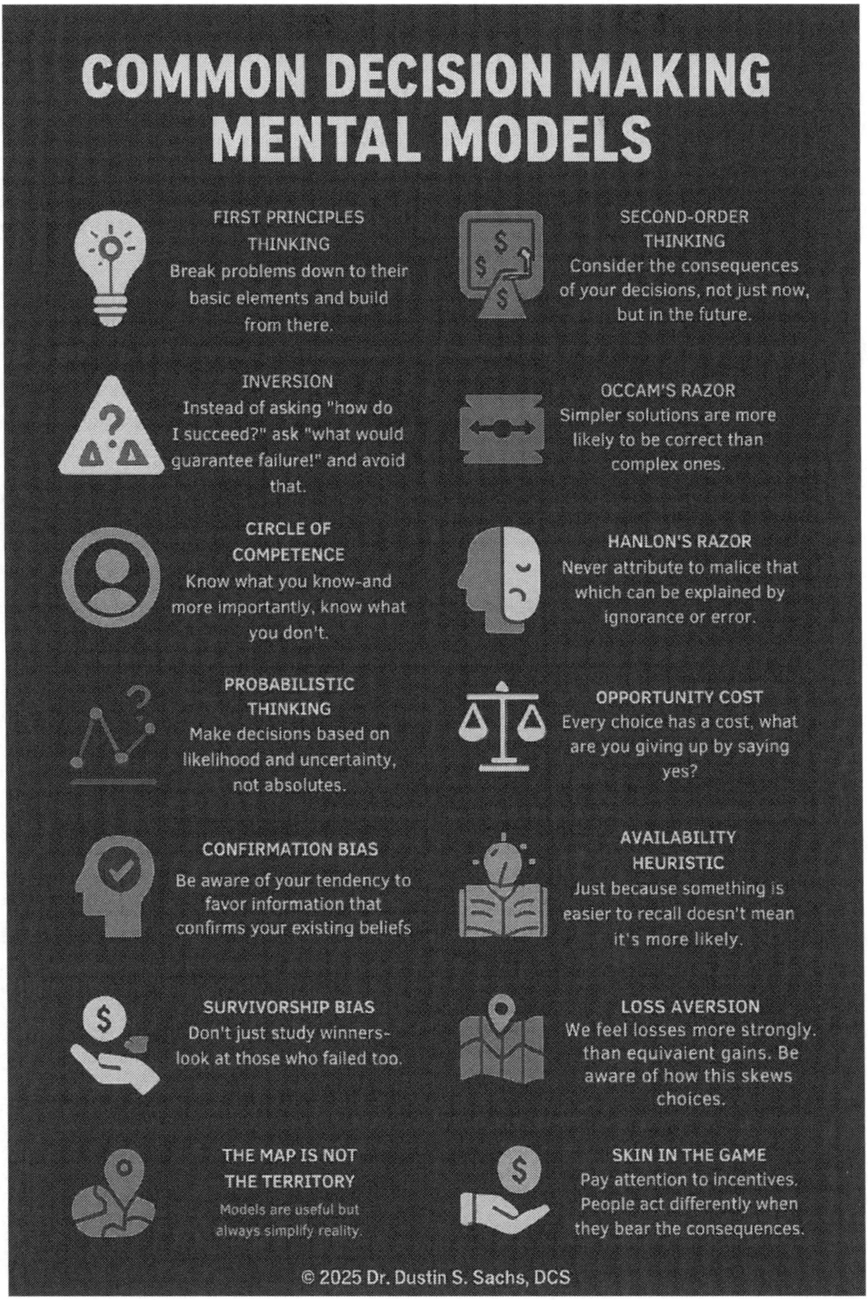


*Figure 6.2* Common Decision-Making Mental Models

## Decision Support Systems

DSS are digital platforms that help users analyze data, evaluate risks, and make structured decisions. In cybersecurity, DSS can be used to guide incident response, prioritize threats, and allocate resources. However, to be effective in reducing bias, DSS must be designed with cognitive limitations in mind. Lai et al. (2020) emphasize the importance of bias-aware DSS, which incorporate probabilistic models to detect and adjust for human decision distortions, such as anchoring or default bias, especially in high-stakes environments like security checkpoints or access control systems.

For example, visual dashboards that present risks using multiple frames (absolute values, probabilities, and historical comparisons) can help counteract framing effects. Similarly, prompting users to provide justification for their choices within the system can encourage reflective thinking and discourage snap judgments. As shown by Chen et al. (2024), machine learning-enhanced DSS can simulate humanlike reasoning based on previous decisions and offer contextual nudges to improve judgment, without overwhelming users.

## Premortems and Red Teaming

Premortem analysis is a structured technique in which teams imagine that a failure has already occurred and then work backward to identify what might have caused it. This tool is especially useful in cybersecurity, where high uncertainty and fast-paced decisions can lead to overconfidence and narrow thinking. By simulating future failure, premortems expose assumptions, challenge dominant narratives, and broaden the range of risks considered (Bone, 2021).

Red teaming, the practice of simulating adversaries to test system defenses, is another behavioral tool that mitigates cognitive bias. Red teams act as "devil's advocates," forcing defenders to reconsider their assumptions and adopt an attacker's perspective. These exercises not only test technical systems but also reveal flaws in human threat modeling and response protocols. They counteract confirmation bias, groupthink, and optimism bias by creating a psychologically safe space for dissent and imaginative thinking.

## Thoughtfully Reflective Decision-Making

As introduced in prior sections, TRDM is a cognitive style that emphasizes deliberate thinking, option evaluation, and reflection on past decisions. Howell et al. (2024) found that individuals high in TRDM are more likely to adopt secure behaviors and less likely to fall for phishing attempts or ignore security warnings. Integrating TRDM into cybersecurity training involves more than just telling users what to do, it requires teaching them how to think critically about security decisions.

Training interventions can include decision-making simulations, journaling about past responses to threats, and structured scenario walkthroughs where users must weigh multiple options before selecting a course of action. Over time, these reflective exercises foster mental habits that align with secure behavior and improve resilience to manipulation or cognitive overload. TRDM-based approaches also encourage users to take ownership of security decisions rather than viewing them as imposed or irrelevant.

## Choice Architecture and Behavioral Nudges

Borrowed from behavioral economics, choice architecture refers to the way choices are presented to users. Subtle changes in wording, layout, or default settings can have significant impacts on behavior. In cybersecurity, nudges can steer users toward safer behaviors without requiring mandates or heavy cognitive effort.

For example, making MFA opt out rather than opt in takes advantage of the default effect, significantly increasing adoption rates. Similarly, phrasing password requirements in terms of protecting loved ones rather than complying with policy taps into emotional framing and improves compliance (Purnamawati, 2024). Systems can also present users with immediate feedback, such as warnings about reused passwords or expired patches, that gently prompt reconsideration.

Critically, nudges must be tested and ethically implemented. Koshiya (2025) warns that poorly designed nudges can backfire or create user fatigue if overused. Organizations should adopt nudge transparency principles and measure behavioral outcomes to ensure interventions improve security without undermining trust or autonomy.

## Cognitive Bias Checklists and Bias-Aware Playbooks

Just as pilots use checklists to avoid omission errors, cybersecurity teams can use bias checklists to detect and correct flawed thinking. These checklists remind users to consider alternative explanations, revisit early assumptions, or consult with others before finalizing a decision. Bias checklists are particularly helpful during high-pressure tasks such as incident triage or root cause analysis (Sachs, 2024) (Figure 6.3).

In parallel, bias-aware playbooks are predefined response guides that embed bias mitigation into procedural steps. These playbooks help ensure that best practices are followed consistently, even under stress or cognitive load. They can be adapted to reflect evolving threats and new bias research.

## Bias Audits and Decision Debriefs

Bias mitigation should not end with a single decision; it must be part of continuous learning. Bias audits are structured reviews of past decisions to identify

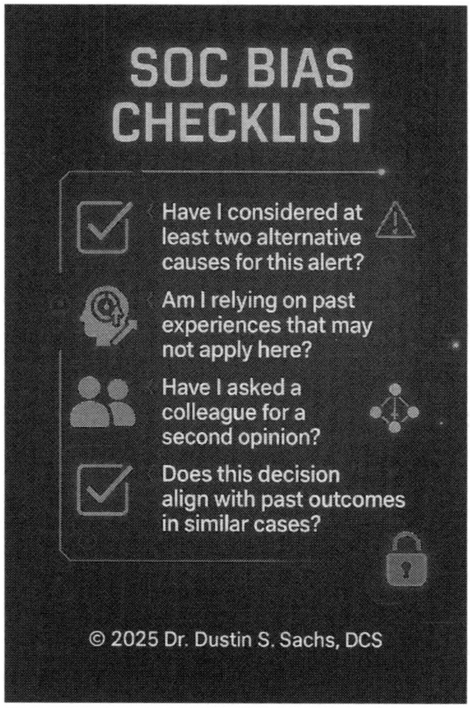


*Figure 6.3* SOC Bias Mitigation Checklist

where cognitive biases may have played a role. This practice, common in aviation and healthcare, is gaining traction in cybersecurity as well. During post-incident reviews, teams should not only analyze technical failures but also reflect on human decision patterns: Were early warnings ignored? Did groupthink distort judgment? Was risk underestimated due to familiarity?

Pharmer et al. (2024) suggest integrating **behavioral forensics** into security audits to track decision paths and identify bias signatures, such as consistent underestimation of novel attack vectors or repeated reliance on outdated threat models. Combined with anonymized behavioral metrics and decision logs, bias audits can inform better training and system redesigns.

Decision debriefs take this a step further by incorporating team reflections after key choices, whether in threat hunting, patch management, or vendor risk scoring. These debriefs reinforce learning, surface assumptions, and institutionalize reflection as part of the decision culture.

## Embedding Bias Mitigation in Organizational Culture

Tools alone are not enough. To have sustained impact, decision hygiene must be woven into the culture and leadership practices of cybersecurity teams. Leaders play a key role by modeling humility, openness to dissent, and willingness to revise judgments. Teams that value psychological safety, where questioning assumptions is encouraged, are better at detecting and correcting bias (Aggarwal et al., 2024).

Organizations should formalize bias literacy as part of cybersecurity certification, leadership development, and onboarding. Creating communities of practice, running tabletop exercises focused on decision errors, and celebrating examples of revised thinking all contribute to a culture of continuous improvement. When bias mitigation is seen not as a burden but as a professional discipline, it becomes part of organizational identity.

Cybersecurity is as much about human judgment as it is about technical defense. Cognitive biases are pervasive, but not immutable. By applying tools such as DSS, premortems, TRDM-based training, nudges, bias checklists, and post-incident debriefs, organizations can foster more consistent, rational, and secure decision-making. The most successful interventions are those that integrate seamlessly into workflows and reflect a deep understanding of human psychology. Ultimately, decision hygiene should be viewed not as a corrective patch but as a core design principle for cybersecurity systems and strategy.

## APPLICATION IN DAILY OPERATIONS AND CASE STUDIES

While the theoretical foundations and frameworks of decision hygiene provide a strong starting point, their real value lies in how they can be integrated into everyday cybersecurity operations. This section explores how decision hygiene is applied in practice, using concrete examples and case studies to illustrate its relevance and impact. From threat detection to incident response, vendor management to user behavior, cognitive bias mitigation must be embedded in the operational fabric of security decision-making.

### Incident Response Under Cognitive Load

Incident response is among the most cognitively demanding aspects of cybersecurity. Analysts must quickly gather evidence, diagnose root causes, coordinate with stakeholders, and make real-time decisions, often under stress and time pressure, and with incomplete information. In such environments, the conditions are ripe for bias: availability heuristics (relying on the last incident), anchoring (fixating on the first alert), or groupthink (conforming to the lead responder's view).

In a case study described by Sachs (2024), a financial institution suffered a ransomware attack. The initial triage team assumed the point of entry was phishing, based on prior incidents, and built their response around that theory. However, the true entry point was a remote desktop protocol (RDP) vulnerability, which was overlooked due to confirmation bias and availability effects. It wasn't until a third-party forensic team conducted a postmortem that the bias became evident. As a result, the organization adopted structured bias debriefs and added "alternative hypothesis checklists" to its response protocol.

This case shows that decision hygiene must be embedded in real-time workflows. Templates for incident response should include prompts to consider multiple explanations, check for common bias triggers, and assign a "devil's advocate" to challenge prevailing assumptions.

## Secure Configuration and System Defaults

Another daily operational domain where decision hygiene is critical is in secure system configuration. Administrators frequently make choices about firewall rules, authentication settings, patch schedules, and access controls. These decisions often appear routine but are highly susceptible to the default effect and complexity aversion. Without deliberate effort, admins may leave settings unchanged, skip complex options, or prioritize convenience over security.

In the study by Kankane et al. (2018), researchers explored how different types of nudges could influence users' password management behaviors, a domain where users often make insecure choices due to convenience or lack of awareness. Among the five nudges tested (incentives, norms, defaults, salience, and ego), the salience nudge proved most effective. A *salience nudge* is a behavioral design technique that draws users' attention to important information, often by making risks or consequences more visible or emotionally impactful, to influence their decisions. In this case, the salience nudge made users more aware of the risks of using auto-generated passwords, leading them to feel less comfortable keeping them and instead nudging them toward stronger, self-created passwords without requiring complex decision-making (Kankane et al., 2018).

## Cybersecurity Training and TRDM in User Behavior

Cyber hygiene among nontechnical users is also a critical front in bias mitigation. While many organizations conduct annual training, evidence suggests that static, one-size-fits-all modules have limited effectiveness. Instead, programs that foster TRDM, by engaging users in active reflection, decision simulations, and consequence modeling, are far more effective.

Howell et al. (2024) implemented a TRDM-based training model in a university setting, showing that users with higher TRDM scores were significantly more likely to update software, enable 2FA, and scrutinize suspicious links. These users also expressed greater personal responsibility for cybersecurity. One notable outcome was that phishing susceptibility dropped by 35% after TRDM training compared to only 8% for the control group.

Daily security operations should incorporate TRDM principles. For instance, interactive phishing simulations followed by reflective debriefs can help users internalize lessons more deeply. Likewise, tools like "risk reflection popups" (brief questions that ask users why they chose to click a link or ignore a warning) are subtle ways to build decision hygiene without creating fatigue.

## Vendor and Supply Chain Risk Assessment

Third-party risk management is another area where biases can cloud judgment. Many organizations use scoring systems or standardized frameworks (e.g., National Institute of Standards and Technology (NIST) or International Organization for Standardization (ISO)) to assess vendor risk, but human decision-makers still interpret these scores and make final calls. Here, anchoring, halo effects, and optimism bias often influence assessments. A well-known vendor might be seen as inherently more secure, even if recent audits suggest otherwise.

In a case analyzed by Vajpayee and Hossain (2024), a telecommunications firm experienced a breach that stemmed from a misconfigured third-party Application Programming Interface (API). The vendor had a long-standing relationship with the company, and its risk score was based on outdated data. Due to anchoring on the vendor's prior "safe" label, security teams did not reevaluate its systems after a major acquisition, a missed opportunity. Following the breach, the company introduced a cognitive bias checklist into its third-party review process and required multiple independent evaluations before vendor onboarding.

This case illustrates that mitigating bias in vendor decisions involves institutionalizing friction: requiring cross-team input, regular reassessment of high-trust vendors, and rotation of evaluators to avoid overfamiliarity.

## Cognitive Risk in SOCs

SOCs are ground zero for fast-paced decision-making. Analysts must triage a high volume of alerts, identify true threats, and escalate incidents, all while avoiding fatigue and bias. Tools like SOAR (Security Orchestration, Automation and Response) platforms can reduce bias by automating routine decisions and forcing structured analysis. However, these tools must be designed to avoid reinforcing existing heuristics or assumptions.

Pharmer et al. (2024) show how asymmetric dominance and anchoring biases affected attacker behavior in experimental cyber scenarios. This same cognitive framing applies to defenders as well. If an alert presents limited context or highlights one threat vector disproportionately, analysts may anchor on that path and ignore others.

One SOC case study showed that implementing a "bias audit button," which allowed analysts to flag decisions they believed were potentially biased, helped increase awareness and led to better documentation of thought processes. Analysts reported feeling more empowered to reconsider assumptions, and over time, false positive rates decreased.

## Real-World Organizational Deployment of Bias Frameworks

In recent years, the deployment of bias frameworks within real-world organizations has become an urgent focus across industries relying on artificial intelligence (AI) and machine learning systems. As models transition from research environments to live operational contexts, the stakes of biased predictions, such as unfair hiring decisions, discriminatory credit assessments, or unequal healthcare access, become profoundly consequential. This reality has prompted organizations to integrate bias mitigation practices throughout their model development lifecycle. However, the gap between theoretical fairness metrics and practical deployment often reveals unforeseen complexities in adapting these frameworks to diverse, real-world data and workflows.

One critical development in bridging this gap has been the introduction of structured bias mitigation toolkits and deployment models, such as the Aequitas toolkit and the DEPLOYR framework. These systems allow organizations to audit models for disparate impact and performance discrepancies before full-scale deployment, thereby enabling early intervention when biased behaviors are detected (Saleiro et al., 2020), (Corbin et al., 2023). At healthcare institutions, for example, DEPLOYR has enabled silent model deployment for evaluation prior to real-time use, highlighting performance shifts that are often invisible in retrospective validation. This kind of proactive monitoring represents a paradigm shift from traditional development-focused fairness strategies to those embedded within dynamic deployment environments.

Equally important is the emergence of comprehensive frameworks that guide organizations through each phase of machine learning development and deployment with fairness in mind. A four-stage model proposed by Hickman et al. outlines the journey from data generation to model release, identifying potential bias at each stage and recommending mitigation methods accordingly (Hickman et al., 2024). These frameworks are particularly valuable in industries such as employment and education. Moreover, studies show that countries vary in their regulatory responses, with some adopting risk assessment and conformity checks for high-stakes applications (Ness et al., 2024). This global disparity reinforces the need for organizations to tailor their bias frameworks not only to technical requirements but also to cultural and legal contexts.

Ultimately, deploying bias frameworks in real-world organizations requires more than technical fixes; it demands a cultural shift toward transparency, accountability, and ethical foresight. As Vijayan emphasizes, Machine Learning Operations (MLOps) strategies must embed responsible AI practices, such as continuous monitoring, model governance, and ethical deployment protocols, into the infrastructure of production environments to ensure models remain fair and effective post-deployment (Vijayan, 2024). Bias frameworks must therefore evolve beyond static checkpoints to become living components of the deployment pipeline, interacting with live data, responding to user behavior, and adapting to emerging ethical risks. With increasing awareness and tooling, organizations are better equipped than ever to deploy models responsibly but doing so effectively remains a collaborative and ongoing challenge.

## RECOMMENDATIONS

The evolving cybersecurity threat landscape requires more than technical expertise; it demands cognitive agility, reflective judgment, and a deep understanding of how human decision-making is shaped by bias. Decision hygiene offers a scientifically grounded and operationally relevant path to improving cybersecurity decision-making across all organizational levels. This section provides a set of actionable recommendations for organizations seeking to embed decision hygiene practices and concludes the chapter by synthesizing key takeaways.

### Establish a Bias-Aware Cybersecurity Culture

Creating a culture of bias awareness starts with leadership. Cybersecurity leaders should actively promote reflection, humility, and continuous learning as core values. Encourage open dialogue around past decision failures and normalize the practice of revisiting assumptions. Teams that feel psychologically safe to challenge decisions are more likely to correct errors early (Aggarwal et al., 2024). Leaders must model these behaviors by acknowledging their own blind spots and supporting decisions grounded in evidence, not hierarchy.

### Integrate Bias Training into Security Education

Cybersecurity training should go beyond technical checklists to include modules on cognitive bias, decision-making frameworks, and psychological factors. Use real-world breach scenarios to show how specific biases (e.g., anchoring, overconfidence) contributed to failures. As Howell et al. (2024) demonstrated, TRDM-based training significantly improves protective behavior. These training programs should be periodic, role-specific, and incorporate active elements like phishing simulations, decision walkthroughs, and scenario-based reflection.

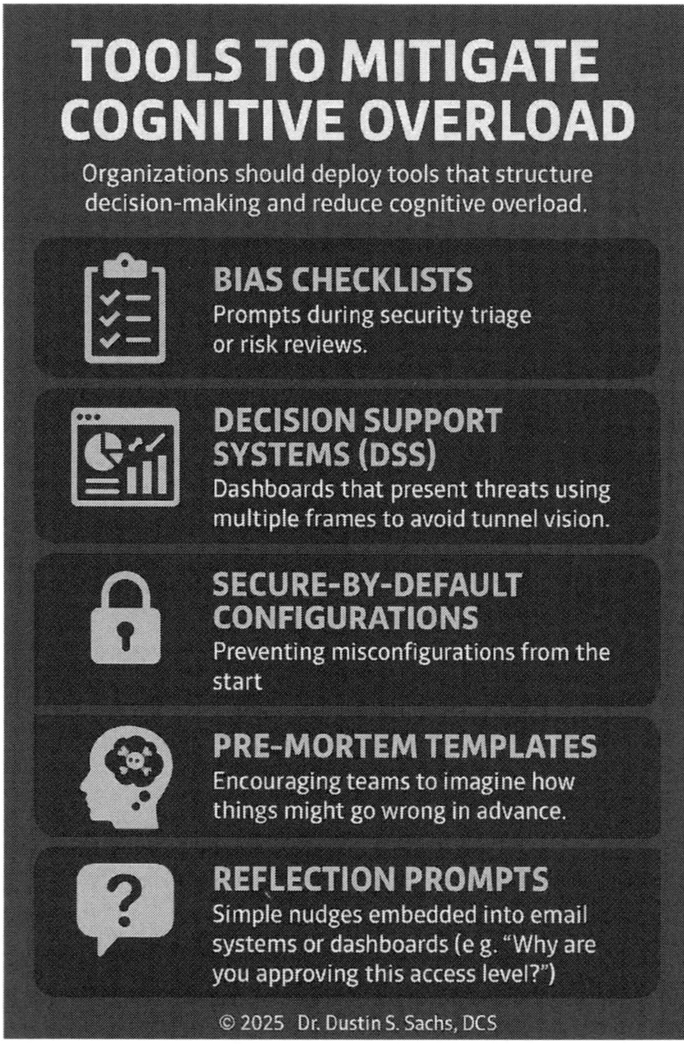


*Figure 6.4* Tools to Mitigate Cognitive Overload

## Use Decision Tools That Scaffold Reflective Thinking

Organizations should deploy tools that structure decision-making and reduce cognitive overload (Figure 6.4).

These tools reinforce deliberate, bias-aware reasoning without overwhelming users or disrupting workflow (Lai et al., 2020).

## Formalizing Post-Incident Bias Debriefs

Incorporate structured bias debriefs into all post-incident reviews and near-miss evaluations (Figure 6.5).

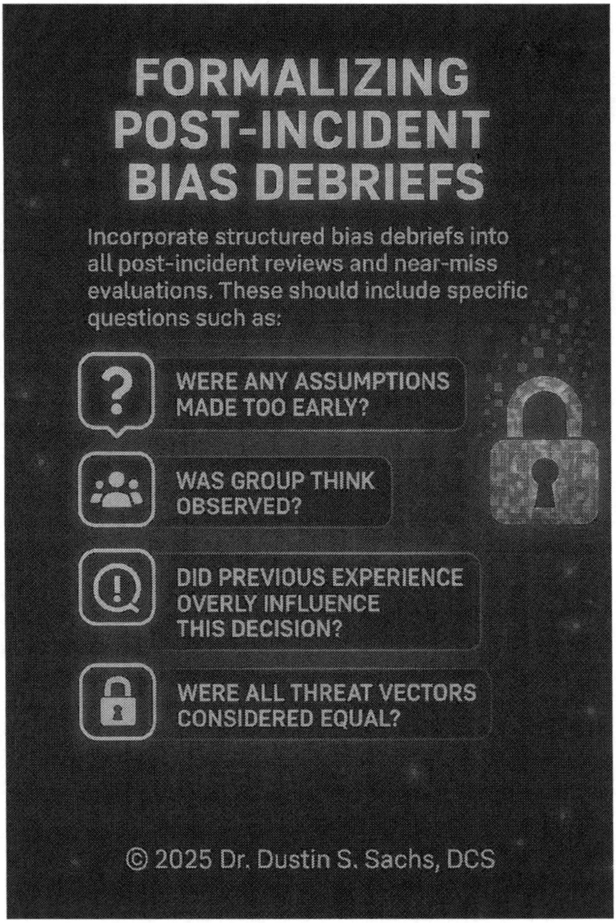


*Figure 6.5* Formalizing Post-Incident Bias Debriefs

Documenting this analysis allows organizations to track patterns and improve over time. In larger enterprises, aggregated data from bias debriefs can feed into training, automation design, and policy updates (Pharmer et al., 2024).

## Align Security Policies with Behavioral Design Principles

Design policies that recognize human behavior rather than assuming perfect compliance. For instance, rather than requiring users to create strong passwords from scratch, offer password managers with auto-generated credentials. Use opt-out defaults for MFA, simplify user interfaces, and ensure security warnings are contextual, brief, and actionable. These choice architecture principles increase compliance by removing friction and guiding users toward better choices (Purnamawati, 2024).

## CHAPTER SUMMARY

Across this chapter, several critical insights have emerged about the intersection of cognitive science and cybersecurity decision-making. Most notably, cognitive biases are not flaws to be eliminated, but realities to be managed. Decision hygiene, an approach to improving the conditions under which decisions are made, does not promise to remove bias altogether. Instead, it aims to create structures and habits that reduce the influence of bias, allowing leaders and teams to make more accurate, ethical, and strategic decisions in high-stakes environments.

Security decisions are often shaped by mental shortcuts like anchoring, availability bias, and overconfidence. These heuristics, while sometimes useful, become especially dangerous when choices must be made quickly or with limited information. In incident response or risk acceptance discussions, the pressure to act can lead to decisions that feel intuitive but are misaligned with the best available evidence. Recognizing and counteracting these tendencies requires a deliberate shift toward more reflective processes and team-based decision-making frameworks.

Research shows that reflective thinking significantly improves cybersecurity behavior. Individuals who score high on TRDM are more likely to question assumptions, resist social pressure, and take proactive security measures (Howell et al., 2024). This insight is particularly important for security leaders, whose example sets the tone for organizational culture. By fostering a mindset of critical inquiry and reflective skepticism, they can enhance team performance and reduce susceptibility to preventable incidents.

Tools are essential for sustaining decision hygiene in practice. While training lays the foundation, lasting change comes from embedding bias-aware tools into the workflows and technologies people use daily. Examples include premortem risk analyses, bias checklists in incident postmortems, and secure default settings that guide users toward safer actions. These tools reduce the cognitive load required for good decision-making, shifting the burden from memory and vigilance to systems and design.

Equally important is the role of organizational culture in reinforcing these habits. When organizations value curiosity, dissent, and thoughtful reflection, they normalize behaviors that contribute to better decisions. Leaders who reward thoughtful pushbacks and make space for uncertainty signal that security is not just about technical controls but about critical thinking. This kind of culture doesn't just reduce incidents; it accelerates learning from them, leading to smarter, faster, and more resilient teams over time.

As cybersecurity threats grow more complex, defenders must evolve, not just technically, but cognitively. The future will likely bring AI-driven DSS that recognize when a human is likely to err and intervene with real-time nudges. Behavioral analytics and biometric cues may help detect stress-induced bias, while immersive simulations will serve as "cognitive gyms" for practicing decision hygiene in realistic scenarios. These developments promise to scale human judgment with the precision and adaptability cybersecurity demands.

Ultimately, the greatest vulnerability in cybersecurity is not the code; it's the way people think under pressure, uncertainty, and complexity. Firewalls can block malware, but they can't stop a rushed decision, a skipped step, or a flawed mental model shaped by cognitive bias. These human factors are often the root cause of incidents that technical defenses alone cannot prevent. Like patching a system or conducting regular audits, promoting cognitive hygiene should be a core element of every organization's risk strategy, ensuring that decision-making processes are as resilient as the technologies they support.

## REFERENCES

Abdallah, M., Woods, D., Naghizadeh Ardabili, P., Khalil, I. M., Cason, T., Sundaram, S., & Bagchi, S. (2020). BASCPS: How does behavioral decision making impact the security of cyber-physical systems? *arXiv*. https://arxiv.org/abs/2004.01958

Aggarwal, P., Venkatesan, S., Youzwak, J., Chadha, R., & Gonzalez, C. (2024). Discovering cognitive biases in cyber attackers' network exploitation activities: A case study. In A. Moallem (Ed.), *Human factors in cybersecurity* (Vol. 127, pp. 115–126). AHFE International. http://doi.org/10.54941/ahfe1004771

Bone, J. (2021). Cognitive risks. *EDPACS, 64*(1), 1–8. https://consensus.app/papers/cognitive-risks-bone/4f3a9078e76c5e2ebf5ccf0ab5232450/

Chen, C., Chirra, S. R., Ferreira, M. J., Gonzalez, C., Sinha, A., & Varakantham, P. (2024). *Towards neural network based cognitive models of dynamic decision-making by humans. arXiv*. https://arxiv.org/abs/2407.17622

Corbin, C. K., Maclay, R., Acharya, A., Mony, S., Punnathanam, S., Thapa, R., Kotecha, N., Shah, N., & Chen, J. H. (2023). DEPLOYR: A technical framework for deploying custom real-time machine learning models into the electronic medical record. *Journal of the American Medical Informatics Association, 30*(8), 1532–1542. https://doi.org/10.1093/jamia/ocad114

Hickman, L., Huynh, C., Gass, J., Booth, B., Kuruzovich, J., & Tay, L. (2025). Whither bias goes, I will go: An integrative, systematic review of algorithmic bias mitigation.*Journal of Applied Psychology, 110*(7), 979–1000. https://doi.org/10.1037/apl0001255

Howell, C., Maimon, D., Muniz, C. N., Kamar, E., & Berenblum, T. (2024). Engaging in cyber hygiene: The role of thoughtfully reflective decision-making and informational interventions. *Frontiers in Psychology, 15*. https://doi.org/10.3389/fpsyg.2024.1372681

Kahneman, D., Sibony, O., & Sunstein, C. R. (2021). *Noise: A flaw in human judgment*. Little, Brown Spark.

Kankane, S., DiRusso, C., & Buckley, C. (2018). Can we nudge users toward better password management?: An initial study. In *Extended Abstracts of the 2018 CHI Conference on Human Factors in Computing Systems* (pp. 1–6). Association for Computing Machinery. https://doi.org/10.1145/3170427.3188689

Koshiya, P. (2025). The human element in cybersecurity: Exploring cognitive biases while working remote. *Journal of Technology and Systems*, 7(1), 1–5. https://doi.org/10.47941/jts.2477

Lai, K., Oliveira, H. C. R., Hou, M., Yanushkevich, S., & Shmerko, V. (2020). Assessing risks of biases in cognitive decision support systems. In *European Signal Processing Conference (EUSIPCO)* (pp. 840–844). https://doi.org/10.23919/Eusipco47968.2020.9287384

Ness, S., Sarker, M., Volkivskyi, M., & Singh, N. (2024). The legal and political implications of AI bias: An international comparative study. *American Journal of Computing and Engineering*, 7(1), 37–45. https://doi.org/10.47672/ajce.1879

Pharmer, R., Martey, R., Henery, G., Myers, E., Ray, I., & Clegg, B. (2024). Mental firewall breached: Leveraging cognitive biases for enhanced cybersecurity. In A. Moallem (Ed.), *Human factors in cybersecurity* (Vol. 127, pp. 94–104). AHFE International. http://doi.org/10.54941/ahfe1004769

Purnamawati, R. F. (2024). The role of cognitive bias in principal decision making: A narrative analysis of the literature. *PPSDP International Journal of Education*, 3(2), 213–219. https://doi.org/10.59175/pijed.v3i2.310

Sachs, D. (2024). Deciphering the supply chain chessboard: The science of decision-making in risk management. *The Pinnacle: A Journal by Scholar-Practitioners*. https://doi.org/10.61643/c30815

Saleiro, P., Rodolfa, K. T., & Ghani, R. (2020). Dealing with bias and fairness in data science systems: A practical hands-on tutorial. In *Proceedings of the 26th ACM SIGKDD International Conference on Knowledge Discovery & Data Mining* (pp. 3551–3552). Association for Computing Machinery. https://doi.org/10.1145/3394486.3406708

Vajpayee, P., & Hossain, G. (2024, May). Cognitive bias in cyber-value-at-risk: Identification and mitigation approach. In *Proceedings of the 2024 Computers and People Research Conference* (Article 12). Association for Computing Machinery, Murfreesboro, TN, USA. https://doi.org/10.1145/3632634.3655861

Berthet, V. (2022). The impact of cognitive biases on professionals' decision-making: A review of four occupational areas. *Frontiers in psychology*, *12*, 802439.

Vijayan, N. E. (2024). Building scalable MLOps: Optimizing machine learning deployment and operations. *International Journal of Scientific Research in Engineering and Management*, 8(10), https://doi.org/10.55041/ijsrem37784

Zhu, R. (2023). The influence of cognitive bias on risk decision-making under uncertain conditions: A case study of 1986 Challenger. In *Lecture Notes in Education Psychology and Public Media* (Vol. 18, pp. 8–15). Clausius Scientific Press.

Chapter 7

# Applying Artificial Intelligence and Emerging Tech to Behavioral Insights

## LEARNING OBJECTIVES

- Gain insights into how artificial intelligence (AI) and machine learning (ML) technologies are transforming cybersecurity by identifying patterns in human behavior, detecting anomalies, and enhancing threat detection.
- Examine the use of behavioral biometrics, such as keystroke dynamics, mouse movements, and touchscreen interactions, as a layer of identity verification.
- Develop an understanding of predictive modeling techniques used to forecast potential security incidents based on historical and real-time data.

## INTRODUCTION

Cybersecurity has become a frontline concern for organizations, governments, and individuals alike. The volume, variety, and velocity of cyber threats have made it increasingly difficult for traditional defense systems to keep up. Consequently, AI and ML technologies are transforming the cybersecurity landscape, enabling practitioners to analyze behavior-based risks, detect anomalies, and implement preventive strategies with greater precision and scale. These innovations not only enhance technical defenses but also offer practical avenues for operationalizing behavioral science within cybersecurity workflows (Edmund & Enemosah, 2024).

At the heart of this transformation is the potential of AI to support cybersecurity professionals in applying behavioral science without needing advanced degrees in psychology. AI systems can identify, analyze, and learn from human behavior, effectively translating behavioral science concepts into actionable insights. These insights help detect insider threats, phishing schemes, and social engineering tactics, all of which rely heavily on human behavior. By automating this complex interpretation process, AI ensures

DOI: 10.1201/9781003606345-7

that practitioners can stay focused on strategy and implementation while minimizing errors rooted in cognitive biases (Muheidat et al., 2024).

As society becomes increasingly dependent on digital infrastructure, the cost of cybersecurity breaches, financial, reputational, and operational, continues to escalate. Legacy systems based on static rules or signature detection struggle to keep up with sophisticated threats like zero-day exploits, ransomware, and advanced persistent threats (APTs). AI-powered platforms offer dynamic, real-time monitoring and predictive analytics, allowing cybersecurity teams to anticipate attacks before they occur. These systems are particularly effective when combined with behavioral analytics, which helps identify deviations from normal user behavior that may signify a breach (Patel, 2023).

One of the most significant advantages of integrating behavioral science into cybersecurity via AI is the move from reactive to proactive security postures. Traditionally, cybersecurity systems respond after a threat has been detected, which can lead to costly delays. In contrast, AI enables predictive threat modeling, using historical and real-time data to identify potential risks before they manifest. This shift enhances organizational resilience and responsiveness, empowering teams to mitigate threats with strategic foresight rather than scrambling in the aftermath (Hasan et al., 2025).

AI also plays a pivotal role in simplifying complex behavioral science theories into usable formats for cybersecurity applications. ML algorithms can parse through massive volumes of data to identify subtle behavioral cues, such as unusual login times, typing patterns, or device usage, that may indicate malicious activity. These models can then generate alerts or even automate responses, significantly reducing the burden on human analysts. As a result, cybersecurity teams are empowered to make quicker and more informed decisions without getting bogged down in theoretical analysis (Chen et al., 2024).

The fusion of human behavioral patterns and ML has also led to more intuitive and adaptive security systems. Advanced AI methods like deep learning and reinforcement learning allow systems to continuously learn from data, enhancing their ability to detect novel threats that might elude traditional tools. For example, AI can recognize context-aware deviations in user behavior, adjusting risk scores accordingly and triggering preemptive actions. These features reduce detection-to-response times and minimize damage during breaches (Rishad, 2025).

Another major benefit of AI in cybersecurity is its unparalleled scalability. As organizations grow and accumulate vast amounts of user data, manual monitoring becomes infeasible. AI systems can manage enormous datasets in real time, filtering out noise and highlighting the most relevant anomalies. This capability prevents analyst fatigue and ensures that critical threats receive timely attention without overwhelming the human workforce (Razzaq & Shah, 2025).

Importantly, AI-driven systems can function as partners to cybersecurity professionals, rather than as mere tools. By continuously analyzing patterns and generating recommendations, AI systems help limit decision-making biases, such as confirmation bias or availability heuristics, which can skew human judgment. For instance, anomaly detection systems powered by ML are far more consistent in evaluating behavioral deviations than human observers, especially when dealing with large-scale environments like enterprise networks (Siam et al., 2025).

Moreover, explainable AI (XAI) is emerging as a crucial area of focus to ensure that security decisions made by machines are transparent and interpretable. This development is particularly important in regulatory environments where justification and accountability are necessary. XAI techniques offer human-readable justifications for AI decisions, allowing cybersecurity teams to audit AI behavior and maintain control. These explanations help build trust in AI systems and ensure that human oversight remains a core component of cybersecurity strategy (Nnamani, 2024).

AI also enhances security intelligence modeling by assimilating data from threat intelligence feeds, internal logs, and third-party sources. These models can produce actionable insights that guide cybersecurity policy and investment decisions. When combined with behavioral data, the intelligence becomes even more robust, allowing teams to anticipate threat actor strategies and align defenses accordingly. This data-driven approach is far more agile than relying on outdated playbooks or reactive protocols (Akinade et al., 2023).

Despite these advancements, integrating AI and behavioral science into cybersecurity is not without challenges. Issues like algorithmic bias, adversarial attacks on ML models, and data privacy concerns must be managed carefully. Adversarial actors can manipulate inputs to deceive AI systems, making robustness and security-by-design principles essential. Additionally, ethical AI development practices, such as fairness and transparency, must be upheld to avoid reinforcing systemic inequalities in automated systems (Kamoun et al., 2020).

In parallel, the global shortage of skilled cybersecurity professionals underscores the importance of AI-driven automation. AI tools can perform tasks such as real-time network monitoring, endpoint protection, and threat triage, freeing human experts to focus on high-level strategy and innovation. In this way, AI helps bridge the skills gap while promoting continuous learning through adaptive feedback loops within security systems (Çakır, 2024).

Interestingly, AI is also reshaping cybersecurity education and training. Adaptive learning platforms powered by AI can personalize content delivery based on learner behavior, improving engagement and skill retention. This approach is especially beneficial for training nonspecialists, such as small business owners, who need practical security knowledge without deep technical expertise. AI-driven education democratizes access to cybersecurity knowledge and cultivates a more resilient digital ecosystem (Austin-Gabriel et al., 2024).

Looking ahead, the role of AI in cybersecurity will only expand as both threats and defenses evolve. Hybrid AI models that combine supervised, unsupervised, and reinforcement learning are being developed to improve detection accuracy while reducing false positives. These systems also feature self-learning capabilities that refine detection models based on new data, making them more effective over time. The continuous evolution of AI models ensures that cybersecurity remains responsive to emerging challenges without compromising performance or ethical standards (Edmund & Enemosah, 2024).

## AI AND ML FOR BEHAVIORAL THREAT DETECTION

AI and ML provide powerful mechanisms to analyze and act on behavioral data without requiring cybersecurity teams to become behavioral science experts. These technologies continuously model user behavior, learn baseline patterns, and detect deviations that may signal insider threats, compromised accounts, or anomalous activity. By automating these processes, AI reduces the reliance on manual interpretation, helping analysts make faster, more accurate decisions without the risk of cognitive overload. This abstraction of behavioral complexity enables cybersecurity professionals to focus on strategic response rather than sifting through vast amounts of behavioral data (Edmund & Enemosah, 2024). As these systems mature, they increasingly serve as cognitive extensions of the analyst, surfacing actionable insights with greater precision and timeliness.

AI applications in cybersecurity include behavioral anomaly detection, threat scoring, and real-time alerts, all of which contribute to faster and more accurate threat identification. These capabilities are grounded in both supervised and unsupervised learning algorithms that analyze vast datasets to differentiate between normal and suspicious behaviors. By learning baseline behavioral patterns, AI systems can flag deviations that may indicate insider threats, credential misuse, or evolving attack techniques. For example, deep learning models such as Convolutional Neural Networks (CNNs) can identify nuanced shifts in network traffic or user activity that often serve as early indicators of a cyberattack (Rishad, 2025). As these models continue to evolve, they offer scalable and adaptive defenses that are critical in today's dynamic threat landscape.

Behavioral analytics models powered by AI assess the baseline routines of users and systems, identifying subtle deviations that may indicate insider threats, compromised accounts, or emerging attack patterns. These models leverage clustering and anomaly detection techniques to categorize typical and atypical behaviors, continuously refining their accuracy over time. By contextualizing behavioral anomalies within the broader security environment, they reduce false positives and provide actionable intelligence. As a result, analysts receive concise alerts enriched with behavioral context, enabling faster, more informed responses without the need to sift through overwhelming volumes of raw data (Patel, 2023).

Moreover, AI applications are not static; they continuously evolve through feedback loops and the integration of new data inputs. This dynamic learning process enables AI systems to recognize emerging attack vectors, such as social engineering tactics, zero-day exploits, and previously unseen threat patterns. As adversaries become more sophisticated and unpredictable, the ability of AI to adapt in near real time becomes essential for maintaining an effective security posture. By identifying subtle anomalies and learning from past incidents, AI enhances both the speed and accuracy of threat detection, making it a vital asset in modern cybersecurity strategies (Nyangaresi et al., 2024).

AI also addresses key limitations in human behavioral analysis by offering speed, scale, and precision beyond human capabilities. While human analysts bring contextual understanding and experience, they may inadvertently overlook subtle behavioral cues or fall victim to cognitive biases such as confirmation bias, especially under pressure. AI systems, on the other hand, apply consistent analytical models and remain objective, regardless of external stressors or preconceived notions. This enables a more reliable and scalable assessment of risk across diverse environments, reducing the likelihood of false positives or missed threats (Nnamani, 2024).

To further support practitioners, AI-generated visual dashboards offer intuitive and real-time representations of user behavior, threat patterns, and system anomalies. These tools reduce the reliance on deep behavioral science expertise by translating complex data into clear, actionable insights. As a result, security teams can more effectively prioritize risks, detect emerging threats, and streamline their response efforts. By interpreting and simplifying behavioral data, AI not only improves situational awareness but also enhances the overall efficiency and precision of cybersecurity operations.

The future of AI in behavioral threat detection lies in XAI, which aims to make AI decisions transparent and interpretable. As cybersecurity increasingly relies on ML models to detect subtle patterns in user behavior, the ability to understand why a model flagged certain activity as suspicious becomes critical. XAI not only enhances accountability but also empowers security teams to validate, fine-tune, and trust AI-driven decisions. This development will further bridge the gap between complex AI systems and human understanding, fostering greater collaboration and confidence in human-machine partnerships (Sarker et al., 2024).

## AUTOMATING BEHAVIORAL BIOMETRICS WITH AI

Behavioral biometrics involve identifying users based on unique behavioral characteristics such as typing patterns, mouse movements, gait, and touchscreen dynamics. Unlike traditional authentication methods, behavioral biometrics enable continuous and passive user verification, reducing friction while maintaining security. These patterns are difficult to replicate, making them highly effective in detecting unauthorized access or compromised accounts. AI plays a pivotal role in analyzing this complex and dynamic data in real time, identifying subtle anomalies that may indicate malicious behavior or insider threats (Oduri, 2024).

Traditional biometric systems like fingerprint scanning or facial recognition provide a static form of authentication that is typically effective only at the initial point of access. While these methods can confirm a user's identity at login, they do not continuously verify that the authenticated user remains the one interacting with the system. In contrast, behavioral biometrics offer dynamic, continuous authentication by analyzing unique patterns such as typing rhythm, mouse movement, and touchscreen behavior. These behavioral signals enable AI-driven systems to build ongoing user profiles and detect anomalies in real time, significantly enhancing the ability to identify and respond to potential insider threats or account takeovers (Emiroğlu, 2025).

AI-powered behavioral biometric systems significantly reduce the burden on cybersecurity teams by automating the analysis of vast volumes of user behavior data. These systems leverage deep learning algorithms to identify subtle patterns and anomalies that may signal threats such as account takeovers, bot activity, or credential theft. By continuously monitoring behavioral traits, like typing cadence, mouse movements, or touchscreen gestures, they create dynamic user profiles that evolve over time. The integration of reinforcement learning enables these systems to adapt and improve with each interaction, becoming more accurate at distinguishing between legitimate users and sophisticated adversaries. This adaptive capability enhances both detection speed and precision, helping organizations stay ahead of emerging threats.

Importantly, AI reduces false positives by integrating contextual data with behavioral profiles, allowing security systems to make more informed decisions. For instance, a slightly unusual typing pattern may be considered benign if it aligns with known environmental changes such as a new geographic location, time zone, or device type. This nuanced analysis enhances detection accuracy by distinguishing legitimate anomalies from actual threats. As a result, security teams experience less alert fatigue and can focus their attention on high-priority incidents, improving both response time and overall system efficiency (Finnegan et al., 2024).

Behavioral biometrics, when combined with AI, enable sophisticated risk-based authentication systems that adapt in real time. These systems analyze user behaviors, such as typing patterns, mouse movements, and navigation habits, to continuously assess the likelihood of legitimate access. AI algorithms assign dynamic risk scores based on deviations from a user's typical behavioral profile, allowing security measures to adjust accordingly. As a result, low-risk users enjoy frictionless access, while high-risk anomalies trigger additional verification steps, such as multifactor authentication or temporary access restrictions (Yusop et al., 2025). This approach not only enhances security but also improves the overall user experience by minimizing unnecessary interruptions.

The scalability of AI makes behavioral biometrics not only feasible but highly effective in large-scale environments such as banks, healthcare systems, and government networks. These sectors manage vast numbers of users, each with unique and evolving behavioral patterns that traditional authentication methods struggle to track. AI-driven systems can learn and adapt in real time, continuously refining their understanding of normal behavior to detect anomalies more accurately. This dynamic capability ensures consistent protection, even as user behaviors shift over time, enhancing both security and user experience (Patel, 2023).

The scalability of AI makes behavioral biometrics not only feasible but highly effective in large-scale environments such as banks, healthcare systems, and government networks. These sectors manage thousands of users whose behavioral patterns evolve over time due to changes in routines, devices, and work environments. Traditional authentication methods often struggle to keep pace with such variability, leading to security gaps or user friction. AI-driven behavioral biometrics, however, can continuously learn and adapt to these changes in real time, enabling dynamic risk assessment and frictionless user experiences. By evolving alongside user behavior, AI ensures consistent, personalized protection without sacrificing performance or security (Patel, 2023).

## PREDICTIVE MODELS SUPPORTING SECURITY STRATEGY

Predictive modeling in cybersecurity involves leveraging AI and ML algorithms to forecast future cyber threats by analyzing historical data, user behavior patterns, and real-time threat intelligence feeds. These models can identify subtle indicators of compromise and evolving attack vectors, allowing organizations to detect vulnerabilities before they are exploited. By anticipating threats rather than merely responding to incidents, cybersecurity teams can prioritize resources, harden defenses, and reduce response times. This shift from reactive to anticipatory defense strategies represents a major evolution in cyber risk management (Yusop et al., 2025).

AI-driven models analyze historical security incidents to identify patterns and behavioral indicators that may signal future threats. These models leverage techniques such as classification algorithms, regression analysis, and time-series forecasting to track the evolution of cyber risks over time. By learning from past events, the models can make data-informed predictions and recommend preemptive actions to mitigate potential breaches. For example, if a specific sequence of user behaviors previously correlated with a ransomware attack, the system can recognize similar behavioral trajectories and trigger early alerts to security teams (Finnegan et al., 2024). This proactive approach enhances an organization's ability to respond before an attack fully materializes, shifting cybersecurity from reactive to predictive.

In cloud security, it can proactively identify misconfigurations and access anomalies that are likely to be exploited by attackers. In endpoint security, predictive models can assess device health and configuration states to forecast which endpoints are most at risk. These models are particularly powerful when trained on diverse datasets, including user behavior analytics, access logs, and real-time threat intelligence feeds. By continuously learning from this data, predictive analytics provides a dynamic and evolving defense mechanism that adapts to emerging threats (Nyangaresi et al., 2024).

Rather than overwhelming security analysts with unfiltered alerts and logs, AI-driven models assign risk scores based on factors such as exploitability, threat actor activity, and potential impact. This prioritization enables security teams to focus on the most critical vulnerabilities and allocate resources more efficiently. The result is a more targeted and strategic incident response process, which enhances both operational efficiency and overall security posture. In essence, predictive modeling turns noise into actionable intelligence, driving smarter and faster decision-making (Rishad, 2025).

In practice, predictive modeling supports strategic planning by enabling simulations and scenario analysis. Organizations can use these models to simulate various attack vectors, user behaviors, or policy adjustments to see how they might affect their security environment. This capability helps teams test the effectiveness of controls and improve incident response plans before actual threats materialize. Moreover, predictive insights are invaluable for long-term risk management and communicating cybersecurity posture to executive leadership and board members. By providing data-driven forecasts and evidence-based recommendations, predictive modeling bridges technical insights with strategic business decisions (Nnamani, 2024).

Moreover, predictive models can enhance compliance efforts by identifying gaps in data protection or policy adherence. These models analyze patterns in user activity to flag behaviors that may violate internal policies or external regulatory standards. By linking user behavior to specific compliance requirements, AI provides real-time monitoring that supports both security and governance objectives. This proactive approach helps organizations stay ahead of evolving regulations while reducing the risk of costly violations or data breaches (Patel, 2023).

Despite their complexity, predictive models are becoming more accessible through user-friendly platforms and APIs. These tools abstract much of the technical detail, enabling cybersecurity professionals to deploy sophisticated analytics with minimal coding or algorithm design. As a result, teams can integrate behavioral insights into their workflows without needing deep expertise in data science or behavioral psychology. This democratization of advanced analytics empowers a broader range of practitioners to make informed, data-driven decisions to improve their security posture (Sarker et al., 2024).

## HUMAN-CENTRIC AI DESIGN IN CYBERSECURITY

Effective cybersecurity tools must be designed with human users in mind. Human-centric AI emphasizes usability, interpretability, and collaboration, ensuring that AI complements rather than complicates human decision-making. In the high-stakes environment of cybersecurity, where rapid and accurate judgments are critical, AI tools must support workflows and cognitive processes rather than introduce new burdens (Naseer et al., 2025). Designing with the end user in mind leads to more intuitive interfaces, reduces the learning curve, and facilitates quicker adoption. When AI systems align with how cybersecurity professionals think and act, they become trusted allies in defending digital infrastructure.

AI systems should be transparent and explainable. Cybersecurity analysts must trust AI recommendations, especially in mission-critical scenarios. XAI allows users to understand the rationale behind AI outputs, which improves confidence and promotes more effective integration of AI insights into daily operations. Transparency helps users detect when AI is wrong or uncertain, allowing for human oversight and course correction. This trust also encourages consistent usage and reduces the risk of automation bias, which can occur when users blindly follow AI guidance without question (Sarker et al., 2024).

A key principle of human-centric AI is cognitive load reduction. Cybersecurity professionals often deal with vast amounts of information, high alert volumes, and time-sensitive threats. AI can prioritize alerts, suppress noise, and summarize key threats, enabling faster and more confident decision-making. For example, AI dashboards that visualize anomaly patterns and associate them with specific user actions simplify investigation and response (Emiroğlu, 2025). Reducing information overload allows analysts to focus on high-value tasks, ultimately improving both efficiency and threat response outcomes.

Additionally, AI should support a variety of user experience levels. Not all cybersecurity professionals are data scientists or have deep expertise in ML. Designing interfaces that adapt to different user needs, offering simple summaries for junior analysts and detailed logs for experts, ensures broad accessibility and effectiveness. This inclusive design approach fosters team collaboration, reduces user frustration, and encourages broader adoption across security operations centers. When AI tools accommodate diverse roles and skills, they become more resilient and scalable within dynamic organizational structures (Edmund & Enemosah, 2024).

Human-centered design also includes continuous feedback loops. When cybersecurity teams interact with AI tools, their feedback should be used to improve model performance and contextual relevance. Interactive ML (iML) allows human insights to refine models over time, enhancing accuracy and responsiveness to new or evolving threats (Naseer et al., 2025). These feedback mechanisms not only boost model quality but also increase user engagement by giving professionals a sense of agency. Empowering humans to shape AI outcomes ensures systems stay relevant, adaptive, and aligned with real-world operations.

Ethical considerations are also central to human-centric AI. AI systems must respect privacy, avoid discriminatory outcomes, and align with organizational values and regulatory frameworks. When behavioral data is used, safeguards must be placed to anonymize sensitive information and prevent misuse. Ensuring transparency in data handling practices helps maintain user trust and legal compliance. Cybersecurity teams must also be trained in ethical AI usage and governance to ensure responsible deployment and oversight (Finnegan et al., 2024).

Ultimately, human-centric AI design bridges the gap between technical capabilities and operational needs. It transforms AI from a complex tool into a reliable partner, enabling cybersecurity professionals to do their jobs more effectively, with less stress and greater situational awareness. By aligning AI functionality with human strengths and limitations, organizations can create environments where technology truly augments human performance. This synergy not only improves security outcomes but also enhances job satisfaction and team morale in high-pressure environments.

## INTEGRATING AI DECISION STRUCTURES INTO CYBERSECURITY STRATEGY

As AI continues to evolve in complexity and capability, its integration into cybersecurity operations has moved from experimental applications to core strategy. This integration presents both opportunities and challenges, as the fusion of ML, predictive analytics, and intelligent automation transforms how security teams detect, assess, and respond to threats. One emerging area of focus is understanding and optimizing **AI-human decision structures**, that is, defining how decisions are shared, delegated, or augmented between people and machines. Strategic success in cybersecurity now hinges not only on adopting AI tools but also on structuring their involvement in decision-making processes in a way that enhances, rather than complicates, security governance and response capabilities.

Frameworks such as "Humans + AI: Decision Structures" and "Levels of AI Delegation in Decision-Making" offer a taxonomy for assigning decision roles that balance automation, control, and ethical accountability (Dellermann et al., 2021). These frameworks are especially pertinent in cybersecurity, where decisions span a wide spectrum of risk, complexity, and temporal urgency. Strategic, tactical, routine, and micro-decisions each warrant a distinct delegation model, grounded in considerations of context, explainability, and governance.

### Strategic Decisions

Strategic decisions often involve high-level planning, resource allocation, or policy shifts, such as transitioning to a zero-trust architecture, investing in AI-driven endpoint detection and response (EDR), or preparing for nation-state attacks. These decisions require nuanced contextual understanding and ethical foresight, qualities that remain best handled by human leadership. However, AI can provide critical support by analyzing threat intelligence, projecting attack scenarios, or simulating the outcomes of different strategic choices. For instance, Hassan et al. (2025) notes that AI-driven scenario modeling tools are increasingly used to prioritize budget allocation and policy development based on predictive analytics and real-time data synthesis. While final decisions remain human-led, AI enhances strategic awareness and reduces information overload.

### Tactical Decisions

Tactical decisions involve short-term actions that implement strategic goals, such as determining how to respond to a ransomware attack or prioritizing patch deployment. AI can play a more active role here through tools that assess threat severity, estimate remediation time, and suggest courses of action. While human oversight is still crucial for validating ethical and contextual appropriateness, many of these decisions can be made with AI-generated recommendations and human approval. According to a 2024 report by IBM Security, organizations that integrated AI into tactical threat response reduced their breach lifecycle by 100 days on average compared to those without AI augmentation (IBM Security, 2024). This efficiency reflects AI's ability to optimize decisions under time constraints, making it a powerful partner in tactical contexts.

### Routine and Micro-Decisions

Routine decisions (e.g., triaging common vulnerabilities) and micro-decisions (e.g., flagging suspicious emails) are ideal candidates for full or conditional AI delegation. These are repetitive, low-stakes decisions that benefit from speed and consistency. Automating them allows security professionals to redirect focus toward high-impact areas. AI-powered systems like Microsoft's Defender or Google's Chronicle now routinely manage micro-decisions involving user behavior anomalies or endpoint activity, leveraging reinforcement learning to improve decision accuracy over time (Emiroğlu, 2025). As AI models mature, the scope of safe delegation can expand, provided robust validation mechanisms are in place.

## HUMAN-AI COLLABORATION ACROSS DECISION STAGES

Integrating AI into cybersecurity is not just about replacing human decisions with automation. Instead, it involves crafting a dynamic partnership where humans and AI systems collaborate across every phase of decision-making. A six-stage model, comprising awareness, definition, option generation, assessment, decision, and post-decision, helps structure this interaction in a way that leverages both machine efficiency and human judgment. This hybrid approach reflects a growing body of research emphasizing the value of complementary strengths in human-AI collaboration for high-stakes environments like cybersecurity (Akinnagbe, 2024; Çakır, 2024).

### Awareness

In the awareness phase, AI helps identify emerging threats by scanning vast datasets for anomalies and signs of cyberattacks. These systems often rely on ML techniques that adaptively learn what constitutes "normal" network behavior and flag deviations that may signal a threat. Tools like Darktrace utilize unsupervised learning to detect novel attack vectors, often ahead of traditional rule-based systems (Chowdhury et al., 2023). However, deciding whether flagged anomalies represent false positives or genuine threats still requires human insight and domain expertise (Leitão et al., 2022).

### Define the Decision

Defining the scope of a cybersecurity decision entails outlining its constraints, objectives, and contextual factors. AI can assist by analyzing incident histories, identifying key variables, and surfacing insights from unstructured data through natural language processing. For example, Natural Language Processing (NLP) tools can sift through threat intelligence reports to extract structured, actionable information, helping teams clearly frame the problem (Akinnagbe, 2024). Still, the process of scoping a decision also relies heavily on human-led prioritization and interpretation, particularly when ethical or legal considerations are involved (Kim, 2023).

### Generate Options

In the option generation phase, AI tools simulate different responses such as containment or mitigation plans using generative models and reinforcement learning. These tools can quickly propose a range of strategies based on historical data and predictive algorithms. However, despite their speed, AI lacks the capacity for contextual and creative reasoning that humans contribute. Human experts bring in ethical considerations, company-specific factors, and imaginative problem-solving capabilities that are crucial for selecting viable and responsible solutions (Çakır, 2024; Tariq et al., 2024).

### Assess Options

During this stage, AI evaluates potential outcomes using simulations, probabilistic models, or cost-benefit analyses. These methods help assess the technical merits of each option, such as estimated financial impact or probability of success. Nevertheless, such evaluations often miss qualitative and strategic factors like stakeholder sentiment, brand reputation, or political risks. Here, human judgment is essential to interpret AI output through a broader organizational lens (Akinnagbe, 2024; Westphal et al., 2023).

### Make the Decision

Once options are assessed, decision-making responsibilities can fall on AI, humans, or a hybrid team, depending on the situation. Modern cybersecurity systems increasingly follow a tiered delegation model that defines levels of autonomy based on risk, data quality, and explainability. This enables flexible decision-making structures where AI might propose or even enact decisions under supervision but still defers to human authority when necessary (Jain et al., 2023; Leitão et al., 2022). Trust, transparency, and clarity in role assignments are essential for this process to be effective.

### Post-Decision Analysis

After a decision is made, AI systems can continue to contribute through detailed root-cause analysis and generation of after-action reports. These insights not only clarify what went right or wrong but also feed data back into ML pipelines to improve future performance. This cycle supports continuous learning and enhances organizational resilience by evolving both technical systems and human expertise. Research underscores that integrating human feedback into post-decision evaluations improves long-term system accuracy and adaptability (Chowdhury et al., 2023; Tariq et al., 2024).

## GOVERNANCE OF AI-DRIVEN CYBERSECURITY DECISIONS

With increased AI autonomy comes the need for robust governance mechanisms. As AI systems become more autonomous, organizations must establish clear rules for their deployment and oversight. This includes defining responsibilities, setting boundaries between human and machine decision-making, and implementing continuous monitoring systems. In fields such as cybersecurity, where the stakes are exceptionally high, a failure in governance can lead to devastating consequences including data breaches, system failures, and even national security risks (Basak, 2024). Therefore, robust AI governance is not just an ethical imperative; it's a strategic necessity.

### Accountability

Organizations must clearly define who is responsible for the outcomes of AI-driven decisions, particularly in scenarios involving legal, ethical, or reputational consequences. The European Union's AI Act (2023) explicitly advocates for a human-centric approach, requiring meaningful human oversight for high-risk AI systems, such as those used in cybersecurity. Establishing accountability ensures that AI deployment aligns with existing laws, ethical norms, and organizational values. Recent studies emphasize that incorporating oversight structures and responsibility layers is key to building trust and operational resilience (Kolade, 2024).

### Explainability

Explainability is a cornerstone of responsible AI, particularly in cybersecurity, where actions like quarantining devices or blocking access must be justifiable. If an AI system flags an insider threat, stakeholders, including IT teams, auditors, and regulators, must understand the rationale behind that decision. Tools such as SHAP (SHapley Additive exPlanations) and LIME (Local Interpretable Model-agnostic Explanations) are widely adopted to provide insights into model logic. A lack of explainability not only hampers decision-making but also erodes confidence in the system's integrity (Khan et al., 2024).

### Transparency

Transparency in AI operations is achieved through thorough documentation of models, decision logs, data sources, and system limitations. This is essential for maintaining traceability during compliance audits or incident investigations. Transparent AI systems allow legal, technical, and operational teams to coordinate effectively, reducing friction in multidisciplinary workflows. The growing emphasis on AI auditability supports not only internal trust but also external regulatory compliance (Nageab et al., 2024).

### Bias Mitigation

AI models can perpetuate or even exacerbate bias if not carefully designed and tested. In cybersecurity, biased training data may lead to disproportionate monitoring of certain users or regions, resulting in discriminatory practices. Methods such as regular bias audits, adversarial testing, and inclusion of diverse datasets are essential to minimize unfair outcomes. Research highlights that fairness must be a built-in objective, not an afterthought, in AI development to ensure trust and societal acceptance (Kumar et al., 2023).

## STRATEGIC IMPLICATIONS FOR CYBERSECURITY LEADERSHIP

CISOs must now act as AI strategists, evaluating which decisions can be automated, how AI performance is measured, and how governance is maintained. The "Levels of AI Delegation" model (Dellermann et al., 2021) helps leaders determine the appropriate degree of autonomy based on risk, impact, and explainability.

A tiered delegation strategy allows for both scalability and control:

- **Full AI Delegation**: Used for well-defined, low-risk decisions (e.g., flagging known phishing URLs).
- **Conditional Autonomy**: AI acts unless certain thresholds are crossed (e.g., anomaly detection in privileged accounts).
- **AI with Human Approval**: High-risk actions (e.g., disabling a critical server) require human sign-off.
- **Human-Led, AI-Informed**: For strategic planning and policymaking, AI serves as an advisor.

Leadership should also consider the organizational maturity model for AI use, progressing from basic data automation to predictive modeling, adaptive learning, and eventually trust-based autonomy (Jain et al., 2023). This maturity path enables both efficiency and resilience in navigating evolving cyber threats.

Integrating AI decision structures into cybersecurity is not merely a technological evolution; it is a strategic imperative. By aligning AI involvement with decision types, stages, and governance models, organizations can optimize both agility and accountability. Strategic decisions benefit from AI as an analytical advisor, while routine and micro-decisions can be confidently delegated to AI with the right controls in place. Human-AI collaboration throughout the decision-making process enhances speed, reduces cognitive load, and supports continuous learning. As AI capabilities expand, cybersecurity leaders must adopt a balanced and transparent approach, ensuring that ethical standards, accountability structures, and explainability tools evolve in tandem. The frameworks explored in this chapter offer a roadmap for building resilient, adaptive, and trustworthy cybersecurity strategies in the AI era.

## CONCLUSION

AI and emerging technologies are revolutionizing how cybersecurity professionals integrate behavioral science into threat detection and response. Rather than requiring practitioners to become behavioral science experts, AI systems automate the analysis of user behavior, detect anomalies, and predict potential risks in real time. This shift allows professionals to act more decisively and efficiently, armed with insights that would be difficult to uncover manually. As a result, cybersecurity operations become more proactive, reducing the reliance on reactive measures and lowering the cognitive burden on human analysts.

AI enables seamless, continuous user verification based on patterns such as typing cadence, mouse movement, and device interaction. These subtle yet distinct behavioral markers allow for robust identity validation without disrupting the user experience. Predictive modeling further strengthens security by translating historical user behavior into foresight, helping organizations identify weaknesses and intervene before breaches occur. Together, these tools form a security approach that is not only intelligent and adaptive but also deeply aligned with human usability and ethical considerations.

As cyber threats grow more sophisticated and user environments become increasingly complex, the demand for intelligent, behavior-aware systems is becoming critical. AI plays a key role in meeting this demand by operationalizing behavioral insights across large, diverse environments. It empowers cybersecurity teams to close knowledge gaps, adapt to evolving threats, and manage growing system complexity with confidence. Far from replacing human professionals, AI augments their abilities, serving as an indispensable partner in modern cybersecurity strategy.

Looking forward, organizations must prioritize investments in AI literacy, ethical AI governance, and interdisciplinary collaboration across cybersecurity, behavioral science, and data analytics. These investments are essential to ensure that AI technologies not only defend digital infrastructure but also reinforce human decision-making and resilience. By cultivating a culture of responsible AI use, security teams can harness its full potential while maintaining trust and transparency. With the right frameworks and mindset, cybersecurity professionals will be better equipped to navigate the behavioral complexities of today's digital threat landscape.

## REFERENCES

Akinade, A. O., Adepoju, P. A., Ige, A. B., & Afolabi, A. I. (2023). Evaluating AI and ML in cybersecurity: A USA and global perspective. *GSC Advanced Research and Reviews*, *17*(01), 138–148. https://doi.org/10.30574/gscarr.2023.17.1.0409

Akinnagbe, O. B. (2024). Human-AI Collaboration: Enhancing Productivity and Decision-Making. *International Journal of Education, Management, and Technology*, 2(3), 387–417. https://doi.org/10.58578/ijemt.v2i3.4209

Austin-Gabriel, B., Afolabi, A. I., Ike, C. C., & Hussain, N. Y. (2024). AI and machine learning for adaptive elearning platforms in cybersecurity training for entrepreneurs. *Computer Science & IT Research Journal*, *5*(12), 2715–2729. https://doi.org/10.51594/csitrj.v5i12.1787

Basak, B. (2024). The Impact of Cybersecurity Threats on National Security: Strategies. *International Journal of Humanities Social Science and Management (IJHSSM)*, 4(2), 1361–1382.

Çakır, A. M. (2024). *Human-AI collaboration in decision-making auto systems with AI*. Human Computer Interaction. https://doi.org/10.62802/b4z5p105

Chen, H., Shen, Z., Wang, Y., Ke, H., & Xu, J. (2024). Threat detection driven by artificial intelligence: Enhancing cybersecurity with machine learning algorithms. *World Journal of Innovation and Modern Technology*, *7*(6), 58–70. https://doi.org/10.53469/wjimt.2024.07(06).09

Chowdhury, A., Nguyen, H., Ashenden, D., & Pogrebna, G. (2023). POSTER: A teacher-student with human feedback model for human-AI collaboration in cybersecurity. *Proceedings of the 2023 ACM Asia Conference on Computer and Communications Security*. https://doi.org/10.1145/3579856.3592829

Edmund, E., & Enemosah, A. (2024). AI and machine learning in cybersecurity: Leveraging AI to predict, detect, and respond to threats more efficiently. *International Journal of Science and Research Archive*, *11*(01), 2625–2645. https://doi.org/10.30574/ijsra.2024.11.1.0083

Emiroğlu, B. G. (2025). AI-driven threat detection and response systems: Enhancing cybersecurity in the digital era. In S. U. Rehman (Ed.), *Challenges and solutions for cybersecurity and adversarial machine learning* (pp. 227–270). IGI Global Scientific Publishing. https://doi.org/10.4018/979-8-3373-2200-1.ch008

Finnegan, O. L., White, J. W., Armstrong, B., et al. (2024). The utility of behavioral biometrics in user authentication and demographic characteristic detection: A scoping review. *Systematic Reviews*, *13*, 61. https://doi.org/10.1186/s13643-024-02451-1

Hasan, K., Hossain, F., Amin, A., Sutradhar, Y., Jeny, I. J., & Mahmud, S. (2025). Enhancing proactive cyber defense: A theoretical framework for AI-driven predictive cyber threat intelligence. *Journal of Technologies Information and Communication*, *5*(1), 33122. https://doi.org/10.55267/rtic/16176

IBM Security. (2024). *Cost of a Data Breach Report 2024*. IBM. https://www.ibm.com/reports/data-breach

Jain, R., Garg, N., & Khera, S. N. (2023). Effective human–AI work design for collaborative decision-making. *Kybernetes*, *52*(11), 5017–5040. https://doi.org/10.1108/K-04-2022-0548

Kamoun, F., Iqbal, F., Esseghir, M. A., & Baker, T. (2020). AI and machine learning: A mixed blessing for cybersecurity. In *2020 International Symposium on Networks, Computers and Communications (ISNCC)* (pp. 1–7). IEEE. https://doi.org/10.1109/ISNCC49221.2020.9297323

Khan, M. M., Shah, N., Shaikh, N., Thabet, A., Alrabayah, T., & belkhair, S. (2024). Towards secure and trusted AI in healthcare: A systematic review of emerging innovations and ethical challenges. *International Journal of Medical Informatics*, *195*, 105780. https://doi.org/10.1016/j.ijmedinf.2024.105780

Kim, H. (2023). Suggestions for ethical decision-making model through collaboration between human and AI. *J-INSTITUTE*. https://doi.org/10.22471/ai.2023.8.12

Kolade, T. M. (2024). Artificial Intelligence and Global Security: Strengthening International Cooperation and Diplomatic Relations. *Archives of Current Research International*, *24*(11), 23–47. https://doi.org/10.9734/acri/2024/v24i11945

Kumar, K., & Bhushan, B. (2023). Augmenting cybersecurity and fraud detection using artificial intelligence advancements. In *2023 International Conference on Computing, Communication, and Intelligent Systems (ICCCIS)* (pp. 1207–1212). IEEE. https://doi.org/10.1109/ICCCIS60361.2023.10425069

Leitão, D., Saleiro, P., Figueiredo, M. A. T., & Bizarro, P. (2022). Human-AI collaboration in decision-making: Beyond learning to defer. *ArXiv*. https://doi.org/10.48550/arXiv.2206.13202

Muheidat, F., Abu Mallouh, M., Al-Saleh, O., Al-Khasawneh, O., & Tawalbeh, L. (2024). Applying AI and machine learning to enhance automated cybersecurity and network threat identification. *Procedia Computer Science*. https://doi.org/10.1016/j.procs.2024.11.112

Nageab, W., Alrasheed, R., & Khalifa, M. (2024). *Cybersecurity in the era of artificial intelligence: Risks and solutions*. In *2024 ASU International Conference in Emerging Technologies for Sustainability and Intelligent Systems (ICETSIS)* (pp. 240–245). https://doi.org/10.1109/ICETSIS61505.2024.10459584

Naseer, A., Ahmad, N. R., & Chishti, M. A. (2025). Psychological impacts of AI dependence: Assessing the cognitive and emotional costs of intelligent systems in daily life. *Review of Applied Management and Social Sciences*, *8*(1), 291–307. https://doi.org/10.47067/ramss.v8i1.458

Nnamani, C. C. (2024). Exploiting AI Capabilities: An in-Depth Analysis of Artificial Intelligence Integration in Cybersecurity for Threat Detection and Response. *International Journal of Education, Management, and Technology*, *2*(3), 268–286. https://doi.org/10.58578/ijemt.v2i3.3904

Nyangaresi, V. O., AlRababah, A. A. Q., Yenurkar, G., Chinthaginjala, R., & Yasir, M. (2024). Anonymous authentication scheme based on physically unclonable function and biometrics for smart cities. *Engineering Reports*. https://doi.org/10.1002/eng2.13079

Oduri, S. (2024). Continuous authentication and behavioral biometrics: Enhancing cybersecurity in the digital era. *International Journal of Innovative Research in Science, Engineering and Technology*, *13*(7), 13632–13640. https://www.ijirset.com/upload/2024/july/140_Continuous.pdf

Patel, U. (2023). Leveraging AI and machine learning for cyber threat analysis. *Journal of Artificial Intelligence & Cloud Computing*, *2*(2), 1–5. https://doi.org/10.47363/JAICC/2023(2)E205

Razzaq, K., & Shah, M. (2025). Advancing Cybersecurity Through Machine Learning: A Scientometric Analysis of Global Research Trends and Influential Contributions. *Journal of Cybersecurity and Privacy*, *5*(2), 12. https://doi.org/10.3390/jcp5020012

Rishad, S. M. S. I. (2025). Leveraging AI and machine learning for predicting, detecting, and mitigating cybersecurity threats: A comparative study of advanced models. *International Journal of Computer Science & Information System*, *10*(01), 06–25. https://doi.org/10.55640/ijcsis/Volume10Issue01-02

Sarker, I. H., Janicke, H., Mohsin, A., Gill, A., & Maglaras, L. (2024). Explainable AI for cybersecurity automation, intelligence and trustworthiness in digital twin: Methods, taxonomy, challenges and prospects. *ICT Express*, *10*(4), 935–958. https://doi.org/10.1016/j.icte.2024.05.007

Siam, A. A., Hassan, M. M., & Bhuiyan, T. (2025). Artificial intelligence for cybersecurity: A state of the art. In *2025 IEEE 4th International Conference on AI in Cybersecurity (ICAIC)* (pp. 1–7). IEEE. https://doi.org/10.1109/ICAIC63015.2025.10848980

Tariq, S., Chhetri, M. B., Nepal, S., & Paris, C. (2024). A2C: A modular multi-stage collaborative decision framework for human-AI teams. *ArXiv.* https://doi.org/10.48550/arXiv.2401.14432

Westphal, M., Vössing, M., Satzger, G., Yom-Tov, G., & Rafaeli, A. (2023). Decision control and explanations in human-AI collaboration: Improving user perceptions and compliance. *Computers in Human Behavior, 144*, 107714. https://doi.org/10.1016/j.chb.2023.107714

Yusop, M. I. M., Kamarudin, N. H., Suhaimi, N. H. S., & Hasan, M. K. (2025). Advancing passwordless authentication: A systematic review of methods, challenges, and future directions for secure user identity. *IEEE Access*, *13*, 13919–13943. https://doi.org/10.1109/ACCESS.2025.3528960

Chapter 8

# Ethical Considerations and Privacy

## LEARNING OBJECTIVES

- Evaluate ethical concerns in applying behavioral science to cybersecurity contexts.
- Balance privacy rights with organizational security mandates.
- Build user trust through transparent, ethical design of behavioral interventions.
- Preserve user autonomy while using behavioral techniques to reduce risk.

## INTRODUCTION FOR SECURITY LEADERS

In an era where cyber threats are increasingly complex and persistent, cybersecurity professionals are embracing behavioral science to strengthen organizational defenses. From phishing simulations to behavioral analytics that predict insider threats, these methods aim to enhance security outcomes by influencing human behavior. However, the adoption of behavioral science introduces pressing ethical questions: Are these techniques respecting user autonomy? Where is the line between persuasion and manipulation? And how can CISOs and security leaders ensure transparency and accountability?

The growing use of behavioral interventions in cybersecurity brings with it the responsibility to balance security objectives with ethical integrity. Behavioral tools such as nudges, warnings, and interface design can increase compliance and reduce risky actions, but if applied without ethical oversight, they risk infringing on users' rights and trust (Mersinas et al., 2025). For instance, a default setting that opts users into extensive monitoring may technically increase visibility but could do so at the cost of violating privacy expectations or undermining autonomy.

This tension is especially critical for CISOs, who must align technical safeguards with organizational ethics, legal compliance, and long-term trust. Without clear ethical guidelines, interventions that aim to "nudge"

 DOI: 10.1201/9781003606345-8

users may devolve into dark patterns or manipulative practices, eroding both morale and legitimacy. As noted in recent literature, cybersecurity practitioners often lack access to institutional ethical oversight (like research ethics boards), making it essential that they proactively build ethical principles into their operational decision-making (Macnish & Ham, 2020).

Furthermore, the complexity of ethical decision-making in cybersecurity mirrors that found in medicine or legal practice, fields that have long employed structured ethical frameworks. Borrowing from biomedical ethics, researchers have proposed a tailored set of principles for cybersecurity behavior change, including respect for autonomy, beneficence, transparency, and justice (Mersinas et al., 2025). These principles are particularly relevant in corporate environments, where ethical missteps can lead to regulatory penalties, employee backlash, or erosion of public trust.

For today's CISOs, embedding ethics into the design, implementation, and communication of behavioral tools is no longer optional. As behavioral science continues to integrate with security operations, leaders must ensure these tools are not only effective but also just transparent and respectful. This chapter explores how ethical principles can be practically applied by security leaders to navigate this rapidly evolving space.

## CORE ETHICAL PRINCIPLES FOR CYBERSECURITY PRACTITIONERS

As cybersecurity teams increasingly rely on behavioral interventions, such as nudges, predictive analytics, and adaptive security prompts, ethical considerations must be at the forefront of decision-making. Unlike purely technical solutions, behavioral interventions directly affect human autonomy, perceptions of fairness, and trust. For CISOs and security leaders, understanding the ethical landscape is essential to designing and deploying responsible security strategies.

### Respect for Autonomy

Respect for autonomy means enabling users to make informed and voluntary decisions without manipulation. In cybersecurity, this applies to how policies, prompts, and interventions are structured. For example, users should understand what data is being collected and why, and they should have meaningful choices about participation in behavioral monitoring or feedback systems. Ethical frameworks consistently prioritize autonomy as a core principle (Formosa et al., 2021), and research confirms that users value autonomy even when faced with security trade-offs (Fenech et al., 2024). Nudging users toward secure behaviors should not involve hidden choices or preselected defaults that undermine freedom of action.

### Justice and Fairness

Justice in behavioral cybersecurity means treating all users fairly, without bias, discrimination, or unjustified surveillance. Predictive models used for insider threat detection, for instance, must avoid perpetuating workplace inequalities by flagging individuals based on irrelevant characteristics or incomplete data. Profiling tools that score users' risk must be carefully assessed for fairness, especially when used in high-stakes environments like finance or healthcare. Research shows that ethical concerns about justice are often shaped by users' cultural values, personality traits, and perceptions of organizational trustworthiness (Mersinas et al., 2025).

### Transparency and Explainability

Security professionals must ensure that behavioral interventions are understandable to the people they affect. This is where the principle of explainability, introduced from artificial intelligence (AI) ethics, plays a crucial role. Users should not only be informed about what the system is doing but also be able to understand why a decision was made, such as why a particular action was flagged as suspicious. Transparent practices improve user trust and can enhance compliance. A principlist approach that combines transparency with justice and autonomy is increasingly recognized as best practice (Formosa et al., 2021).

### Beneficence and Non-maleficence

Behavioral interventions should aim to reduce harm (non-maleficence) and promote user well-being (beneficence). For example, well-designed phishing simulations help users build confidence and security awareness. But excessive simulations, fear-based messaging, or punitive interventions can cause stress, reduce morale, or even stigmatize individuals. Cybersecurity professionals must weigh these consequences when designing behavioral systems. A 2024 study proposed six clusters of ethical principles for behavior change, emphasizing the importance of minimizing harm while maximizing user benefit (Mersinas et al., 2025).

## PRACTICAL IMPLEMENTATION FOR CISOS

For CISOs and practitioners, ethical principles are not abstract; they must be operationalized into tools and policies.

- **EIAs**: Evaluate behavioral tools using checklists based on autonomy, justice, and harm.
- **Informed Consent Mechanisms**: Ensure transparency about what behavioral data is collected and how it will be used.

- **Bias Audits**: Regularly review predictive models for signs of discriminatory outcomes.
- **Training and Culture Building**: Educate staff on ethical risks of behavioral tools and establish an ethics-first mindset across security teams.

Ultimately, embedding these principles into practice ensures that behavioral interventions support, not undermine, organizational integrity and public trust.

## BALANCING SECURITY WITH PRIVACY: STRATEGIC DECISIONS

For CISOs, few challenges are more complex, and more consequential, than balancing organizational security needs with the privacy rights of users and employees. Behavioral cybersecurity interventions add a new layer of complexity: while they can be effective in reducing insider threats, phishing susceptibility, and data loss, they often involve monitoring, influencing, or predicting user behavior, raising legitimate ethical and legal concerns.

### The Tension Between Surveillance and Autonomy

Security mechanisms that involve user behavior monitoring, such as keystroke analysis, behavioral biometrics, or risk scoring, often require invasive data collection. While these methods can improve threat detection, they also pose risks to user autonomy and privacy if implemented without clear justification or transparency. This tension is at the heart of ethical cybersecurity governance. Organizations must decide not just what they *can* do with behavioral data but what they *should* do. As noted in recent legal and ethical analyses, while cybersecurity is a critical imperative, so too is the right to privacy, a fundamental human right recognized across democratic legal systems (Allahrakha, 2023).

### Rethinking the "Trade-Off" Model

The traditional framing of privacy and security as opposing forces, where increasing one necessarily reduces the others, is increasingly being challenged. Scholars argue that this binary is overly simplistic and counterproductive. Instead, organizations should pursue *privacy-respecting security*, solutions that protect systems without unnecessarily encroaching on individual rights (Del-Real et al., 2025). For example, behavior-based phishing simulations can be run without identifying individuals, focusing instead on team- or department-level trends. Similarly, anomaly detection systems can be designed with differential privacy techniques to prevent the de-anonymization of individual behavior (Figure 8.1).

*Figure 8.1* Strategic Recommendations for CISOs

### Privacy-Enhancing Behavioral Technologies

- **Differential Privacy:** Adds statistical noise to behavioral data to preserve anonymity while still identifying meaningful trends.
- **Federated Learning:** Enables behavioral models to be trained on-device, so user data never leaves the endpoint.
- **Role-Based Monitoring:** Limits behavioral surveillance to only those roles with elevated risk profiles (e.g., privileged users)

## DESIGNING ETHICAL BEHAVIORAL INTERVENTIONS

Behavioral interventions in cybersecurity, such as nudges, alerts, simulations, and predictive scoring, are powerful tools to shape safer user behaviors.

However, when these tools are poorly designed, they risk becoming manipulative, discriminatory, or opaque. For CISOs and cybersecurity teams, ethical design is not just the best practice; it's essential for protecting user trust, legal compliance, and organizational integrity.

## Recognizing the Line Between Nudging and Manipulation

Nudges, derived from behavioral economics, influence decision-making by altering the choice environment. In cybersecurity, examples include default security settings, persuasive alerts, and warnings about unsafe websites. While effective, these tools can easily cross ethical lines.

For instance, forcing users into security behaviors without clear explanation (e.g., opt-out surveillance) undermines autonomy. Interventions must avoid "dark patterns," designs that trick users into unwanted actions, such as misleading default options or time pressure to accept security policies. Ethical behavioral design involves supporting *informed* decision-making, not subtly coercing users (Mersinas et al., 2025).

## Designing for Transparency and Understanding

Users are far more likely to accept and engage with behavioral interventions when they understand the reasoning behind them. This understanding hinges on clear, accessible communication about what behavior is being tracked, why the intervention exists, and what choices the user has in response. When users are informed, the intervention becomes a collaborative effort rather than an imposed directive. This concept, often referred to as a "justified nudge," makes the promoted behavior feel logical and aligned with user goals, rather than coercive or manipulative.

In contrast, interventions that are hidden or poorly explained can erode user trust and foster resistance. Research highlights the critical role of explainability in the ethical design of cybersecurity interventions. It's not enough for nudges or controls to be visible; they must also be understandable and justifiable. In fact, explainability is now recognized as one of the five foundational principles for ethical cybersecurity decision-making, standing alongside autonomy, justice, beneficence, and non-maleficence (Bajwa et al., 2023). These principles help ensure that behavioral design is aligned with both user rights and organizational integrity.

## Avoiding Harm and Ensuring Fairness

While behavioral interventions can drive positive change, they also carry the potential for unintended harm if not carefully designed. For instance, the overuse of fear-based messaging in phishing simulations might seem effective in the short term, but it can create a culture of anxiety and diminish overall morale. Similarly, automated risk scoring systems that flag behaviors such as accessing sensitive data after hours might inaccurately classify legitimate users as threats, leading to reputational harm or a sense of mistrust between teams.

To prevent these issues, behavioral interventions should be proportionate, inclusive, and designed to avoid bias. This means thoroughly testing systems for potential disparities in how different user groups are affected, as well as evaluating psychological side effects like stress, fatigue, or disengagement. It's also important to monitor for behavioral adaptations, such as users avoiding efficient workarounds out of fear of being flagged, that may undermine productivity or innovation. To proactively address these concerns, designers should incorporate ethical audits and scenario-based testing as part of their development process (Saeidnia et al., 2024). This not only protects users but also strengthens the long-term efficacy and credibility of cybersecurity programs.

## OPERATIONALIZING ETHICS IN BEHAVIORAL DESIGN

As cybersecurity leaders increasingly leverage behavioral tools to guide user decision-making and strengthen security culture, the responsibility to ensure ethical integrity cannot be an afterthought. Ethical design isn't just about compliance or optics; it's about building trust, preserving autonomy, and safeguarding long-term effectiveness. To embed ethics into everyday design, CISOs should take the lead in institutionalizing best practices across their teams and processes.

### Start with Ethical Design Checklists

Before any behavioral intervention is deployed, whether it's a nudge, prompt, or predictive system, its ethical implications should be thoroughly vetted. Tools should be assessed against core principles such as autonomy (does it respect user agency?), transparency (is the intention clear?), fairness (are all users treated equitably?), and proportionality (is the intervention appropriate to the risk?). An ethical design checklist helps teams stay grounded in these guiding values.

### Conduct EIAs

Much like a privacy impact assessment, an EIA evaluates the potential risks, benefits, and unintended harms of behavioral tools, especially those powered by AI or predictive analytics. This process encourages critical reflection and proactive risk mitigation, ensuring interventions align with both organizational values and societal expectations.

### Design Iteratively with User Feedback

No matter how well intentioned a design may be, its real-world impact can vary. CISOs should champion iterative testing that incorporates feedback from diverse user groups. This helps refine clarity, identify unforeseen effects, and build systems that are not only secure but also intuitive and respectful.

### Involve Interdisciplinary Perspectives Early

Ethical design requires more than just technical savvy. By involving behavioral scientists, legal professionals, and ethicists from the outset, CISOs can ensure that solutions are not only functionally sound but also ethically robust. These perspectives can help balance security goals with the lived experiences and rights of users.

### Monitor, Reassess, and Evolve

Behavioral interventions are not static. What begins as a well-meaning nudge can evolve into coercion if left unchecked. Establishing regular review cycles allows teams to monitor effectiveness, identify drift, and adapt designs in response to emerging ethical considerations or societal norms.

## THE CASE FOR PROACTIVE ETHICAL DESIGN

Ethical design in behavioral cybersecurity is not a one-time event; it's a continual process of reflection, refinement, and responsiveness. As behavioral interventions become more integrated into cybersecurity tools and practices, the cost of getting ethics wrong increases: legal liability, user backlash, and reputational damage. By embedding ethics from the start, CISOs can turn behavioral tools into assets for both security and trust, delivering not just safer systems but more respectful and resilient ones.

## BUILDING AN ETHICAL SECURITY CULTURE

The long-term success of ethical behavioral interventions in cybersecurity depends not only on individual design choices but also on the broader organizational culture that shapes decision-making, communication, and trust. For CISOs and cybersecurity leaders, fostering an **ethical security culture** is both a strategic imperative and a moral responsibility. Organizational culture governs what people perceive as acceptable, what they expect from leadership, and how they interpret policies. In cybersecurity, culture determines how seriously people take ethical risks, whether they view security

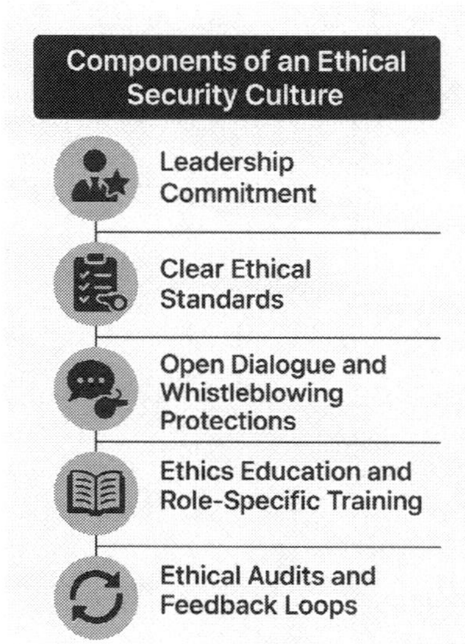


*Figure 8.2* Ethical Security Culture Components

behaviors as compliance obligations or as shared responsibilities rooted in mutual respect. A 2019 analysis argues that ethics and cybersecurity are not in opposition but fundamentally intertwined. The organization's commitment to confidentiality, integrity, and availability (CIA) is deeply dependent on how it understands and prioritizes ethical responsibilities (Al-Mukhtar, 2024) (Figure 8.2).

## ***Components of an Ethical Security Culture***

An ethical security culture starts with leadership. When senior executives and cybersecurity leaders consistently demonstrate ethical behavior, it sets the tone for the rest of the organization. Their commitment to integrity, whether in decision-making, incident response, or policy enforcement, signals that ethics are not just abstract values but critical components of operational excellence. Ethical cybersecurity begins at the top, where leaders prioritize transparency, fairness, and accountability, influencing how risk is managed and how behavior is modeled throughout the organization.

Clear ethical standards are the backbone of this culture. Organizations must develop and maintain codes of conduct that explicitly address security practices and the responsible use of behavioral tools. These standards need to be more than check-the-box documents; they must be dynamic, accessible, and regularly reinforced through targeted training. When integrated into cybersecurity education, especially for roles like developers, analysts, and system administrators, ethical guidance helps teams move beyond compliance and toward a sense of shared responsibility for user safety and trust.

Equally important is cultivating a workplace environment where employees feel empowered to raise ethical concerns without fear of retaliation. Protections for whistleblowers, secure reporting channels, and open dialogue about surveillance, manipulation, and privacy are nonnegotiables. Regular ethical audits and feedback loops, like anonymous surveys or integrity "quick tests," ensure that organizational practices stay aligned with ethical intentions. When these elements work together, they form a culture that is not only secure but principled and resilient.

### *Ethical Failure as a Cultural Breakdown*

Cybersecurity failures rooted in ethics, such as unjust surveillance, poor transparency, or discriminatory AI, are often not the result of technical flaws but of cultural neglect. A 2020 study highlights the lack of ethical governance in many corporate cybersecurity teams compared to the academic sector, which often has more rigorous review boards. Practitioners, therefore, must take the lead in creating their own ethics oversight structures (Macnish & Ham, 2020).

## STEPS CISOS CAN TAKE TO LEAD ETHICAL CULTURE CHANGE

To embed a strong ethical foundation into cybersecurity practices, organizations should begin by establishing a Cybersecurity Ethics Council, a cross-functional team comprising legal experts, HR representatives, behavioral scientists, and technical leads. This council serves as the guiding body for the responsible use of data and behavioral tools, ensuring decisions are grounded in ethical principles. Ethics must also be seamlessly integrated into incident response plans, expanding the scope beyond technical containment to include ethical considerations and transparent user communication, particularly when behavioral interventions fall short. To reinforce this culture, organizations should celebrate ethical decision-making, recognizing and rewarding employees who raise concerns or reject insecure or unethical solutions, even when such actions slow down delivery. Leadership should model transparency by openly discussing ethical dilemmas, sharing audit findings, and regularly updating stakeholders on evolving policies. Finally, benchmarking against recognized standards, such as the CSEC2017 model or the Menlo Report principles, can help organizations assess and advance their ethical maturity in cybersecurity, ensuring practices remain aligned with broader societal expectations (Figure 8.3).

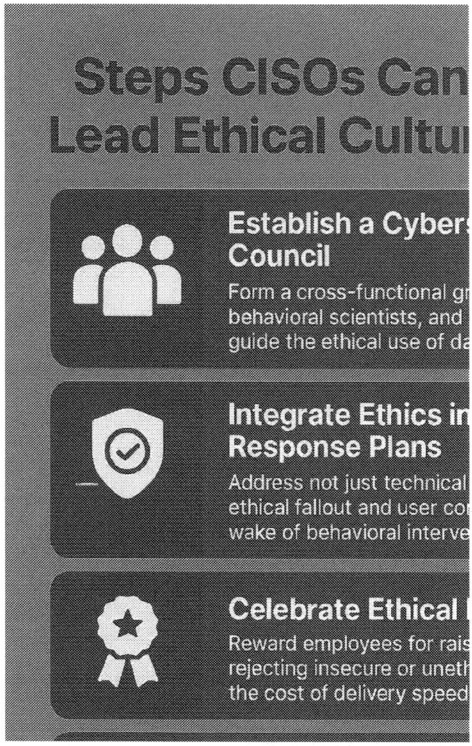


*Figure 8.3* CISOs Lead Ethical Culture Change

## ETHICS AS A STRATEGIC ASSET

Organizations that cultivate strong ethical cultures are not only meeting the moment. They're shaping the future. By embedding ethics into their operations, these organizations are better equipped to navigate complex regulatory environments. They attract and retain values-driven talent. They sustain long-term trust among users and stakeholders. As digital risks evolve, particularly with the rise of AI-driven behavioral prediction and biometric surveillance, a well-established ethical foundation becomes critical. It empowers leaders to respond thoughtfully and responsibly to emerging challenges. Ethical culture is no longer just a matter of compliance. It is a strategic differentiator that fuels resilience. It drives innovation. It builds credibility in an era of accelerating digital transformation.

## CASE STUDIES AND REAL-WORLD APPLICATIONS

To illustrate the importance of ethical decision-making in behavioral cybersecurity, this section presents real-world examples, both successful and problematic. These case studies provide lessons on what works, what can go wrong, and how organizations can ethically manage human-centered security interventions.

## Positive Application: Ethical Phishing Simulation

A large financial institution implemented an ongoing phishing awareness program using behavioral nudges, contextual warnings, simulated phishing emails, and real-time feedback. Importantly, the program was transparent, voluntary, and included training based on user risk profiles.

### *Ethical Strategy*

- Users received clear communications about the purpose of the simulation and how results would be used.
- The organization avoided punitive consequences for failures and instead offered tiered support for high-risk groups.

### *Outcome*

- Phishing click rates declined by over 40% within six months.
- Employee trust remained high due to the opt-in model and personalized support.

This example illustrates how behavioral tools, when designed with respect for autonomy and transparency, can drive security outcomes without coercion or fear-based messaging. It aligns with emerging guidance advocating nonpunitive, user-centric design (Mersinas et al., 2025).

## Ethics Gone Wrong: Predictive Risk Scoring for Insider Threats

A tech firm implemented behavioral analytics to flag potential insider threats using keylogging, email monitoring, and behavior pattern recognition, without fully disclosing the scope of surveillance to employees.

### *Ethical Failures*

- No informed consent process was implemented.
- The algorithm flagged several employees based on statistically normal behavior (e.g., late-night work hours) but with severe consequences.
- A whistleblower revealed the system's opacity and bias, causing employee backlash and reputational damage.

#### *Consequences*

- The program was paused following internal investigation.
- Legal action followed, citing violations of labor protections and privacy rights.

This case reflects ethical lapses in transparency, fairness, and explainability, highlighting the dangers of unregulated behavioral surveillance in workplace security settings (Macnish & Ham, 2020).

### Sector-Specific Case: Cybersecurity in Healthcare

In a health system rollout of electronic health cards, user behavior was monitored to reduce account hijacking. However, the intervention raised ethical concerns regarding informed consent and the trade-off between usability and surveillance.

#### *Ethical Dilemma*

- Balancing the need for behavioral monitoring to prevent data breaches vs. ensuring patient and clinician autonomy.
- Developers failed to provide adequate control or communication about what was being monitored.

#### *Resolution*

- A revised system introduced opt-in consent, user logs, and clearer justifications for behavior-based security decisions.
- Trust levels increased, and the platform met compliance standards while retaining security integrity.

This example demonstrates how case-by-case ethical assessment can resolve value conflicts in high-risk environments (Panadés & Yuguero, 2025).

## LESSONS FOR CISOS

For today's CISOs, ethical leadership in cybersecurity goes beyond technical controls. First, transparency is nonnegotiable. Users have a right to know when and how their behaviors are monitored or influenced, particularly in systems involving behavioral nudges or surveillance. Building resilience starts with consent; opt-in models not only comply with regulations but also encourage user engagement and trust. CISOs must also anticipate the potential for bias and harm, especially in predictive systems. Finally, deploying responsible technology requires a cross-disciplinary

*Figure 8.4* Key Lessons for CISOs

ethics review. Involving legal, technical, and behavioral science experts ensures that cybersecurity solutions are not only secure but also equitable and human-centered (Figure 8.4).

## EMERGING TECHNOLOGIES AND EXPANDING RISKS

As cybersecurity evolves in tandem with emerging technologies, CISOs and practitioners must prepare for a new wave of ethical challenges. Behavioral interventions, already powerful tools in shaping user decisions, will become even more sophisticated with the integration of AI, biometrics, and predictive algorithms. While the potential to preempt threats and tailor defenses grows, so too does the risk of ethical overreach.

The integration of AI and machine learning into behavioral cybersecurity systems is expected to revolutionize security, but not without consequence. These systems can autonomously assess risk based on user actions, identify anomalous behavior, and dynamically adapt defenses. However, algorithmic opacity and bias remain serious concerns, particularly when AI systems make judgments that affect individuals' employment or reputation without transparency or recourse.

Researchers warn that many ethical concerns are going unaddressed, especially in early adoption stages, because the speed of innovation outpaces ethical reflection. These include unintended discrimination in behavioral scoring, surveillance creep, and the normalization of manipulation as part of everyday digital experience (Pawlicka et al., 2023). The next generation of behavioral monitoring is increasingly focused on biometric data, such as typing rhythms, facial expressions, voice patterns, and even emotional states. These tools promise more personalized and accurate threat detection but raise red flags about bodily autonomy and emotional privacy. Some researchers predict that neurosecurity, monitoring brain signals or emotional responses, may one day be used to assess user intent or detect deception. While not yet mainstream, the ethical implications are vast: How much intrusion is justifiable in the name of cybersecurity? And what safeguards should be in place to prevent psychological manipulation or surveillance of affective states? (Kritika, 2025).

## AUTONOMY IN AN AGE OF AUTONOMOUS SYSTEMS

With the rise of autonomous security systems, such as self-healing networks and AI-powered policy enforcement, questions of accountability grow murky. If a behavioral model flags an employee incorrectly or locks a user out of a system unfairly, who is responsible, the developer, the AI, or the security officer who approved it? These scenarios introduce novel ethical considerations about delegated decision-making. Systems that automatically enforce policy without human intervention risk denying users the chance to explain their actions, appeal decisions, or contest surveillance. A growing body of research calls for clear ethical governance frameworks to guide the use of autonomous tools in cybersecurity (Azer & Samir, 2024).

## PREPARING FOR THE NEXT ETHICAL WAVE: RECOMMENDATIONS FOR CISOS

To meet future ethical challenges, CISOs should:

1. **Anticipate Black Swan Ethical Events**
   Invest in horizon scanning and ethics foresight to identify low-probability, high-impact risks before they materialize (Pawlicka et al., 2023).
2. **Institute Ethical Risk Assessments for Emerging Tools**
   Include behavioral ethics considerations in all AI, biometric, and adaptive system implementations.

3. **Develop Multi-stakeholder Governance Models**
   Involve users, legal experts, ethicists, and behavioral scientists in the development and approval of new security technologies.
4. **Push for Regulatory and Industry Standards**
   Advocate for policy frameworks that define acceptable boundaries for behavioral surveillance and algorithmic decision-making in security contexts.
5. **Treat Ethics as Ongoing Practice, Not a One-Time Review**
   Create feedback loops that monitor ethical outcomes over time and enable rapid response to harm or misuse.

The future of behavioral cybersecurity will be shaped not just by what is *technologically* possible but by what is *ethically* sustainable. CISOs who lead with foresight and ethical clarity will ensure that innovation advances not only security but human dignity as well.

## CHAPTER SUMMARY

Even with strong ethical guidelines on paper, an organization's culture ultimately determines whether ethical cybersecurity practices truly take hold. The values and norms promoted within a company will influence how employees make day-to-day security decisions and whether they put ethics first. A culture of integrity and respect for privacy, starting from leadership, empowers staff to act responsibly even when no one is looking. Leaders (such as the CISO and executive team) play a pivotal role by demonstrating a commitment to ethical practices and by rewarding principled behavior. When the "tone at the top" emphasizes doing what is right over just what is expedient, it creates a moral compass for the entire security team.

Regular training and open dialogue about ethical dilemmas further reinforce this environment, helping team members internalize the importance of privacy, fairness, and transparency. By contrast, if an organization's culture is overly aggressive about security at all costs or tolerates dubious practices, employees may feel pressure to cut corners ethically. For example, overly intrusive monitoring of employee activity in the name of security can backfire, and it can also erode trust and morale (employees may view it as an invasion of privacy and even consider leaving). Thus, fostering an ethical cybersecurity culture is not just a "nice to have" but a core part of ensuring that behavioral science techniques are applied in a responsible way. It creates the social framework where doing the ethical thing is the norm, and it gives ethical policies real traction in practice.

The rapid emergence of technologies like artificial intelligence (AI) and biometrics is expanding both the capabilities of cybersecurity and the ethical challenges involved. AI can analyze vast amounts of behavioral data to improve threat detection and response, but it also introduces new risks that organizations must address. AI algorithms may inadvertently learn or amplify biases present in data, potentially leading to unfair or unethical outcomes if, say, certain users are treated with more suspicion than others. The use of AI in monitoring user behavior at scale also raises significant privacy concerns—advanced AI-powered surveillance could encroach on personal freedoms if not kept in check.

Likewise, biometric security technologies (such as fingerprint scanners, facial recognition, and iris scans) offer powerful new ways to authenticate users and prevent fraud. They promise convenience and stronger identity verification, yet they "present significant ethical and legal challenges" alongside their benefits. Biometric systems inherently involve sensitive personal data, one's fingerprints or face is deeply personal, and misuse or breaches of this data can be especially harmful. Experts have voiced concerns about privacy invasions, errors (like false matches), and potential abuse of biometric information if it falls into the wrong hands.

For instance, a stolen biometric identifier is not something a person can simply change like a password, making the consequences of compromise far more severe and lasting. As biometric data becomes more deeply integrated into authentication systems, the stakes for ethical missteps grow exponentially. The growing use of AI and biometrics in security highlights the urgent need for proactive ethics: organizations must anticipate emerging risks and evolve their ethical frameworks accordingly. This includes implementing bias audits for AI systems, enforcing strict governance over biometric data, and ensuring compliance with rapidly developing privacy laws to protect rights, dignity, and individual autonomy in the digital age.

Given the complexity of these considerations, what can CISOs and other security leaders do in practical terms to uphold ethics in behavioral cybersecurity?

- **Establish Ethical Review Processes:** Behavioral cybersecurity initiatives should undergo formal ethics reviews to assess potential impacts on privacy and user rights. Involving privacy officers and legal counsel helps ensure interventions are both effective and ethically sound.
- **Foster Interdisciplinary Collaboration:** Security leaders should work with behavioral scientists, ethicists, and legal experts to identify ethical blind spots. This cross-functional input strengthens ethical decision-making and aligns interventions with diverse stakeholder values.
- **Maintain Transparency with Users:** Clearly communicate what data is collected, why it's used, and how behavioral tools support security goals. Transparency builds trust, encourages user cooperation, and deters manipulative practices.

- **Promote an Ethical Security Culture:** CISOs should champion ongoing ethics training, open dialogue, and reward systems that reinforce principled behavior. A culture rooted in ethical accountability ensures that everyone plays a role in protecting user rights and organizational integrity.

Stepping back from the organizational level, it becomes clear that ethical behavioral cybersecurity carries a broader societal and moral significance. Cybersecurity measures today affect millions of people's daily lives, from the privacy of personal communications to the integrity of critical services, so the ethical choices made by security professionals have far-reaching implications. Practicing ethical cybersecurity is essential to maintaining public trust in the digital society and to operating in a way that consistently demonstrates respect for individual rights and human dignity. When companies and governments handle our data and shape our online behaviors, they are implicitly taking on a duty of care that goes beyond mere compliance; it is a responsibility to uphold the values that free and secure societies are built on. This means that the moral compass guiding cybersecurity (the principles of fairness, transparency, accountability, and empathy for users) has never been more important. By championing these principles, cybersecurity leaders and practitioners serve not only their own organizations but the public at large, positioning themselves as guardians of digital trust, freedom, and well-being.

## REFERENCES


Allahrakha, N. (2023). Balancing cyber-security and privacy: Legal and ethical considerations in the digital age. *Legal Issues in the Digital Age*, *4*(2), 78–121. https://doi.org/10.17323/10.17323/2713-2749.2023.2.78.121

Al-Mukhtar, W. N. M. (2024). AI in cybersecurity: Transformative approaches to safeguarding information technology systems. *Turkish Journal of Computer and Mathematics Education (TURCOMAT)*, *15*(3), 391–412. https://doi.org/10.61841/turcomat.v15i3.14945

Azer, M. A., & Samir, R. (2024). Overview of the complex landscape and future directions of ethics in light of emerging technologies. *International Journal of Advanced Computer Science and Applications (IJACSA)*, *15*(7), 1459–1481. http://doi.org/10.14569/IJACSA.2024.01507142

Bajwa, M. H. A., Richards, D., & Formosa, P. (2023). Evaluation of embodied conversational agents designed with ethical principles and personality for cybersecurity ethics training. *Proceedings of the 23rd ACM International Conference on Intelligent Virtual Agents*. https://doi.org/10.1145/3570945.3607359

Del-Real, C., De Busser, E., & van den Berg, B. (2025). A systematic literature review of security and privacy by design principles, norms, and strategies for digital technologies. *International Review of Law, Computers & Technology*, 1–32. https://doi.org/10.1080/13600869.2025.2457227

Formosa, P., Richards, D., & Bajwa, M. H. A. (2021). Principlist ethical frameworks for cybersecurity decision-making: Autonomy, justice, beneficence, non-maleficence, and explainability. *Journal of Cyber Ethics*, *13*(2), 76–91. https://doi.org/10.1016/j.cose.2021.102382

Fenech, J., Richards, D., & Formosa, P. (2024). Ethical principles shaping values-based cybersecurity decision-making. *Computers & Security*, *140*, 103795. https://doi.org/10.1016/j.cose.2024.103795

Kritika, E. (2025). Ethical frontiers: Navigating the intersection of neurotechnology and cybersecurity. *Journal of Experimental Neurology*, *6*(1), 21–25. https://doi.org/10.33696/Neurol.6.106

Macnish, K., & Ham, M. (2020). Ethics in cybersecurity practice: Bridging the gap between research and operations. *Journal of Information Ethics*, *29*(3), 45–62. https://doi.org/10.1016/j.techsoc.2020.101382

Mersinas, K., Bada, M., & Furnell, S. (2025). Cybersecurity behavior change: A conceptualization of ethical principles for behavioral interventions. *Computers & Security*, *148*, 104025. https://doi.org/10.1016/j.cose.2024.104025

Panadés, R., & Yuguero, O. (2025). Cyber-bioethics: The new ethical discipline for digital health. *Frontiers in Digital Health*, *6*. https://doi.org/10.3389/fdgth.2024.1523180

Pawlicka, A., Pawlicki, M., Kozik, R., & Choraś, M. (2023). What will the future of cybersecurity bring us, and will it be ethical? The hunt for the black swans of cybersecurity ethics. *IEEE Access*, *11*, 58796–58807. https://doi.org/10.1109/ACCESS.2023.3283791

Saeidnia, H. R., Hashemi Fotami, S. G., Lund, B., & Ghiasi, N. (2024). Ethical considerations in artificial intelligence interventions for mental health and well-being: Ensuring responsible implementation and impact. *Social Sciences*, *13*(7), 381. https://doi.org/10.3390/socsci13070381

Chapter 9

# Future Directions in Behavioral Cybersecurity

## LEARNING OBJECTIVES

- Understand how current studies are uncovering the psychological drivers behind user behavior, decision-making, and threat response in digital environments.
- Examine how designing systems around human needs and behaviors can lead to more intuitive, resilient, and effective security measures.
- Consider the practical implications of applying behavioral insights to security policies, training, and technologies amid rapidly changing threat landscapes.

## EMERGING RESEARCH AREAS IN BEHAVIORAL CYBERSECURITY

Behavioral science is rapidly gaining prominence in cybersecurity, as researchers and practitioners recognize that technical defenses alone are insufficient without considering human behavior. Cyberattacks increasingly exploit human errors rather than purely technical vulnerabilities, emphasizing the need for integrated approaches. This section explores the cutting-edge developments in behavioral cybersecurity, including behavioral analytics, biometrics, psychological profiling, nudging techniques, and interdisciplinary research approaches. These emerging domains show great promise in creating more adaptive, resilient, and human-centric cybersecurity strategies that align with how individuals think, act, and make decisions in digital contexts.

## BEHAVIORAL ANALYTICS AND THREAT DETECTION

User and Entity Behavior Analytics (UEBA) leverages machine learning and statistical analysis to identify deviations in user behavior that may signal potential threats. By continuously monitoring patterns such

DOI: 10.1201/9781003606345-9

as login frequency, access to sensitive files, and device usage, UEBA systems help detect anomalies associated with insider threats or account compromise. Behavioral analytics are particularly useful in identifying subtle, non-signature-based attacks that evade traditional detection systems, making them critical in modern security environments. Research highlights the value of integrating behavioral insights with adaptive defense systems to model user behaviors and identify threats early, with cognitive-information technologies like UEBA playing a pivotal role in enhancing cybersecurity resilience in artificial intelligence (AI)-powered ecosystems (Andrade et al., 2022).

## BEHAVIORAL BIOMETRICS AND CONTINUOUS AUTHENTICATION

Behavioral biometrics, such as typing patterns, mouse movements, gait, or touchscreen gestures, provide a noninvasive, continuous authentication method. These systems enhance security by learning how users interact with devices rather than relying on static credentials like passwords. This approach adds a personalized and adaptive layer of defense that continuously validates identity throughout a session. Recent studies demonstrate the effectiveness of behavioral biometrics in cybersecurity; for example, Long Short-Term Memory (LSTM) models significantly outperform traditional machine learning algorithms, achieving authentication accuracy above 95% (Madavarapu et al., 2024). Additionally, behavioral biometrics offer strong security with minimal user friction, especially valuable in high-security environments like banking and military operations (Rybka et al., 2022). However, issues around data quality, sensor reliability, and user privacy remain critical concerns for widespread adoption.

## PSYCHOLOGICAL PROFILING IN CYBERSECURITY

Psychological profiling aims to identify threat actors based on cognitive and emotional characteristics, enhancing threat prediction and response. The rise of Large Language Models (LLMs) and psycholinguistic analysis tools enables the detection of linguistic patterns that correlate with malicious intent. These approaches provide deeper insights into attacker motivations, cognitive biases, and behavioral markers that traditional tools may overlook. Emerging research shows that psychological profiling can be effectively applied to both internal and external threats through the analysis of textual communication and behavioral cues (Tshimula et al., 2024). This enables early identification of high-risk individuals, including potential malicious insiders or those susceptible to social engineering.

## NUDGING AND BEHAVIORAL INTERVENTIONS

Behavioral nudging applies insights from psychology and behavioral economics to influence secure decision-making without coercion. Nudges can range from subtle prompts and warning messages to default settings that guide users toward more secure behaviors. A 2024 study highlights how behavioral economics—including cognitive bias exploitation—can be used to reduce susceptibility to phishing and impersonation attacks (Tsanov, 2024). Techniques such as real-time feedback, personalized training simulations, and adaptive messaging have proven effective in fostering more resilient user behavior in digital environments. These interventions are increasingly embedded in software interfaces, security training, and corporate communication strategies.

## INTERDISCIPLINARY RESEARCH APPROACHES

Cybersecurity has evolved into an interdisciplinary field, intersecting with psychology, behavioral science, criminal justice, political science, and social science. This convergence is essential for addressing complex, human-centric challenges that arise in cybersecurity today. Recent workshops and conferences, such as the CySSS (Cybersecurity and Social Sciences) workshop, highlight how cross-disciplinary collaboration is shaping future research agendas (Chan-Tin & Kennison, 2022). Additionally, bibliometric analyses show a surge in behavioral cybersecurity research, signaling that these integrative efforts are now central to the field's progression (Sajikumar & Ajithkumar, 2024). Interdisciplinary work fosters holistic strategies that account for both technological and human dimensions of security.

## CHALLENGES IN BEHAVIORAL INTEGRATION

While behavioral science offers transformative potential in cybersecurity, its integration into security frameworks is fraught with persistent challenges. These range from cultural and organizational barriers to ethical dilemmas, measurement difficulties, and user fatigue. Many organizations are still structured around siloed operations, with technical teams and behavioral experts rarely collaborating. Understanding and overcoming these barriers is essential for creating effective, human-centered security strategies that can evolve with changing digital landscapes and threats.

A major barrier to integrating behavioral science in cybersecurity is organizational resistance, often rooted in a culture of technological determinism and rigid hierarchies. Security teams frequently prioritize traditional tools over human-centric approaches, leading to underinvestment in behavioral interventions. Additionally, interdisciplinary collaboration is often limited due to institutional structures and communication gaps. This lack of integration hampers innovation and weakens the potential for developing adaptive, people-focused defenses.

Research highlights that many businesses lack an internal culture that values behavioral insight due to difficulty in communicating its value, limited managerial buy-in, and the absence of clear success metrics (Young, 2024). Without tangible evidence of behavioral return on investment (ROI), it becomes difficult to justify the required investment to key stakeholders. Moreover, a tertiary review of behavioral cybersecurity studies indicates that this field remains under-theorized and fragmented, leading to inconsistent implementation across organizations (Khan et al., 2022). These challenges highlight the need for standardized frameworks and collaborative strategies that bridge disciplinary divides.

## PRIVACY AND ETHICAL CONCERNS

As behavioral cybersecurity often involves collecting and analyzing detailed user behavior, privacy concerns emerge as a major ethical roadblock. Users may perceive behavioral monitoring as invasive, especially when transparency around data usage is lacking. Organizations must carefully navigate data protection regulations, balancing the need for behavioral insights with respect for individual privacy. Without clear ethical frameworks, even well-intentioned security tools can erode trust and reduce compliance.

In metaverse environments, studies show that privacy concerns and perceived risks significantly reduce cybersecurity compliance among users, particularly when they lack understanding of how their behavioral data is being used (Al-Emran et al., 2024). The immersive nature of these platforms introduces new layers of data vulnerability, further complicating privacy management. Similar findings in biometric systems demonstrate the challenges of aligning continuous behavioral monitoring with ethical and legal standards (Shuford, 2024). To move forward, organizations must adopt privacy-by-design principles and engage users transparently to foster ethical data practices.

## COMPLEXITY OF HUMAN BEHAVIOR AND VARIABILITY

Human behavior is inherently dynamic, context-sensitive, and culturally diverse, making it difficult to model reliably in cybersecurity frameworks. Individuals behave differently across situations, platforms, and timeframes, creating challenges in developing universally applicable behavioral models. This variability can lead to false positives or missed threats in behavioral detection systems. Consequently, cybersecurity solutions must be flexible and adaptive to account for the nuances of human behavior.

Researchers emphasize that the absence of a consistent theoretical foundation in behavioral cybersecurity makes it hard to generalize findings, particularly in nonorganizational settings (Khan et al., 2022). The private sector faces unique challenges due to diverse employee roles, varying levels of technical literacy, and different motivational drivers (Young, 2024). These complexities necessitate more granular, context-aware models that can be tailored to specific environments and user profiles. Failure to account for variability can diminish the effectiveness of even the most advanced behavioral tools.

## TECHNOLOGY OVERLOAD AND SECURITY FATIGUE

Repetitive security prompts, frequent policy updates, and constant threat warnings can lead to user fatigue and disengagement. This cognitive overload reduces the likelihood that users will consistently follow secure behaviors, particularly when they perceive these measures as interfering with productivity. Over time, even well-designed security protocols can become background noise, ignored or bypassed by overwhelmed users. Organizations must therefore balance vigilance with usability.

Though not specific to cybersecurity, behavioral research in digital systems has shown that users become demotivated when overwhelmed by complexity, alert frequency, or redundant tasks (Balan, 2024). In security-specific contexts, studies have identified "response cost"—the perceived inconvenience of taking security actions—as a major inhibitor to proactive behavior (Al-Emran et al., 2024). To combat this, companies must streamline security protocols, introduce adaptive prompts, and consider user experience in policy design. Reducing friction is key to maintaining consistent user engagement and compliance.

## MEASUREMENT AND ROI CHALLENGES

One of the most persistent barriers in behavioral cybersecurity is the difficulty of measuring success and ROI. Unlike technical controls that can be evaluated using precise metrics, behavioral interventions often rely on subjective or indirect indicators, such as survey responses, user feedback, or incident frequency. These methods can be unreliable or inconsistent, making it harder to justify long-term investment. As a result, organizations may deprioritize behavioral strategies in favor of quantifiable technical measures.

There is a notable lack of standardized frameworks for assessing behavioral cybersecurity outcomes. Most efforts in the field remain exploratory, with empirical studies often producing conflicting or nonreplicable results (Khan et al., 2022). Without clear benchmarks, it becomes difficult for cybersecurity leaders to evaluate the effectiveness of training programs, nudging techniques, or awareness campaigns. Future progress will depend on developing validated tools and metrics that can quantify the behavioral impact of security interventions in diverse organizational settings.

While behavioral science offers transformative potential in cybersecurity, its integration into security frameworks is fraught with persistent challenges. These range from cultural and organizational barriers to ethical dilemmas, measurement difficulties, and user fatigue. Understanding these barriers is essential for creating effective, human-centered security strategies that can evolve with changing digital landscapes.

A major barrier to integrating behavioral science in cybersecurity is organizational resistance, often rooted in a culture of technological determinism and siloed departments. Many security teams still prioritize technical tools over human factors, leading to underinvestment in behavioral interventions and interdisciplinary collaboration.

Research highlights that many businesses lack an internal culture that values behavioral insight due to difficulty in communicating its value, limited managerial buy-in, and the absence of clear success metrics (Young, 2024). Moreover, a tertiary review of behavioral cybersecurity studies indicates that this field remains under-theorized and fragmented, leading to inconsistent implementation across organizations (Khan et al., 2022).

## THE FUTURE OF CYBERSECURITY CULTURE

As the cybersecurity landscape evolves, the role of human factors and organizational culture has become increasingly central to defense strategies. Culture influences how individuals perceive risks, respond to policies, and engage with security practices, making it a critical factor in shaping long-term cyber resilience. Moving forward, an organization's cybersecurity posture will depend not only on technological defenses but also on the values, norms, and behaviors embedded in its culture. This section explores the emerging shifts in cybersecurity culture, the role of leadership, the evolution of awareness practices, and the broader societal transformations shaping the future of digital defense.

## THE NEXT GENERATION OF SECURITY AWARENESS

Traditional security awareness programs often emphasize compliance checklists and policy memorization rather than meaningful behavioral change. However, the future of training lies in sustained engagement, personalized learning, and behavior-driven outcomes that empower users to make secure decisions intuitively. Innovative approaches such as gamification, scenario-based simulations, and microlearning modules are making security education more relevant and impactful. Research shows that when security training is tailored to organizational context and delivered through interactive platforms, small and medium-sized enterprises (SMEs) experience up to 65% fewer incidents caused by human error (Ugbebor et al., 2024). Furthermore, multilayered training architectures that incorporate continuous feedback loops lead to cultural transformation and more resilient threat responses (Rongala, 2025).

## PREDICTIVE CULTURE MODELING AND METRICS

Looking ahead, organizations will increasingly adopt data-driven frameworks to anticipate cultural trends and proactively manage cybersecurity behavior. Predictive models such as the Cybersecurity Culture Maturity Model (CCMM) and the Cyber Trust Index (CTI) enable organizations to assess key dimensions like accountability, communication, and employee buy-in (Dornheim & Zarnekow, 2023), (Silva, 2024). These tools combine behavioral analytics, user feedback, and incident data to generate actionable insights. Over time, organizations can use such metrics to identify cultural weak spots and implement targeted interventions. As more firms embrace this approach, cybersecurity culture may become as measurable and optimizable as any technical performance indicator.

## THE ROLE OF LEADERSHIP AND BEHAVIORAL CHAMPIONS

Leadership plays a critical role in shaping organizational attitudes and behaviors around cybersecurity. Transformational and servant leadership styles have been shown to foster trust, motivation, and shared responsibility—traits essential for building a strong security culture (Feraru & Bacali, 2024). Leaders must go beyond top-down enforcement and model desired security behaviors themselves, sending a clear message about expectations and accountability. Consistent communication, recognition of positive behavior, and inclusion of security in organizational values are all necessary for embedding cybersecurity into daily operations. Studies underscore that without visible and active leadership support, even the most well-designed cybersecurity initiatives struggle to gain lasting traction (De Silva, 2023), (Triplett, 2022).

## DECENTRALIZED AND DEMOCRATIZED SECURITY MODELS

Future cybersecurity cultures will move toward decentralized models where frontline employees and end users are empowered to make security decisions. This shift recognizes that users are often the first line of defense and that centralized command structures can slow down response times and innovation. By involving employees in policy design and implementation, organizations can foster greater ownership, trust, and accountability (Waiganjo et al., 2024). This approach aligns with behavioral theories such as Self-Determination Theory, which emphasizes autonomy, competence, and relatedness as key motivators for sustained behavioral change (Feraru & Bacali, 2024). Ultimately, democratizing security fosters a shared responsibility model that increases adaptability and resilience.

## SOCIETAL AND GLOBAL INFLUENCES ON CYBERSECURITY CULTURE

Cultural values, national policies, and global events are increasingly shaping cybersecurity behaviors and organizational responses. The COVID-19 pandemic and rapid adoption of remote work accelerated the demand for adaptive and culturally sensitive cybersecurity measures. Studies indicate that SMEs with strong cybersecurity awareness and adaptability fared better in maintaining digital resilience during crises (Kassar, 2023). Frameworks like Protection Motivation Theory and Dynamic Capabilities Theory offer valuable tools for cultivating security cultures that can evolve during uncertainty. Additionally, cross-cultural differences such as individualism vs. collectivism or power distance influence how users interpret and comply with security policies (Collier et al., 2023), underscoring the importance of localizing training and awareness efforts.

## OPPORTUNITIES FOR INNOVATION USING BEHAVIORAL INSIGHTS

As cybersecurity evolves from a purely technical discipline into a human-centric endeavor, the integration of behavioral science is unlocking new avenues for innovation. Understanding how users perceive, interact with, and respond to digital systems provides critical insights for designing more secure and intuitive tools. This section highlights five key domains where behavioral insights are catalyzing innovation: user-centered design, AI-augmented cyber defense, personalized training, behavior-based threat intelligence, and policy development. These domains demonstrate that aligning cybersecurity solutions with human psychology not only enhances effectiveness but also increases user trust and long-term engagement.

Traditional cybersecurity tools often prioritize technical robustness over user experience, resulting in systems that may be secure but are difficult to use. Human-centered design (HCD) shifts this focus by ensuring that security systems align with how users think, behave, and make decisions under pressure. By integrating principles from behavioral science, HCD can improve usability, reduce cognitive load, and prevent security errors caused by user confusion. Research shows that aligning interface design with psychological cues—such as clarity, simplicity, and feedback—can significantly enhance engagement and reduce risky behavior (Van Rooy & Vaes, 2024). This approach is particularly valuable in high-stress environments where intuitive decision-making is crucial.

Integrating HCD into AI applications helps align systems with diverse user needs, leading to more ethical and intuitive designs. This approach enhances user trust and reduces security errors triggered by confusion or complexity (Van Rooy & Vaes, 2024). Effective human-AI synergy can result in more adaptive and inclusive cybersecurity experiences, especially when behavioral insights inform system development.

## AI-AUGMENTED BEHAVIORAL CYBER DEFENSE

AI is revolutionizing cybersecurity by enabling faster, more adaptive threat responses. When combined with behavioral analytics, AI systems can monitor baseline user behavior and detect subtle anomalies indicative of compromise. This creates a powerful defense mechanism that not only reacts to known threats but anticipates them through predictive modeling. Recent research shows how integrating machine learning with real-time behavioral data enhances the precision of anomaly detection and allows for more efficient incident prioritization (Nnamani, 2024), (Al-Mukhtar, 2024). These AI-powered tools represent a shift from reactive security to proactive defense, offering a critical edge in a rapidly evolving threat landscape.

## PERSONALIZED CYBERSECURITY TRAINING

Generic, one-size-fits-all security training programs often fail to engage users or produce lasting behavioral change. Personalized training leverages behavioral science and immersive technologies to create adaptive learning paths tailored to an individual's risk perception, motivation, and cognitive style. These programs often incorporate gamified environments, virtual simulations, and AI-driven feedback to enhance learning outcomes. For instance, new platforms using extended reality (XR) and generative AI can simulate real-world attack scenarios while tracking user responses to refine training in real time (Chandrashekar et al., 2024). Such tailored approaches improve engagement and retention, making users more resilient under real-world cyber stress.

## BEHAVIORAL THREAT INTELLIGENCE

Traditional Cyber Threat Intelligence (CTI) focuses on known indicators of compromise (IOCs), but behavioral threat intelligence expands this by analyzing how users interact with systems to predict threats before they manifest. Behavioral CTI integrates data on user patterns, emotional cues, and decision-making behaviors to detect early warning signs of cyber risk. These insights are especially effective for identifying insider threats or detecting social engineering attacks that bypass technical controls. Advanced machine learning platforms can continually update behavioral models, enabling systems to adapt dynamically to changing behaviors (Ofoegbu et al., 2023). As collaboration between industries improves, shared behavioral threat data will further strengthen predictive capabilities across sectors.

## POLICY AND REGULATION TAILORED TO HUMAN BEHAVIOR

Cybersecurity policies are often framed in technical or legal language that fails to resonate with users. By integrating behavioral science into policy design, regulators can create frameworks that align with how individuals perceive and react to risks. Techniques such as nudges, default options, and visual cues can guide secure behavior without requiring coercion. Studies suggest that policies rooted in behavioral principles lead to higher compliance and more ethical user engagement with digital systems (Sajikumar & Ajithkumar, 2024). Policymakers who understand behavioral tendencies can better align incentives, reduce friction, and foster long-term adherence to security standards.

## CONCLUSION

As the cybersecurity landscape becomes increasingly complex and intertwined with human behavior, the integration of behavioral science offers one of the most promising paths forward. This chapter explored emerging research areas, the barriers to adoption, the evolution of security culture, and innovative applications poised to transform the field. The consistent theme is clear: human behavior must be treated not as a vulnerability to be mitigated but as a strategic asset in building stronger security systems. By acknowledging and incorporating human factors into design, detection, and defense, organizations can develop truly adaptive cybersecurity infrastructures.

Human error continues to be a leading cause of breaches, and addressing it requires a paradigm shift toward seeing users as active defenders. A human-centered cybersecurity model includes behavioral monitoring, adaptive policies, and personalized interventions that evolve with user behavior. Studies show that such approaches can cut phishing susceptibility, shorten response times, and reduce breach costs by up to 50% (Tambe-Jagtap, 2023).

Integrating technologies like behavioral biometrics and UEBA moves cybersecurity from a static system to a dynamic, context-aware defense ecosystem (Andrade et al., 2022).

Effective behavioral cybersecurity demands interdisciplinary collaboration—drawing from psychology, sociology, computer science, and policy. Projects like ADVANCES show how genomics, behavioral modeling, and technology can combine to form holistic strategies (Majore et al., 2023). Human factors such as cognitive load, stress, and emotion must be embedded into system design to reflect the real-world complexity of user decision-making (Hakimi et al., 2024).

To build resilient next-generation cybersecurity systems, we must train professionals not just in coding or infrastructure but in behavioral literacy. Education must include adaptive thinking, ethical reasoning, and the skills needed to collaborate with AI systems (Familoni, 2024). Governments and institutions have a role to play by supporting interdisciplinary programs and funding human-centric research. Ultimately, cybersecurity must evolve into a living, adaptive ecosystem that is shaped by and for the people it protects.

## REFERENCES

Al-Emran, M., Al-Sharafi, M. A., Foroughi, B., Iranmanesh, M., Alsharida, R. A., Al-Qaysi, N., & Ali, N. (2024). Evaluating the barriers affecting cybersecurity behavior in the Metaverse using PLS-SEM and fuzzy sets (fsQCA). *Computers in Human Behavior, 159*, 108315. https://doi.org/10.1016/j.chb.2024.108315

Andrade, R. O., Fuertes, W., Cazares, M., Ortiz-Garcés, I., & Navas, G. (2022). An Exploratory Study of Cognitive Sciences Applied to Cybersecurity. Electronics, 11(11), 1692. https://doi.org/10.3390/electronics11111692

Al-Mukhtar, W. N. (2024). AI in cybersecurity: Transformative approaches to safeguarding information technology systems. *Turkish Journal of Computer and Mathematics Education (TURCOMAT)*, 15(3), 391–412. https://doi.org/10.61841/turcomat.v15i3.14945

Balan, O. (2024) "The Changing Paradigm of Behavioral Economics: Removing Barriers to Behavioral Change." *Business Inform* 7:14–20. https://doi.org/10.32983/2222-4459-2024-7-14-20

Chandrashekar, N., Lee, A., Azab, M., & Gracanin, D. (2024). Understanding User Behavior for Enhancing Cybersecurity Training with Immersive Gamified Platforms. *Information*, *15*(12), 814. https://doi.org/10.3390/info15120814

Chan-Tin, E., & Kennison, S. (2022). CySSS '22: 1st International workshop on cybersecurity and social sciences. *Proceedings of the 2022 ACM on Asia Conference on Computer and Communications Security.* https://doi.org/10.1145/3488932.3517203

Collier, H., Morton, C., Alharthi, D. N., & Kleiner, J. (2023). Cultural influences on information security. *European Conference on Cyber Warfare and Security.* https://doi.org/10.34190/eccws.22.1.1127

De Silva, B. (2023). Exploring the relationship between cybersecurity culture and cyber-crime prevention: A systematic review. *International Journal of Information Security and Cybercrime*, 12(1), 23–29. https://doi.org/10.19107/IJISC.2023.01.03

Dornheim, P., & Zarnekow, R. (2024). Determining cybersecurity culture maturity and deriving verifiable improvement measures. *Information and Computer Security*, 32(2), 179–196. https://doi.org/10.1108/ICS-07-2023-0116

Familoni, B. T. (2024). Cybersecurity challenges in the age of AI: Theoretical approaches and practical solutions. *Computer Science & IT Research Journal*, 5(3), 703–724. https://doi.org/10.51594/csitrj.v5i3.930

Feraru, I. & Bacali, L. (2024). Explore the intersection of Self-Determination Theory and cybersecurity education - A literature review. *International Journal of Advanced Statistics and IT&C for Economics and Life Sciences*, 14(1), 2024. 55–77. https://doi.org/10.2478/ijasitels-2024-0017

Hakimi, M., Quchi, M. M., & Fazil, A. W. (2024). Human factors in cybersecurity: An in depth analysis of user centric studies. *Jurnal Ilmiah Multidisiplin Indonesia (JIM-ID)*, *3*(01), 20–33. https://doi.org/10.58471/esaprom.v3i01.3832

Kassar. (2023). Exploring Cybersecurity Awareness and Resilience of SMEs amid the Sudden Shift to Remote Work during the Coronavirus Pandemic: A Pilot Study. *ARPHA Conference Abstracts (6, e107358)*. https://doi.org/10.3897/aca.6.e107358

Khan, N., Yaqoob, A., Khan, M. S., & Ikram, N. (2022). The cybersecurity behavioral research: A tertiary study. *Computers & Security*, *120*, 102826. https://doi.org/10.1016/j.cose.2022.102826

Madavarapu, J. B., Mittal, M., Salagrama, S., Adnan, M. M., Rana, A., & Yadav, K. (2024). Behavioral biometrics authentication systems: Leveraging machine learning for enhanced cybersecurity. In *2024 International Conference on Communication, Computer Sciences and Engineering (IC3SE)* (pp. 1478–1483). https://doi.org/10.1109/IC3SE62002.2024.10593247

Majore, G., Bukauskas, L., Sütterlin, S., & Brilingaitė, A. (2023). Advancing human performance in cybersecurity (ADVANCES). *Proceedings of Baltic Cybersecurity Research Collaboration*. https://consensus.app/papers/advancing-human-performance-in-cybersecurity-advances-majore-bukauskas/18aabf70b67b52439b124f4787d38112/?utm_source=chatgpt

Nnamani, C. C. (2024). Exploiting AI capabilities: An in-depth analysis of artificial intelligence integration in cybersecurity for threat detection and response. *International Journal of Education, Management, and Technology*, 2(3), 268–286. https://doi.org/10.58578/ijemt.v2i3.3904

Ofoegbu, K. D. O., Osundare, O. S., Ike, C. S., Fakeyede, O. G., & Ige, A. B. (2023). Data-driven cyber threat intelligence: Leveraging behavioral analytics for proactive defense mechanisms. *Computer Science & IT Research Journal*, 4(3), 502–524. https://doi.org/10.51594/csitrj.v4i3.1501

Rongala, S. (2025). Best practices in cybersecurity training: Enhancing employee awareness to mitigate risks. *International Journal of Scientific Research in Computer Science, Engineering and Information Technology*, 11, 538–547. https://doi.org/10.32628/CSEIT25111251

Rybka, P., Bąk, T., Sobel, P., & Grzechca, D. (2022). Investigation of the Impact of Damaged Smartphone Sensors' Readings on the Quality of Behavioral Biometric Models. *Sensors*, 22(24), 9580. https://doi.org/10.3390/s22249580

Sajikumar, S., & Ajithkumar, N. (2024). Understanding the emergence and significance of behavioral cybersecurity: A bibliometric analysis. *Multidisciplinary Reviews*, 6, 2023ss102. https://doi.org/10.31893/multirev.2023ss102

Shuford, J. (2024). Exploring the Efficacy of Behavioral Biometrics in Cybersecurity. *Journal of Artificial Intelligence General Science (JAIGS) ISSN:3006-4023*, 6(1), 577–593. https://doi.org/10.60087/jaigs.v6i1.285

Da Silva, F. A. (2024). Evolving approaches in cybersecurity: Metrics and human factors. *International Seven Journal of Multidisciplinary*, 1(2). https://doi.org/10.56238/isevmjv1n2-010

Tambe-Jagtap, S. N. (2023). Human-centric cybersecurity: Understanding and mitigating the role of human error in cyber incidents. *SHIFRA*, 2023, 53–59. https://doi.org/10.70470/SHIFRA/2023/007

Triplett, W. J. (2022). Addressing human factors in cybersecurity leadership. *Journal of Cybersecurity and Privacy*, 2(3), 573–586. https://doi.org/10.3390/jcp2030029

Tsanov, I. (2024). Social engineering threats in cybersecurity: Risk mitigation through behavioral insights. In *2024 International Conference Automatics and Informatics (ICAI)* (pp. 136–141). https://doi.org/10.1109/ICAI63388.2024.10851536

Tshimula, J. M., Nkashama, D. K., Muabila, J. T., Galekwa, R. M., Kanda, H., Dialufuma, M. V., … & Intudi, R. K. K. (2024). Psychological profiling in cyber security: A look at LLMs and psycholinguistic features. *arXiv*. https://doi.org/10.48550/arXiv.2406.18783

Ugbebor, F., Aina, O., Abass, M., & Kushanu, D. (2024). Employee cybersecurity awareness training programs customized for SME contexts to reduce human-error related security incidents. *Journal of Knowledge Learning and Science Technology ISSN: 2959-6386 (online)*, *3*(3), 382–409.

Van Rooy, D., & Vaes, K. (2024). Harmonizing human-AI synergy: Behavioral science in AI-integrated design. *Proceedings of the Design Society, 4*, 2287–2296. https://doi.org/10.1017/pds.2024.231

Waiganjo, I., Osakwe, J., & Azeta, A. (2024). Impediments to cybersecurity policy implementation in organisations: Case study of Windhoek, Namibia. *International Journal of Research and Scientific Innovation*, *11*(6), 540–546. https://doi.org/10.51242/ijrsi.v11i6.108

Young, S. (2024). Bridging the divide between the potential and practice of behavioral science in the private sector. *Behavioral Science & Policy*, *10*(1), 19–25. https://doi.org/10.1177/23794607241263414

Chapter 10

# Summary

Cybersecurity has long been perceived as a discipline dominated by technical controls and digital defenses. However, research increasingly emphasizes the vital role of human behavior in both exacerbating and mitigating cyber threats. Behavioral science, a field rooted in psychology, sociology, and cognitive neuroscience, offers critical insights into how individuals and groups perceive risks, make decisions, and interact with technology in the context of cybersecurity. This comprehensive chapter synthesizes the findings from nine foundational documents to present an integrated view of behavioral science in cybersecurity, addressing human factors, organizational culture, decision-making, emerging technologies, ethics, and future directions.

## THE HUMAN ELEMENT IN CYBERSECURITY

Behavioral science underscores that cybersecurity breaches are predominantly caused by human error, with estimates indicating 85%–95% of incidents stem from human behavior (Dawson & Thomson, 2018). Factors such as password reuse, social engineering susceptibility, and cognitive overload illustrate the limitations of relying solely on technical defenses. These vulnerabilities are not merely the result of user negligence but often stem from systemic issues such as poorly designed systems, lack of training, and ineffective communication strategies.

The significance of cognitive biases cannot be overstated when evaluating security outcomes. Cybersecurity professionals are susceptible to the same biases as everyday users, including the availability heuristic, confirmation bias, and optimism bias. These mental shortcuts influence how threats are perceived and prioritized, often leading to flawed decisions. For instance, recent threats may receive disproportionate attention compared to more likely but less visible risks.

Behavioral science provides tools to recognize and mitigate these biases through structured decision frameworks and awareness training. Leaders are encouraged to foster environments where critical thinking is promoted, and diverse perspectives are valued. By addressing the cognitive and


DOI: 10.1201/9781003606345-8

environmental underpinnings of poor cybersecurity behavior, organizations can reduce their attack surface. This human-centric approach enhances the efficacy of technical solutions by aligning them with natural behavioral tendencies.

## FOUNDATIONS OF BEHAVIORAL SCIENCE IN CYBERSECURITY

Simon's concept of bounded rationality illustrates that people make decisions within constraints of limited time, information, and cognitive resources (Simon, 1955). In cybersecurity, this explains common behaviors like choosing weak passwords or postponing software updates. These decisions, while seemingly irrational, are pragmatic responses to the complexity and volume of modern security demands. Understanding this can inform the design of systems that accommodate rather than resist human limitations.

Dual-process theory adds another layer of insight, differentiating between System 1 (fast and intuitive) and System 2 (slow and analytical) thinking. In high-pressure environments such as cybersecurity operations, System 1 often dominates, increasing susceptibility to social engineering and misjudgments. Training and interface design that encourage the activation of System 2 can help users make more deliberate and secure decisions. This might involve cues that prompt reconsideration or highlight potential risks.

Social and organizational factors also shape behavior significantly. Concepts like social proof, loss aversion, and perceived behavioral control explain why individuals conform to group norms, resist change, or overestimate their ability to manage risks. Cybersecurity interventions must therefore consider these psychological and social dynamics. Encouraging visible security behaviors, framing policies around loss prevention, and improving users' confidence in their abilities are key strategies for fostering secure practices.

## HUMAN FACTORS: PROFESSIONALS UNDER PRESSURE

Cybersecurity professionals are often required to make critical decisions under pressure, particularly during incidents such as data breaches or ransomware attacks. Stress impairs cognitive function, leading to errors in judgment or delayed responses. Understanding how individuals perform under duress can inform the development of training programs and support structures that enhance resilience. Incorporating stress management techniques and predefined protocols can help reduce mistakes.

Team dynamics play a vital role in how security operations unfold. Effective collaboration, trust, and communication are essential for coordinating responses and making well-informed decisions. When these elements are lacking, even technically sound teams may struggle to contain threats. Organizational investments in leadership development and communication training can mitigate these challenges.

Cognitive biases among professionals are another persistent issue. Biases such as the Peltzman Effect, consensus bias, and the ostrich effect can lead to risky assumptions and overlooked vulnerabilities. These biases distort perception and reduce the effectiveness of security measures, particularly when overconfidence in tools or team consensus goes unchallenged. Encouraging critical evaluation and diverse perspectives within teams is crucial to maintaining a vigilant and adaptive posture.

## ORGANIZATIONAL CULTURE AS THE BEDROCK

Organizational culture influences cybersecurity at every level, from executive decision-making to frontline compliance. A strong culture promotes security as a shared value and integrates it into everyday business processes. In contrast, a weak culture treats security as a separate, often inconvenient obligation, increasing the risk of breaches and noncompliance. Leaders must recognize culture as a strategic asset in cybersecurity management.

Culture is defined by dimensions such as risk awareness, accountability, adaptability, and communication. These values shape how teams perceive threats, share information, and respond to incidents. A culture that prioritizes transparency and continuous learning encourages proactive threat detection and mitigation. Conversely, environments that suppress dialogue or penalize disclosure can allow vulnerabilities to persist undetected.

Leadership is instrumental in shaping and reinforcing culture. Chief Information Security Officers (CISOs) and other executives must model the behaviors they wish to see, reward compliance, and create avenues for feedback and improvement. Regular training, visible engagement with cybersecurity initiatives, and alignment of security goals with business objectives all contribute to building a resilient and security-conscious organization. When culture supports security, both human and technical defenses become more effective.

## THE TECHNOLOGY STRATEGY NEEDS PYRAMID: APPLYING MASLOW

The Technology Strategy Needs Pyramid presents a human-centric model for understanding and prioritizing cybersecurity through five ascending levels: Reliable Access, Secure Systems, Trusted Identity, Ethical Compliance, and Collective Impact. This framework integrates behavioral science with technical strategies, recognizing that effective cybersecurity isn't just about systems and controls, but about how people interact with those systems. At its foundation, reliable access ensures users have dependable and secure digital infrastructure. This reduces frustration and the temptation to bypass security, promoting secure behavior by aligning systems with natural human tendencies. As organizations reduce barriers to technology use, they foster environments where security practices are more likely to be adopted and sustained.

Progressing up the pyramid, Secure Systems and Trusted Identity emphasize minimizing friction and fostering psychological safety, enabling users to engage securely without fear or excessive complexity. Behavioral science principles—like reducing hyperbolic discounting or utilizing secure defaults—make security feel supportive, not restrictive. Trusted Identity extends this by teaching users to recognize manipulation tactics such as social engineering, while implementing tools like multifactor authentication and zero trust architectures to reinforce secure access. By addressing both technological and behavioral aspects of identity protection, organizations build trust and increase resilience against human-centric threats.

At the top levels, Ethical Compliance and Resilient Maturity push organizations beyond regulatory obligations toward a proactive, ethically driven security culture. Ethical Compliance ensures cybersecurity is embedded in values and decision-making, reducing the risk of moral licensing where compliance breeds complacency. Resilient Maturity, the final stage before Collective Impact, represents the continuous adaptation needed to counter evolving threats through training, simulation, and a growth mindset. Finally, Collective Impact highlights cybersecurity as a shared societal challenge, advocating for collaboration across industries and governments. Through information sharing and policy alignment, organizations can collectively fortify the digital ecosystem, reaching the highest expression of cybersecurity maturity.

## DECISION HYGIENE: MAKING BETTER SECURITY CHOICES

Decision hygiene refers to practices that reduce cognitive errors and improve the quality of choices made under uncertainty. In cybersecurity, where decisions often carry high stakes, this concept is particularly relevant. Errors caused by heuristics, biases, and environmental pressures can compromise threat detection, incident response, and risk prioritization. Understanding these pitfalls is the first step in avoiding them.

Several common biases affect cybersecurity decision-making, including the availability heuristic, anchoring, and confirmation bias. These distortions can lead to overconfidence, misjudgment of threat likelihood, or reliance on outdated assumptions. By applying frameworks that encourage critical reflection and structured analysis, organizations can reduce the impact of these biases.

Training and decision support tools are practical ways to institutionalize these improvements.

Implementing decision hygiene involves both individual and organizational changes. On a personal level, cybersecurity professionals can benefit from reflective practices and cognitive bias training. At the organizational level, promoting diverse team input, using decision matrices, and embedding decision checkpoints into workflows all contribute to better outcomes. Together, these practices support a proactive and resilient security posture.

## ARTIFICIAL INTELLIGENCE AND BEHAVIORAL SCIENCE INTEGRATION

Artificial intelligence (AI) and machine learning (ML) are reshaping cybersecurity by enabling real-time behavioral analysis and adaptive defenses. These technologies analyze large datasets to detect anomalies, predict threats, and automate responses. Behavioral analytics powered by AI can identify deviations in user activity that may indicate insider threats or account compromise, enhancing detection accuracy.

AI also helps operationalize behavioral science insights at scale. By automating the interpretation of behavioral data, AI reduces the burden on human analysts and improves response times. For instance, behavioral biometrics, such as keystroke dynamics or mouse movements, provide continuous authentication without disrupting user experience. These tools enhance security while maintaining usability.

Explainable AI (XAI) is gaining traction to ensure transparency and accountability in machine decision-making. In regulatory environments or high-stakes sectors, understanding why an alert was triggered or a decision made is essential. XAI supports user trust and enables oversight, making AI a true partner rather than a black box tool. This partnership between human judgment and machine precision enhances cybersecurity capabilities across the board.

## ETHICS AND PRIVACY IN BEHAVIORAL CYBERSECURITY

The use of behavioral science in cybersecurity raises important ethical questions. Techniques such as nudging, behavioral analytics, and monitoring must be implemented with respect for user autonomy and privacy. Without proper safeguards, these tools can become manipulative or invasive, undermining trust and compliance. Ethical design is thus not optional; it is foundational.

Cybersecurity leaders must balance organizational security needs with individual rights. This includes conducting ethical impact assessments, ensuring informed consent for data collection, and regularly auditing systems for bias. Transparency in how behavioral data is used fosters user trust and reduces resistance. Ethical principles adapted from fields like biomedicine, such as beneficence, non-maleficence, justice, and autonomy, provide a useful framework.

Operationalizing ethics requires actionable steps. Organizations should train security teams in ethical considerations, establish internal review boards or protocols, and prioritize fairness in algorithmic design. These measures are particularly important as AI and behavioral tools become more pervasive. By embedding ethics into cybersecurity strategies, leaders can enhance both effectiveness and legitimacy.

## FUTURE DIRECTIONS AND EMERGING TRENDS

Behavioral science is poised to become a cornerstone of future cybersecurity strategies. Innovations in behavioral analytics, biometrics, and psychological profiling are transforming how threats are detected and managed. For example, continuous authentication using behavioral cues provides a seamless layer of security that adapts to user behavior in real time. These tools offer both enhanced protection and improved user experience.

Psychological profiling and nudging are gaining traction as proactive security measures. By analyzing language patterns or emotional cues, systems can identify potential threats before they manifest. Similarly, nudges, such as warning prompts or adaptive training, help guide users toward secure behaviors without restricting freedom. These methods are becoming integral to user-centric security strategies.

Interdisciplinary collaboration is essential for advancing the field. Integrating insights from psychology, sociology, computer science, and ethics allows for more holistic solutions. Standardized frameworks and cross-functional teams can help overcome barriers to implementation, such as siloed departments or lack of executive buy-in. As the threat landscape evolves, human-centric approaches grounded in behavioral science will be key to building resilient and adaptive cybersecurity systems.

## CONCLUSION

Behavioral science represents a transformative force in the evolution of cybersecurity strategy. By highlighting the psychological, cognitive, and social dimensions of security practices, it challenges traditional assumptions that technical tools alone can safeguard digital environments. Instead, it calls attention to how human errors, habits, and heuristics influence risk exposure and threat response. Recognizing and addressing these behavioral factors is fundamental to building more resilient organizations.

One of the most critical contributions of behavioral science is its illumination of cognitive biases and decision-making flaws that affect both users and cybersecurity professionals. These biases distort threat perception, hinder policy compliance, and lead to reactive rather than proactive responses. Structured decision frameworks and reflective practices can help mitigate these issues. In doing so, organizations empower their teams to make informed, strategic, and timely decisions that reduce risk.

Organizational culture also plays a defining role in cybersecurity outcomes. A culture that values transparency, continuous learning, and ethical behavior fosters engagement and accountability across all levels of an organization. When cybersecurity becomes part of the organizational identity, not just a checklist or compliance requirement, employees and leaders alike are more likely to act responsibly and vigilantly. Behavioral science offers the tools to diagnose cultural weaknesses and implement targeted improvements.

Furthermore, the integration of emerging technologies such as AI and behavioral analytics marks a new era in adaptive security. These innovations enable personalized, context-aware defenses that align closely with user behavior. However, the ethical implications of these technologies must be carefully managed to avoid infringing on privacy or autonomy. Balancing effectiveness with transparency and fairness ensures that cybersecurity strategies remain both effective and trusted.

Ultimately, the future of cybersecurity lies in bridging the gap between technical innovation and human behavior. Behavioral science equips leaders with a nuanced understanding of how people think, decide, and interact with digital systems. When combined with sound ethics and supportive organizational structures, this approach enhances security outcomes, promotes user trust, and prepares organizations to face evolving cyber threats with agility and confidence.

# Index

Made in the USA
Las Vegas, NV
19 September 2026

97d2f70b-4d57-4f3f-a766-754b70d091f6R02